Positioning Yoga

Positioning Yoga

Balancing Acts Across Cultures

Sarah Strauss

Oxford • New York

First published in 2005 by
Berg
Editorial offices:
1st Floor, Angel Court, 81 St Clements Street, Oxford, OX4 1AW, UK
175 Fifth Avenue, New York, NY 10010, USA

Berg is the imprint of Oxford International Publishers Ltd.

Library of Congress Cataloging-in-Publication Data
Strauss, Sarah.
    Positioning yoga : balancing acts across cultures / Sarah Strauss.– 1st ed.
        p. cm.
    Includes bibliographical references and index.
    ISBN 1-85973-734-X (hardcover) –ISBN 1-85973-739-0 (pbk.) 1. Yoga–History. I. Title.
    B132.Y6S765 2004
    181′.45–dc22

                                                                            2004023169

British Library Cataloguing-in-Publication Data
A catalogue record for this book is available from the British Library.

ISBN 978 1 85973 734 7 (hardback)
        978 1 85973 739 2 (paperback)

Typeset by JS Typesetting Ltd, Wellingborough, Northants.
Printed in the United Kingdom by Biddles Ltd, King's Lynn.

www.bergpublishers.com

In memory of Wilhelm Halbfass (1940–2000),
a great soul and an inspiring teacher.

Contents

List of Figures   ix

Acknowledgements   xi

Glossary and Orthographic Note   xiii

"Lineage" of Swami Sivananda of Rishikesh   xvii

Preface: A Note to Anthropologists and Interested Others . . .   xix

1   Re-Orienting Yoga   1

2   Lives and Histories: Rishikesh, Sivananda, and the Divine Life
          Society   23

3   Balancing Acts: Doing Yoga in Rishikesh   53

4   Moving Out: Yoga for a Transnational Community of Practice   87

5   Yoga: A Global Positioning System   115

Afterword: Virtual Yoga   141

Notes   145

Bibliography   157

Index   177

Figures

1	Yoga with "props"	6
2	Sumit: The Headstand	7
3	Map of India, showing Uttaranchal and Rishikesh	25
4	Rafting on the Ganga River above Rishikesh	29
5	Swami Sivananda Commemorative Postage Stamp	37
6	*Sannyasins* at Tea Stall, Rishikesh	54
7	Swamiji	62
8	Dancing Siva at the DLS, a.k.a Sivananda Ashram	64
9	DLS from Ram Jhula	64
10	Ganga Dawn	136

Acknowledgements

This book (and the dissertation from which it is derived) was made possible through the help and support of a number of individuals and institutions over the last dozen years; its strengths are a direct result of this support, and the deficiencies which remain are my own. Throughout the endeavor, Arjun Appadurai offered intellectual sustenance as well as the encouragement required to pursue a research topic which often seemed untamable. The interdisciplinary community of scholars linked through Arjun and Carol Breckenridge's first Public Culture reading group at Penn in the late 1980s provided an incredibly stimulating environment for a new student with an un- (or perhaps trans-) disciplined mind to begin the transformative process that is graduate school. Peter van der Veer constantly forced me to evaluate and defend my ideas, and his challenges improved my thinking immensely. Rebecca Huss-Ashmore provided a firm anchor in the Anthropology department through all of my transnational traverses. Wilhelm Halbfass is sorely missed; he helped me sort out the tangled relationships between European and Hindu Indian philosophy, and kept me honest.

A great debt of gratitude is owed fellow Penn students and friends, now colleagues, Carolyn Behrman, Amy Trubek, Mark Liechty, Sanjay Joshi, Cecilia van Hollen, Ritty Lukose, Maneesha Lal, Stuart Kirsch. Field research was funded by a Fulbright-Hays Doctoral Dissertation Award for work in India in 1992 (Amiya Kesevan at USEF/I helped my work in India go far more smoothly than it might have), and by a Travel Grant from the School of Arts and Sciences at Penn for work in Germany in 1993. Visiting Scholar status granted by both the Swiss Federal Institute of Technology/EAWAG (1993–94) and the Center for Comparative Research in History, Society, and Culture at the University of California at Davis (1994–95) was essential to writing up.

To the people of Rishikesh, especially Arun Bhattacharya, Mohan Dang and his family, Swamiji, Rudra Gowda, the Issars, Marcel and Pauline, and the many individuals, both in India and elsewhere, who shared their understandings of yoga with me – with special thanks to Sharon, Tom, Astrid, and Claudia. In Delhi, Veena Das, and in Calcutta, Partha Chatterjee, helped to clarify my thoughts. My fellow Rishikesh researchers Lise McKean and Richard Castillo both offered insights and commentaries I could not have done without. Joan appeared in Rishikesh at exactly the right moment, giving me confidence and making me believe that everything was unfolding as it should.

Acknowledgements

Peter Schreiner, Joanna Pfaff-Czarnecka, Cornelia Vogelsanger, Christian Fuchs and Shalini Randeria drew me into the Swiss/German south Asian scholarship network. In America, Lilias, Swami Gurudevananda and Samarpana, and other folks associated with the DLS welcomed me, and rounded out my understanding of the international Sivananda community. Since arriving at the University of Wyoming in 1995, I have benefited from the extraordinarily supportive working environment in the Department of Anthropology; thanks especially go to colleagues Lin Poyer, Audrey Shalinsky, Michael Harkin, and Anne Slater. Other colleagues in Anthropology-land, most notably Vered Amit, Helena Wulff, Hugh Gusterson, and Ben Orlove, have provided excellent advice and much appreciated support over the years. Thanks are also due to my Writing Group colleagues – Susanna Goodin, Jean Schaefer, Kathy Jensen, Cathy Connolly, Colleen Denney, and Bonnie Zare, among others – for reading assorted chapters over the years. More recently, Kathryn Earle and the entire highly competent team at Berg have ensured a smooth passage to publication, with good humor. Nancy Ford has contributed materially to the final product, providing both an outstanding index and a skilled copyediting eye.

Some previously published portions of this work are included here with permission:

Strauss, S. (2000) Locating Yoga: Ethnography and Transnational Practice. In V. Amit, ed. *Constructing the Field*, pp. 162–194. New York: Routledge.

Strauss, S. (2002) "Adapt, Adjust, Accommodate": The Production of Yoga in a Transnational World. *History and Anthropology* 13(3): 231–251.

Strauss, S. (2002) The Master's Narrative: Swami Sivananda and the Transnational Production of Yoga. *Journal of Folklore Research* 39(2/3).

Strauss, S. (2002) Swamiji: A Life in Yoga. In L. Walbridge and A. Sievert, eds. *Personal Encounters in Anthropology: An Introductory Reader*. Mountain View, CA: McGraw-Hill Publishing Co.

My whole family has borne the weight of my distraction patiently over the years – a mere "thank you" seems insufficient, but I have little more to offer. To Carrick I can only say that I could not have made it through without your constant presence; the knowledge that you were always with me in spirit made the years of commuting (California-Pennsylvania-Zurich-Rishikesh!) possible. To Rory and Lia: you are the reason for everything that has been, and the purpose for all that is to come.

Glossary and Orthographic Note

I have not used diacritic markings for transliteration of Hindi and Sanskrit words throughout the text, but have provided them in the glossary below, along with definitions of all significant words and phrases.

abhyās	practice
advaita	non-duality of atman and brahman
ahiṃsā	non-violence
āsana	posture, position, pose; Patanjali's 3rd stage of astanga system
aśram	monastery
aṣṭāṅga yoga	Patanjali's eight-fold path to realization
ātman	soul, self
bhadrālok	"decent people" of Calcutta
bhakti	devotion, worship
bhakti yoga	realization through worship
bhukti	pleasure
brahmacharin	student
brahmacharin-sannyasin	student-renouncer
brahmachārya	first stage of Hindu life cycle; also a life of celibacy
brahman	the Universal soul/spirit
darśan	seeing and being seen by god or guru
darśana	philosophy or school of thought; lit. way of seeing
dharamsala	rest house
dhāraṇa	concentration/Patanjali's sixth stage of astanga system
dharma	biomoral duty
dhyānā	meditation/Patanjali's seventh stage
ghats	riverbank landing places
guna	quality or constituent of nature
guru–shishya	teacher or student master–disciple pair
gurubhaī	students of the same guru
haṭha yoga	realization through physical discipline
japa	repetitive prayer
jīvanmukhti	living liberation
jñāna yoga	realization through intellectual knowledge

kaivalya	isolation, release
kāma	lust, desire
karma	fate, work
karma yoga	realization through work
kuṇḍalinī	divine, cosmic force/energy; Sankskrit "coiled up", refers to the primordial energy located in the sacrum, invoked through a variety of meditative practices
maya	illusion
mahasamādhi	euphemism for death; transition to higher state; see *Samādhi*
mīmāṃṣā	one of the six schools of Hindu thought
moks(h)a	release, absolute freedom
muk(h)ti	see *moks(h)a*
niyama	self-purification/Patanjali's second stage
prāṇa	breath, vitality, energy
praṇāyama	breathing techniques/Patanjali's fourth stage
pratyāhāra	retreat from the senses/Patanjali's fifth stage
pujas	acts of spiritual devotion
rāja yoga	"kingly" yoga/Patanjali's eight-stage yoga
rajas	mobility, activity/one of the three *gunas*
rishis	seers, sages
sādhak	seeker, aspirant
sādhanā	spiritual practice, quest
samādhi	highest altered state of consciousness
samatva	equilibrium, disinterest
saṃsāra	the endless cycle of life
sāṃkhya	one of the six schools of Hindu thought
sampradāya	tradition, sect, ideological community
sannyās	fourth stage of Hindu life cycle; renouncing of *samsāra*
sannyasin	one who has taken vows of *sannyas* (female version: *sannyasini*)
satsang	spiritual fellowship
sattva	clarity, purity/one of the three *gunas*
satya	truth, truthfulness
siddhis	unusual and seemingly magical powers
swara	use of breathing techniques
tamas	darkness, dullness/one of the three *gunas*
tantra	esoteric ritual practices in Hindu and Buddhist traditions, sometimes involving sexual union
tat tvam asi	"that thou art"

vairāgya	absence of worldly desires
vanaprastha	forest-dwelling third life stage before *sannyās*
vedanta	one of the six Darsanas of classical Hinduism, focused on the teachings of the Upanisads and particularly the Brahma Sutras
yama	moral observance/Patanjali's first stage in Astanga system
yogabhyās	yoga practice
yūj	to yoke or join/Sanskrit root of the word "yoga"

"Lineage" of Swami Sivananda of Rishikesh

Note: Not an exhaustive list (by any means!), but rather a genealogical representation of those members of the Sivananda *sampradaya* (tradition or sect) who are discussed in this book.

Ramakrishna (b. 1836 – d. 1886)

    Vivekananda (b. 1863 – d. 1902)

    [*Sivananda was inspired by Vivekananda's writings.*]

Sivananda – considered "self-realized" saint;

    given *sannyas* upon arrival in Rishikesh (b. 1887 – d. 1963)

    Mircea Eliade (early student, pre-Divine Life Society (DLS) incorporation; b. 1907 – d. 1986)

    Chidananda (current president of DLS in Rishikesh; b. 1916)

        Jayananda*, DLS – USA

        Lilias Folan, TSI (Town Sports International)-Yoga

    Krishnananda (general secretary of DLS in Rishikesh; b. 1922 – d. 2001)

        Sumit* (Yoga Center in Rishikesh)

            Ram* (Rishikesh; also heavily influenced by Vivekananda's writings)

    Vishnudevananda (Sivananda Yoga Vedanta Centers/Ashrams – HQ Val Morin, Quebec, but many other global locations; b. 1927 – d. 1993)

        Swamiji* (1990s – hotel in Rishikesh; now living in United States)

    Satchidananda (Integral Yoga Institutes/Yogaville Ashram, Virginia, b. 1914 – d. 2002)

        Dean Ornish, MD (Sausalito, CA, USA)

    Omkarananda (Divine Light Zentrum, Winterthur, Switzerland; Omkarananda International Ashrams/Schools, Europe and India; b. 1930 – d. 2000)

    Sivananda-Radha (Yasodhara Ashram, BC, Canada; b. 1911 – d. 1995)

    Chinmayananda (started Chinmaya Mission as well as VHP; b. 1916 – d. 1993)

    Venkatesananda (DLS – South Africa, b. 1921 – d. 1982)

    Jyotirmayananda (Yoga Research Foundation, Miami, FL, USA; b. 1931)

    Satyananda (Bihar School of Yoga, India, and other international affiliates; b. 1924)

    * = *pseudonym, based on request or other need for protection from publicity*

Preface
A Note to Anthropologists and
Interested Others . . .

In this book, I have tried to tell a fairly simple story about the ways that certain ideas and practices of yoga, primarily those of Swami Sivananda of Rishikesh, have moved from India to elsewhere in the world and back. In the telling, I explain how, over the past century, the practice of yoga has transformed from a regional, male-oriented religious activity to a globalized and largely secular phenomenon. The story can be read in different ways that make it useful to different kinds of readers – both those who are at home in the academic circles that comprise the social sciences, and those rooted more squarely in the wider world.

Students of anthropology who may be reading this book for a class will find descriptions of multi-sited ethnographic fieldwork that follow the paths of trans-national cultural flows of the ideas, practices, and people who comprise one particular "brand" of yoga, that of Swami Sivananda of Rishikesh, India. If I have succeeded in my task, you will feel that you have come to inhabit a world that is both similar to and quite different from the one you wake up to on a daily basis. You will recognize the value of cultural anthropology's primary methodology, participant-observation, as well as the necessity of informed historical context for making sense of the richness of ethnographic data. By following the twists and turns of the ethnographer's path, you will come to understand that, for any given subject, many different stories could be told. You will, I hope, look at the ordinary world around you in a slightly different way for having read this book, and see that in order to make peace with ourselves and others, we need to be able to put into practice that fundamental tenet of anthropology, cultural relativism, and see the world from another vantage point.

Anthropologists and other scholars may find utility in learning the details of one specific example of a transnational cultural process that shares both similarities and differences with other instances of that which is often reduced to the simple rubric of "globalization." By telling the story of Sivananda's yoga as it was developed and disseminated through India and other parts of the world, I try to convey the ways that a variety of what Raymond Williams (1988) has called "keywords" – modern, nationalist, liberation, wealth (in its original sense of well-being) – have converged to produce a particular cultural form that is recognizable in many parts of the world today as "yoga." The peculiarly transnational construction of this cultural form, dependent as it has been on the forces of colonialism, nationalism, and globalization, sheds light on the distinctive values and remedies that resonate with people who call themselves modern.

Readers who are also yoga practitioners, many of whom are my colleagues in academia as well as the production staff who assembled this book, may seek histories both personal and practical that will help them understand things that they have learned in various yoga classes. In addition to the theoretical and methodological points highlighted earlier, those who have practiced yoga may find in this book an extended community to which they themselves belong, and find value in that membership.

To all, I wish you the lessons that I have learned through the lengthy process (now at fourteen years and counting) of engaging in research on yoga and yoga practitioners: that breathing (really, truly, deeply) makes a difference; that like-minded others can be found in the most surprising places; and that by staying with it, following through, and embracing that which may seem at first too different, too meaningless, too ordinary, we can find ourselves engaged in a bear hug with the essence of our own humanity.

–1–

Re-Orienting Yoga

Bombay, India – March, 1992

The train pulled out of the station. I was riding in the famed *Rajdhani Express*, on the way back from Bombay to Delhi. Across from me in the compartment, two middle-aged, middle-class businessmen looked hot and uncomfortable in their standard Western style business attire – jackets, ties, the works. They wondered what a young, unaccompanied, non-Indian woman was doing dressed in *salwar-kameez* (women's dress of long tunic and loose trousers) and studying a Hindi grammar book. When I explained that I was an anthropologist, and had come to India to study yoga in Rishikesh, they became quite attentive, and began to discuss the subject. Their primary sentiments were regret and amazement: regret that they knew so little of their heritage themselves, and what they knew derived solely from hearsay; amazement that I should travel so far from home, learn Hindi, and wear Indian clothing out of preference, all to study a subject they considered important to their own past, but not likely to loom large in anyone's future. Nevertheless, they agreed that Rishikesh was an ideal place to carry out such a study, since it was well known as a site of great spiritual power. As was often the case when I mentioned yoga, the businessmen inquired whether I had met any "real" yogis in my travels, and speculated that there were very few left in the country. In the time of the *Mahabharat* and the *Ramayan*, the great epics of India, they mused, there had been many yogis across the land. Perhaps, one said, if I went south to Tamil Nad, where people were still in touch with the traditions, I could find some there. The other commented that he had once encountered a man lying on a bed of nails, unscathed: "Was that yoga?"

Locating Yoga

Yoga. The word evokes a range of images and ideas, from white-bearded Indian mystics on mountaintops to cross-legged hippies burning incense and urban business people at a lunchtime fitness class. Although there is no single "correct" version of yoga, a close examination of the variety of ideas and practices that is identified with yoga yields a common core. This book asks how the set of ideas and practices known as yoga has moved from its birthplace on the Indian subcontinent to become a global phenomenon, and how this transnationally produced yoga has come home to change the practice of yoga in India itself. What are the values, in India or elsewhere in the world, that have supported the popularity of yoga over the past century? Following a specific form of yoga developed in Rishikesh, India, by Swami Sivananda and his disciples, we will explore how ideas and practices are transformed as they traverse cultural boundaries; and how certain values, like those of "health" and "freedom," have shifted in meaning over time, allowing them to be used in the service of such practices.

Yoga can be defined in many ways – as an attitude, a philosophy, a set of practices, a way of being in the world – but its definition is always located within a particular historical context. Although yoga has been studied extensively as a philosophical and religious system,[1] it has less often been researched ethnographic-ally, as a system of bodily practices within a sociocultural context.[2] Yoga offers an excellent example of the inseparability of mind and body. The eight stages of Patanjali's classical yoga begin with the practice of morality in social life (*yama, niyama*: universal and personal rules for living – see Iyengar 1979: 31–36), proceeding to physical practices (*asana, pranayama*: physical poses and breathing techniques), and then to different states of mental attention or consciousness (*pratyahara, dharana, dhyana, samadhi*: gradual removal of external sensory input, focusing attention on a single point, uninterrupted meditative state, and, depending on the school of thought, perfect isolation or union with the Absolute (Fort and Mumme 1996). Patanjali's yoga takes as one of its primary goals the maintenance of physical fitness of the body, which is a preliminary requirement for eventual spiritual enlightenment (Varenne 1976). In contrast with one well-studied south Asian health system, Ayurvedic medicine (which also has a long-standing textual and popular tradition: see Langford 2002; Leslie 1976; Zimmerman 1987), yoga has received far less academic attention.[3] Yet like Ayurveda, yoga has attracted attention in the West as an Eastern path to health and well-being.

Here, I explore not only the shifts in how yoga itself has been understood, but also the factors that have contributed to changing the demographics of yoga practitioners. Although there were a few scholars outside of India during the seventeenth and eighteenth centuries who were interested in the classical yoga texts, it was only in the late nineteenth century that wider audiences of people in the United States and Western Europe began to learn about yoga. Much of this exposure derived from a series of public lectures given by the Indian Swami Vivekananda. Vivekananda developed his ideas about yoga while he was traveling in the United States and Europe, and later promoted them in India from his home base in Kolkata (formerly Calcutta). Previously known to his friends and family (but few others) as Narendranath Datta, the young swami had taken the new name of Vivekananda for his voyage west. Young Narendranath/Vivekananda, child of a judge and trained in European-style philosophy and law, had overcome his extreme skepticism of religious power through his interactions with Sri

Ramakrishna, one of the most famous figures of the nineteenth-century Hindu world, and still one of the most revered spiritual teachers in all of India. Although Ramakrishna was himself an untutored mystic, in his foremost disciple, Vivekananda, he acquired an eloquent spokesman.

Yoga, described in Vivekananda's lectures as well as printed pamphlets, became a commodity, something of value that could be acquired and circulated among the literate middle class people of both India and the West. Swami Vivekananda presented yoga as a spiritual commodity that had an explicit exchange value for people in America and Europe: he said that India had an abundance of spiritual wealth, and that yoga was a method that could help people to achieve spiritual well-being. In return, the West – well known for its material resources – could pay cash for the privilege of learning yoga. Vivekananda reasoned that the West lacked spirituality, and so a fair trade could be made (Raychaudhuri 1989; Vivekananda 1990c). Vivekananda influenced many other middle-class people like himself (not only in India but also around the globe) to pursue an ascetic lifestyle, or at least to incorporate aspects of classical Hindu religious philosophy and practice in their daily lives (Joshi 2001). One of those strongly influenced by Vivekananda's teachings was Swami Sivananda of Rishikesh, India. As we will see, Sivananda, formerly a secular medical doctor from south India, left his successful career to become one of India's best known twentieth-century religious figures. This book traces a path out from Sivananda's Divine Life Society in Rishikesh, through Germany and the United States, and back to Rishikesh, to explore how the practice of yoga – though clearly of Indian origin – has come to embody the values of health and freedom in a transnational context.

The Historical Context of Yoga – in a Nutshell

The Sanskrit root of the word yoga, *yuj*, means to yoke or join together; the most common English translation is "union," usually referring to the union of the individual self with the Absolute or Universal Self. I use the general term "yoga" to refer to the broad philosophical perspective (*yoga-darsana*) normally considered to constitute one of the six *darsanas* (philosophies) of Hinduism (Eliade 1973 [1958]). One way to begin a discussion of yoga would be to review the ancient Indian texts. Of these, the most famous are the *Yoga Sutras* of Patanjali, dated tentatively to the period 200 BC to AD 200 and considered to be the master text for "classical" yoga. The yoga sutras are somewhat cryptic verse forms, easy for the disciples of the yoga masters to learn, but difficult to analyze. The critical/interpretive tradition which developed around the original texts continues to the present day. The verses outline what are considered the eight basic stages of the yoga system, including guidelines for moral living, physical postures, breathing techniques, meditative practice. Much has been said about this textual tradition (see Aranya 1983; Das Gupta 1989[1920]; B.S. Miller 1996; Werner 1977, among others); here, I will discuss elements of such textual theories of yoga only as they apply to the specific teachings of Swamis Vivekananda and Sivananda.

The original goal of classical yoga, *kaivalya*, or isolation of the self, is a far cry from the contemporary goals of health, stress reduction, and flexibility that are frequently encountered within both Indian and non-Indian communities. There are numerous other Upanishadic and Puranic treatises that also discuss some facet of yoga philosophy and practice within the confines of "orthodox" Hinduism,[4] and generally fall within the 400 BC to AD 400 period. In addition the divergent paths of Buddhism and Jainism have generated a substantial body of early literature.[5] These ancient writings are certainly important; in this chapter, however, they will be considered only in so far as they paint a backdrop for the events of the past century.

Before I delve more deeply into the theoretical concerns of this book, a few clarifications and definitions are in order. The most common usage of the term "yoga" – as seen in Government of India tourist brochures or local television guides, or heard around college campuses – has typically referred to the eight-fold or *astanga* path of *Raja yoga*, the classical yoga of Patanjali's *Yoga Sutras*, described previously. In recent years, however, a proliferation of different yogas have appeared on the scene, from Beryl Birch's Power Yoga to various styles labeled Flow Yoga and beyond. Many, if not most, of these styles are associated with a particular teacher – B.K.S. Iyengar, K. Pattabhi Jois, Swami Vishnudevananda – though others are framed primarily in terms of a broader emphasis or style, such as *astanga* or *kundalini*. *Raja* yoga includes moral guidelines, meditative techniques, and the *asanas*, or poses, of *hatha* yoga, whose purpose is to discipline the body and mind through physical postures; some consider *hatha* yoga to be a category unto itself. *Raja* yoga, the yoga of self-control, is one of the four paths of yoga into which Swami Vivekananda distilled the multiplicity of yogas in the Hindu tradition when he presented these philosophies and practices to the West in 1893.

Rishikesh, India – April, 1992

It's 4.30 a.m. and my alarm has just sounded. In the small dark room, I begin to hear others moving about the ashram (monastery) courtyard. I reach for my clothes and begin to dress. Time enough for a cup of tea and a quick wash before walking down the road to the Yoga Center on the banks of the Ganga (Ganges River). Sixteen of

continued

---

us converge on the large cement structure at 5.15 a.m. – a dozen non-Indian students, mostly women; a couple of Indian students, both men; the instructor and his assistant, also Indian men. Some sit in silent meditation, while others begin to stretch and twist, warming up their bodies in the cool of dawn, while staring into the mist rising up off the Ganga, the glint of the river barely visible beyond the wire mesh windows. At 5.30, Sumit, the instructor, begins to chant; he invokes the aid of the god Siva, exemplar of yogic practice, as we prepare to spend two and a half hours in vigorous pursuit of the perfect pose. As he barks out the names of *asanas*, followed by detailed explanations, I am called upon to translate for the numerous German students in the class. Although most of them speak English fairly well, Sumit's heavily accented, staccato Indian English is too difficult for some to comprehend, and so I try to help.

From History to Practice

Styles of contemporary yoga practice vary from the gymnastic to the sublime. Most people who see a photograph of the yoga class described above (Figure 1), with its members twisted and stretched on various types of equipment, view it as a variant of a medieval torture chamber. Another typical example (Figure 2), this one of a man standing on his head on an oriental carpet, seems to agree with more people's idea of what one ought to be doing when practicing yoga. Yet both photos were taken within minutes and meters of each other. They reflect the diverse range of yoga practices available to students worldwide. There are, however, many Hindu textual and popular traditions other than yoga whose fame has never reached beyond the borders of the subcontinent. While the term "yoga" has widespread name-recognition, the words *Vedanta* or *Mimamsa* will probably draw only a blank stare from any non-Hindu (other than a Sanskrit scholar). But these three together make up half of the six classical schools of Indian philosophy. Of these six philosophical frameworks, why has yoga alone made it to the status of a major "cultural export"? What makes yoga different?

The title of this chapter, "Re-Orienting Yoga," points to three major reasons for yoga's surge in popularity that I shall outline. We will revisit each of these major points in detail, but for now I simply want to lay out the keys to understanding how yoga has developed over the past century. First, we can think about the shift in the orientation of yoga that began with Vivekananda in 1893, at the Parliament of the World's Religions at the Chicago World's Fair. Originally, yoga was a philosophically grounded set of practices designed to facilitate spiritual enlightenment, and it was mostly considered the domain of Hindu men. The practice of yoga in ancient India was geared primarily toward the male gender and had as its purpose the control of the body in service of the release of the spirit. Vivekananda's later

Figure 1 Yoga with "props" (author photo)

reinterpretation shifted the focus of yoga toward the promotion of two specific values of the modern world: health and freedom. Health, as Jackson Lears (1981) and others have shown, is a primary goal of the self-development process, which is itself a key feature of the modern world. While all people have always enjoyed being healthy and suffered when health is compromised, not all populations see health as a specific end in itself; that is, while illness is always a marked category, "health" is not. Health is not only a central value of modernity (Dubos 1965; Herzlich 1995), but also a marker for modernity, in the sense that development of nations is measured in part by a series of "health indicators" such as morbidity and mortality rates. A second indicator for national development, as established by the United Nations, the Commonwealth of former British colonies, and such private groups as Amnesty International, is the degree of individual freedom available to private citizens. In order to participate in one of these alliances of theoretically equal and free nation-states, a government must ensure a minimal level of human rights, with personal freedom the most fundamental of these. The presentation of yoga in the Western context was seen as a way to reconnect with the spiritual world, reduce stress, and regain health and freedom – all without having to lose the productive capitalist base upon which Americans and Europeans had staked their futures. As the transformed versions of yoga from Vivekananda and others became popular in India, they fostered similarly transformed notions of the values of health and freedom within the context of global modernity.

Figure 2 Sumit: The Headstand (author photo)

Second, the title "Re-Orienting Yoga" refers to the continuing debate on "Orientalism" begun by the Palistinian critic Edward Said (1979). In his book of the same name, Said discusses the problem of a Western colonial power, such as Great Britain or France, reducing members of a colonized Asian society to a stereotypical or "essentialized" character. The tendency to reduce an Oriental or Asian "Other" to a singular essence (e.g. "Spiritual India") is not new. However, I suggest that the study of yoga ideology and practice provides an excellent example of how essentialized images have been used by the colonized people themselves, as a way of literally re-forming the physical body and ideological make-up of both colonizer and colonized.[6] Yoga offered an indigenous strategy for both the physical training to generate the bodily strength necessary to reclaim India after centuries of colonial rule, and also a model of the mental fortitude needed by anyone who wanted to effect change in his or her world. The power and flexibility of the yoga philosophy itself allowed Vivekananda to turn one simplified set of ideas and practices to two very different ends: the spiritual awaking of the Western public, and the spiritual rejuvenation of the Indian people.

The third way that this volume demonstrates the re-orientation of yoga can be seen in the literal fact of recirculation of ideas and practices from one place on our planet to another, and back. The modern period is increasingly characterized by the rapid dissemination of people, goods, ideas, images, and practices around the globe.[7] However, the majority of studies which address these transnational phenomena focus on flows from a center or "core" of political/economic power, usually somewhere in the West, to a "peripheral" locale (Wallerstein 1974). But yoga, originating in India, is now widely recognized and practiced in relatively mainstream and globally available settings, such as youth clubs or public adult education programs in the United States or Canada. In India, yoga's popularity has followed on the heels of its Western dissemination; in some sense, though it had not actually "left" India, yoga was nevertheless "re-Oriented."

Yoga and the "Pizza Effect"

Anthropology, as Appadurai (1988a) reminds us, is replete with concepts that have become metonymous with specific locales or regions; caste in India illustrates this phenomenon well.[8] Some places have become so thoroughly identified with particular ideologies, practices, or types of social structure, that although those features of the sociocultural landscape may be present elsewhere, the ethnographic researcher or interested observer/practitioner feels compelled to go to that original place in order to obtain an "authentic" perspective on the subject.[9] But as Bharati (1970) demonstrates, many objects, processes or ideas that are generally identified as the product of a particular people, culture or place, such as pizza for Italy, were in fact developed or elaborated upon in a very different context, or by very different people than those who supposedly originated the thing in question. Bharati uses the "pizza effect" to demonstrate how the neo-Hindu renaissance itself was constituted in large part through the efforts and influence of people living outside of India. Similarly, Raheja (1996) demonstrates that the modern constitution of "caste" in India was to some extent an artifact of efforts by the British Raj to map out the system they perceived, rather than the actual relationships that existed among members of Indian society. Yoga, as a metonym for spirituality more broadly taken, also retains this artifactual status; its contemporary definition and practice reflects more about modern transnational cultural flows than pristine ancient traditions. One of the central figures in the redefinition of yoga was Vivekananda.

Vivekananda's presentation of yoga to the Western public, and his subsequent re-presentation of yoga to his countrymen in India four years later,[10] marks a turning point in the way this ancient system of ideas and practices has been understood (B.S. Miller 1996). Poised between worlds, Vivekananda drew on both his experiences as a privileged child of the Kolkata elite (the *bhadralok*, or "respectable people"), a well-educated son of a judge, and his commitment to Sri Ramakrishna, devotee of the Goddess and Hindu exemplar-saint for the alienated middle-class youth of Kolkata (Sarkar 1992). Since Vivekananda's time (1863–1902), the term yoga has taken on a life of its own, coming to signify everything from the "Wonder that was India" (Basham 1954) to a method for universal salvation.

Modern yoga, as represented in the writings of Swami Vivekananda at the end of the nineteenth century, is a transnational cultural product. While anthropologists may argue about the centrality of caste for understanding India, the primary trait many people, both non-Indian and Indian alike, imagine as quintessentially Indian is spirituality, often contrasted with the West's stereotypical materialism (R.G. Fox 1989). Another way to understand this attribute is to call it "spiritual capital," a specific type of cultural capital (Bourdieu 1977, 1984; Gouldner 1979) that serves much the same function as standard economic understandings of capital: to support a "good life," however defined (Baritz 1989). Yoga, then, can be understood as a practical method for acquiring spiritual capital. But it can also be understood as a commodity that has value as a bodily technique; yoga can be customized for distribution to specific target audiences. By examining the variable life goals and priorities of both Indian and non-Indian householders and renouncers (those who have joined a monastic community and relinquished the ties of worldly social life and possessions) who share common knowledge and practices of Sivananda's yoga, this research contributes to an ongoing discussion of the relationship between religious ideology and practice and everyday visions of the good life in South Asia (Kumar 1987; Madan 1987), as well as the relationship between India and the Euro-American West.

Rather than trying to represent every version of yoga practice now existing, an impossible task, I instead focus on the *sampradaya*, or ideological community, deriving from the teachings of Swami Sivananda of Rishikesh. Sivananda used Vivekananda's division of the yoga tradition into four major orientations: *Raja* (typically associated with the classical yoga of Patanjali – the "king" of yogas, utilizing techniques of moral, physical, and mental discipline); *Bhakti* (the path love or devotion), *Jnana* (the path of knowledge or intellectual learning); and *Karma* (the path of work or selfless service to others) as the basis for most of his own writings about yoga. He also used Vivekananda's organizations, the Rama-krishna Mission and the Vedanta Societies in the West, as models for his own Divine Life Society in Rishikesh. Born in 1887, Sivananda left his body in 1963,[11] but his writings and disciples continue to transmit the version of yoga practice he promoted. However, in his original crest and motto for the DLS, Sivananda links all of Vivekananda's categories into "Serve, Love, Meditate, Realize" – equivalent to the *Karma, Bhakti, Raja,* and *Jnana* yogas.[12] It is important to note that none of these variants of yoga were "invented" by Vivekananda; rather, what Vivekananda did (and Sivananda further popularized) was to crystallize many different philosophical paths (from hundreds of years of textual traditions) into four key categories (the names of which existed previously) that could be offered to a public eager for practical instruction in spiritual progress.

As proponents of yoga in the global context, Swamis Vivekananda and Sivananda were both well aware of contemporary Euro-American scholarship as well as traditional Hindu thought (Divine Life Society 1985a; Raychaudhuri 1989: 229), but they were also inescapably immersed in the colonial context of the nationalist struggle in India. The particular combination of ideas used initially by Vivekananda in his presentation of yoga reflects an eclectic mix of various traditional Hindu texts ranging from the Bhagavad Gita to Tantrism and Buddhism, from *Advaita* Vedanta to the more dualist classical yoga of Patanjali, as well as European ideas about rationality, charity, equality, and individualism.[13] Vivekananda used *Advaita*, or non-dualist, understandings of the nature of divinity to ground his version of yoga. The *Advaita* tradition was more easily aligned with Christianity and other monotheistic traditions familiar to his non-Indian audiences.[14]

In addition to having specific theoretical agendas relating to universal spirituality and global unity, Vivekananda and, to an even greater extent Sivananda, focused attention on the notion of "practice" (*abhyas* in Hindi). Practice is indeed central to understanding the role yoga has come to play in the lives of its advocates; it entails both the bodily enactment of yoga ideology as well as the specific physical postures and methods for breathing described in the many texts.[15] The first question I was asked by nearly everyone, male or female, Indian or not, practitioner or not, was "What is your practice?".[16] Helena Wulff reports a parallel experience in her comprehensive study of transnational ballet culture, suggesting that a "central dichotomy in the ballet world is the one separating the act of doing ballet from watching ballet" (Wulff 1998: 8). Although ballet is generally thought of as a performing art that by definition includes some kind of audience, and yoga is considered to be more of a personal practice, the transformation of yoga from the student-disciple mode of earlier centuries into the public activities of classes and even competitions has made these parallels even more compelling. For yoga practitioners, the benefits gained through yoga practice can be fully understood only by someone who shares those practices, just as the aesthetic and painful experiences of ballet are shared only by dancers. Although there are a plethora of classical texts on the philosophy of yoga, and countless popular "how-to" guides for all levels of aspiring yogis, yoga remains a form of embodied knowledge, which no amount of reading or telling can impart.[17] Only actual bodily engagement – "doing yoga" – can provide the sensory and muscular memories that are essential to realizing the benefits of this practice. Indeed, I argue that yoga provides an increasingly widespread "*technique du corps*" (Mauss 1973[1936]: bodily techniques) for coping with the stresses of everyday life under the terms of late modernity. In this sense, yoga fills the same role as many other bodily practices, such as aerobics, jogging, tai chi, or organized sports.

Nota Bene: Terms of Representation

A couple of caveats are in order here: First, my discussants use the broad term "yoga" to refer to their own application of *yoga-darsana* to daily life, through both physical *hatha* yoga practices and general outlook.[18] For them, this entails the adoption of a particular attitude, or "somatic mode of attention" (Csordas 1993) toward a given set of practices: focusing one's concentration on the activity in question, not allowing the mind to stray, not worrying about external perceptions of the action, but only about the process of carrying it out. I follow their usage, taking "yoga" as a general term, specifying only if reference to particular aspects of the tradition is meant. Second, in specific portions of this book, I have used an essentializing shorthand, contrasting "the West" with "India." While quite aware of the hornet's nest such a tactic will likely provoke, I find it equally problematic to ignore the active use of this dichotomy by the people whose lives and writings I describe.

Although Said and others' concern for the hegemony of Orientalist discourse is well placed, we need to bear in mind that the story is more complex than that alone might suggest; a volume on Occidentalism edited by James Carrier (1995) attests to the importance of understanding the mutual implications of such dichotomizing discourse. One cannot define the situation simply in terms of being "for" or "against" Orientalism as Said defines it. Rather, it is important to realize that the oppositional pairing of India and the West has been used to strategic advantage (Spivak 1988, 1993) by many prominent Indians over the past century.[19] The "Orientophilia" of various Western intellectuals was put to good use by Asian intellectuals, many of whom had, like Gandhi and Tagore, spent a considerable amount of time abroad. As van der Veer (1994:133) points out, "there was not a one-way imposition of Orientalist discourse on Asian realities, but rather an intense intellectual interaction between Orientalists and Indian scholars." These intellectuals were perhaps more like each other than like their fellow countrymen (Shils 1961).[20]

Further, this Eastern monolith has often been characterized, by both lay and academic commentators, by its spirituality as against the materialism of the West (R.G. Fox 1989; McKean 1996; Spencer 1995). As a member of this group, Swami Vivekananda very deliberately represented yoga and the Vedantic tradition as India's gift to the West, for which monetary assistance to aid the poverty stricken Indian masses would be a most appropriate exchange (Raychaudhuri 1989:

242–249). In his address to the citizens of Kolkata upon returning from his first journey to the West, Vivekananda asked his fellow Indians to join his cause: "we must go out, exchange our spirituality for anything they have to give us: for the marvels of the region of spirit we will exchange the marvels of the region of matter" (Vivekananda 1990c:109).

Vivekananda's emphasis on universal spirituality had much to do with his interests in resolving inequities at the national (caste) and international (colonialism) levels; in a similar fashion, the adoption of his approach by non-Indians in the nineteenth century seems to have been driven to a great extent by concern for class inequities and social problems. But by the 1950s, after the threat of global destruction made possible by the atomic bomb had been clearly understood, Sivananda's message of universal spirituality took on an urgency related less to nationalist and more to global concerns. In both cases, these swamis used an essentialized vision of India to promote a particular modern and ecumenical cause, and to ignore their own usage seems more problematic to me than to expose it for analytic review.

Modern Yoga: Seeking Health and Freedom

With Foucault (1984), I see modernity as an attitude, a society's way of relating to the world. More specifically, I define modernity as a critical mode of engagement in the world – a "project" – that assumes that unlimited progress is both possible and desirable. As a way of approaching the world, modernity directs our attention to certain key values, among them freedom and health. The pursuit of these values occurs, especially in what have been termed "late" or "reflexive" modernities, between two poles: the seemingly opposed trends toward individualization and globalization (U. Beck et al. 1994). Such a vision of modernity acquires its shape through both the reflexive project of the individual self as well as the increasing tendency toward globalization. Over the course of the nineteenth and twentieth centuries, that is, during the transition from early to late modernity, concern with personal health and freedom shifted direction, from serving the interests of the nation to fulfilling the more universal or global agenda which developed in the aftermath of World War II. While these are concepts that are debated in highest levels of philosophical discourse (what is a good life?), for an ordinary person-in-the-world, health and freedom must always be understood in the contexts of local cultures and communities. The perceived benefits of modernity – health, happiness, leisure (Chatterjee 1986:86) – together comprise the increased standard of living that is the expected result of increased productivity through the widespread use of technology and the extensive control of human and other natural resources. Such changes in the standards of comfort were in large part the reason for Gandhi's opposition to modern technology, for he was justly concerned that such expectations of comfort would lead to increased desires and demands, with no end in sight and no way to pay the piper.[21]

The classical social theories of Marx, Weber, and Durkheim described the distinction between traditional and modern societies, and analyzed the social, economic, and political structures that constituted them. But this stark opposition fails to explain much of what we encounter in the contemporary world, where "modernization" projects have been seen to both succeed and fail beyond the expectations of their architects, leaving in their wake entirely different modernities for which the dichotomy of the modern and the traditional has outlived its utility. Instead of examining yoga from the perspective of a "traditional" set of ideas and practices being adopted by "modern" societies, I choose to view the situation as one of alternative modernities, here seen as many "fractured" and perpetual projects (Joshi 2001) reflecting a range of different aspirations. As Knauft (2003: 22) has so eloquently stated, "modernity as a concept is fraught with difficulties, especially in the singular." Yet one can go too far in localizing or regionalizing modernity, losing sight of its still-relevant origins in Western notions of progress and development. In this book, I join many other anthropologists and social theorists in trying to avoid the reification of modernity as a monolithic force, while retaining the impact of its collective past on the yearnings of people living in the present and future.

This effort to reframe what is meant by "modernity" is crucial, because the currently popular way of understanding the transmission of yoga as a unilineal trajectory from (traditional) India to the (modern) West does not permit the complexity of the production of yoga as an explicitly transnational project spanning the period since the 1890s, as described in this book. These various modernities, in India as well as across the West, have exchanged visions of health and freedom with each other, with the actual results in each case dependent upon the particular constellation of participants and histories for a given locale over a specific period of time.

Health has become one of the primary markers for development images of modernity, a way of measuring the progress of development programs. Within the realm of general health indicators are more specialized evaluations, such as those based on the epidemiological transition theory of Omran (1971) and others. Modernization theorists consider causes of death, such as infectious disease, chronic disease, or "lifestyle" diseases (Huss-Ashmore et al. 1991), in order to determine how "modern" a country has become.

Health and freedom therefore became the symbolic cart by means of which yoga could be brought to new audiences in the United States and Europe, as well as to those newly reacquainted with it in India. For the Western audience, the appeal lay in the presentation of a universal spiritual framework that was non-exclusive, "scientific" (testable through personal practice), and seemingly universal. For Indians, yoga was emblematic of a revered precolonial past; it offered not only ideas and practices, but also heroes and success stories, that could be applied to the rising nationalist project. Additionally, yoga offered the kind of physical training that could provide the means to stand tall. As Vivekananda (1990c) pointed out, political freedom depends on moral fortitude, or the "backbone" to stand tall. As a subjugated population, colonial India had lost both its physical and its moral strength, and yoga – rather that British physical training – was the ticket to independence. Yoga therefore offered both a way of being in the world and a system of practices. Reproduced by individual actors, yoga has also been perpetuated by means of written and photographic records. It provides one very good method for achieving the goal of self-development in a global world. Through yoga, the individual attempts to take charge of both body and consciousness, simultaneously focusing the mind and flexing the body.

Sites and Subjects: Methodological Concerns

What constitutes health or freedom for a given person, and how do such perceived states of being relate to everyday practices or broader life goals? Are understandings of personal well-being linked in any way to other social relationships extending beyond the person? How do such understandings differ across cultures? Questions like these first brought me to India to investigate how ideas and practices of health maintenance were represented in the everyday lives of visitors, townspeople, and ashram residents in an Himalayan town. In addition to its long-standing history as a major Hindu pilgrimage site on the banks of the holy Ganga River, Rishikesh has been proclaimed by the state of Uttar Pradesh and the Government of India to be "the place to go for yoga,"[22] as well as the base for a number of adventure tourism organizations which take aspiring trekkers and white water rafters to the higher reaches of the Himalayan rivers and peaks.

Initially, I saw the study of yoga practice as a contribution to understanding the relationship between the householders who came to visit the ashram and the monks and spiritual students who lived there, as well as a way to use a specific set of bodily practices and their accompanying millennia-old textual tradition to understand how such philosophically based ideologies are actually enacted in everyday life. I assumed that the practice of yoga by these people was linked to their quest for health and a generally better life. I therefore expected to focus on the relationship between concepts of physical health and other levels of health – mental, social, spiritual, or however people wanted to define them.

I did not expect to be examining the way that the West took up the idea of yoga, nor did I expect to consider the way that American and German ideas about freedom and well-being would intersect with Hindu ideas of *samsara* (the cycle of worldly life), *karma* (universal causality of actions), *dharma* (duty), and *moksha* (liberation from all of the preceding, which can be achieved through the practice of yoga).[23] As originally conceived, my research project assumed the usual conditions of ethnographic research: a geographically and culturally circumscribed field site and community. Yet, the extremely mobile situation I found in Rishikesh, as well as the responses of my discussants and the ubiquitous media representations of yoga I encountered in India and the West, influenced me to depart from some of the more usual paths anthropologists have followed.

Because both Vivekananda and Sivananda were educated, middle-class professionals who used English as the primary medium for disseminating their teachings, their ideas were most available to a narrowly defined but internationally distributed population. Today, yoga seems to appeal primarily to the educated or professional middle classes of both India and the West, and as a result, the majority of my discussants are from socioeconomic and educational backgrounds similar to my own: politically liberal, highly educated, and "cosmopolitan" in Hannerz's (1992: 252–255) sense, with sufficient interest and discretionary income to travel regularly. Who, then, might I identify as the Other so often sought in anthropological research? Though I came to India thinking that I would study only the Indians who lived in Sivananda's ashram, I quickly learned that such a study, though possible, would not be sufficient to describe the linked communities of middle-class Westerners and Indians whose lives in Rishikesh were centered on yoga practice.

In addition, since my research sites form a network emanating from a hub in Rishikesh out to linked organizations and individuals from New Delhi to Switzerland, Germany, and North America, I found the question of distinguishing a "field site" in the traditional sense of the term a bit problematic. Instead, I followed a network of personal and institutional leads that makes any location into "the field."[24] Such an approach works well with the kind of data available in the contemporary world of multifaceted transnational cultural flows. Rishikesh was the primary field site, and the locus for most of my ethnographic research. However, the time I spent in several other locations, often with the same people in more than one place, enhanced my understanding of the network of Sivananda yoga practitioners immensely. While multi-sited research was not evenly distributed across field sites, this type of project still required a different approach to the concept of "the field" (Amit 2000; Strauss 2000).

One key example can be seen in the problematic category of the "field language." The use of a "local" language, which usually constitutes one of the hallmarks of anthropological fieldwork, was itself an issue. Although I had prepared extensively, studying Hindi for four years before my year in India, and I fully expected to make use of that training, I found that the translocal politics of language use resulted in an almost equal utilization of Hindi, English and German. Because Sivananda was born in the southern state of Tamilnadu, many of the

Indian residents of the ashram, as well as visitors, spoke Tamil or Malayalam as a first language. Although most spoke Hindi as well or better than I, the north–south politics of India, as well as the class concerns of many highly educated Indians, dictated that we spoke English together.

After my initial year of fieldwork based in Rishikesh – reflecting the traditional requisite of non-Western research to qualify for the anthropology PhD at an American university – I pursued ethnographic research in a range of contexts across Germany, Switzerland, and the United States for another fifteen months, making research trips of one to three weeks from my home in Zurich. This "home-base" in the center of Europe allowed me to see yoga centers around the continent, as well as to visit people whom I had first met in Rishikesh at their own homes in Germany and Switzerland. "My home," I say, because it was where I spent most of my days and nights, yet during that time most of my worldly possessions were in storage in three different places in the United States. My husband and I, academic migrant laborers, lived out of suitcases and backpacks for three years. Like many of the people you will meet in these pages, our professional practice took us to many different places, but in each, we found like-minded others with whom to share life.[25] One question I explore here is how anthropology can incorporate the recognition that we are all, to one degree or another, now cosmopolitans in Rabinow's (1986) sense. We cannot place Others in a restricted locale, while we as ethnographers have the freedom to roam. That much has been clear for quite a while now, at least since the mid-1980s and the publication of Clifford and Marcus's *Writing Culture* (1986), the volume in which Rabinow's discussion of cosmopolitans appeared. Appadurai has also worked to define the parameters of a new "cosmopolitan ethnography" (1996:52) which offers a new take on the old subject of micro–macro relations, highlighting the ways that the global and the local are ever intertwined and implicated in each other's pasts and futures. In 2000 a special issue of the journal *Public Culture* (no. 32) took this idea further, suggesting that "the nature of the late twentieth-century nationalism, multi-culturalism, and the globalization of late liberalism has created a new historical context for reconsidering concepts of cosmopolitanism" (Pollock et al. 2000:583).

Seeking Direction: Locating Cosmopolitans in the Field(s)

Cosmopolitan ethnography demands new ways of thinking about "the field," and of actually doing fieldwork. I have come to think about the ways that my field experience developed in relation to a pair of linked concepts. These concepts help define the rather amorphous and sometimes ephemeral spaces – spheres of activity – within which I conducted ethnographic research, and allow me to begin to map out the ways in which individuals, institutions, communities, ideas, practices, and objects interacted in ways that made possible the transformation of yoga over the past century. The term I want to propose for such a "sphere of activity" is a *matrix.* A matrix is comprised of two or more intersecting *vectors.* Drawing on the language of mathematics and physics, a *vector* is defined as a quantity having the properties of both direction and magnitude – force, mass, substance of any sort (Oxford Desk Dictionary); the standard definition of a matrix is a "vector of vectors," that is, an array of intersecting directional forces, each with its own observable characteristics. In the context of ethnographic practice, *vectors can be understood as directional forces capable of transporting ideas, practices, objects or actors along specific pathways.*

A matrix, then, is a set of linked or intersecting vectors. Matrices are by definition multidimensional, but the degree of dimensionality is infinite, as are, potentially, the boundaries of the matrix. The dimensions of a matrix are determined only by the number and scope of the vectors that comprise it. With these terms, we have a framework for defining non-geographically bounded sites of interactive research – field sites that are not necessarily anywhere, but do take place *somewhere.* The concept of a matrix allows us to describe contingent locations for social interaction, in which actors who call other places "home" meet on regular or irregular bases, and create social worlds that in turn have implications for other arenas of sociocultural life, as well as more permanent locations. In this way, the 1893 and 1993 Parliaments of the World's Religions, in Chicago, as well as yoga retreats in rural Maryland or the Bahamas, or even a chatroom on a yoga-focused website, can be seen as a matrix, a shared frame of reference. A matrix can be virtual, or located in geographically defined space; using the terms vector and matrix, we can define any kind of sociocultural form, without requiring that it have a physical boundary. The matrix is defined not only by the individual actors as one type of vector, but also by institutions, paradigms, products, and any other aspect of sociocultural life that can be described; they are all vectors, because they all have magnitude and direction, both of which can change in interaction with other such forces. Not all vectors have equal force in influencing outcomes, and when thinking about using the language of vector/matrix to describe multi-sited fieldwork, we must recall that matrices, too, are of different magnitudes. Rishikesh, for example, carries more significance in this ethnography than do Zurich or Chicago – precisely because more vectors related to Sivananda intersect in that locus than in the other two.

Using other terms, anthropologists and other social theorists have put forth a number of candidates for describing the shifting terrain of the "postlocal" (Appadurai 1996) world: Clifford (1997), Gupta and Ferguson (1997), and Kaplan (1997) have talked about locations; Appadurai (1996) has described cultures as non-Euclidean fractals comprised of various kinds of flows, escapes, localities, and neighborhoods; Augé (1995) presented the notion of non-place as the product of a supermodernity that has taken over large sectors of the modern world, though not completely displaced it; Martin (1997:145) has suggested several metaphors – citadels, rhizomes and string figures – that contribute to a "toolbox" of potential ways to imagine aspects of the world that can be approached by ethnographic research. Even the widely used idea of "virtual reality" or "virtual community" is part of this trend toward redefinition of old or acknowledgement of new socio-cultural forms.

As I have defined them here, the terms vector and matrix can accommodate most, if not all, of these other concepts. I do not want to use vector and matrix as the building blocks for a mathematical model of the world, nor do I see them strictly as metaphors. Rather, I offer them as a pair of hermeneutic devices that can help us to visualize, describe, and understand the shapeshifting locations in which cosmopolitan ethnography takes place. Some of these locations are ephemeral, while others can more easily be revisited. They are all comprised of constituent units that I call vectors, each having certain identifiable characteristics – histories and futures, beliefs and goals, political, economic, social or ideological power that can be defined relative to each other, whether we are speaking of individual actors, institutions or other entities or objects. These vectors interact in spaces I define as matrices; such matrices are both predictable and accidental, in ways that are shaped by the histories and trajectories of their constituent layers and tangents. Messy entities, these matrices yield infinite numbers of connections, but can of course always be truncated for purposes of analysis; they do not, however, assume bounded units. In the pages that follow, I will discuss the applications and limitations of the vector/matrix concept.

A cozy apartment in Bayreuth, Germany – October, 1993

Karen met me at the Bayreuth train station in the early evening. I had just come from Zurich via Munich, where I had visited the Sivananda Yoga Vedanta Center in the university quarter that afternoon. Karen had been one of my companions during an intensive yoga course in Rishikesh in April, 1992, and she had returned home to Germany the following summer. Before going to India, she had been a student at "The First Yoga School in Germany," started by Swami Sivananda of Rishikesh's disciple-by-mail, Boris Sacharow. Since returning from India, Karen had cut back to three-quarter time at her stressful job as a social worker at a battered women's shelter. Stress is a major part of her life – experiencing it, then trying to relieve it through yoga, diet, playing with her cats, and working in her garden. When she was in India, practicing yoga several hours a day in a structured setting, she felt that her general health was much better than at home, when she had the time and self-discipline only on weekends or random days to practice. In a year or two, she hoped to make another trip to Rishikesh and perhaps to southern India for another yoga course.

The Roller Coaster of Modernity

The ways that individuals interpret and incorporate the kind of textual tradition represented by yoga within their everyday lives affects, and is affected by, the activities and practices that they engage in on a regular basis in order to stay well. Staying well, of course, implies avoiding sickness, whether understood as catching a cold, developing cancer, or something more general. One of the primary umbrella terms for non-specific ill health in the popular imagination, whether of Indians, Germans or Americans, is stress.[26] The notion of stress appears frequently in discussions of the problems of "modern living" (Lehrer and Woolfolk 1993; Young 1980), and so leads us to a review of the anthropology of modernity, where efforts to define the "good life" are linked to questions of personal identity, freedom, manipulation of capital – whether material, symbolic or spiritual – tourism, and other characteristic concerns of modern transnational cultures (Appadurai 1996; Bourdieu 1984; Featherstone et al. 1995; Hannerz 1996). Yoga provides a focus for the intersection of these general theoretical concerns within the context of contemporary south Asia.

Karen, described previously, sees stress as an inevitable result of life under conditions of modernity. Yoga provides her with a way of alleviating stress and the health problems it creates, while allowing her to keep her job and all of its other benefits. Although Karen does not want to give up modern living entirely – nor is that really an option – she is acutely aware of the need to deal with its downside, whose primary symptom is stress. Yoga, as an individual or personal strategy for living under conditions of modernity, supports the concept of "unlimited progress" as self-realization. To "realize" the self is to recognize the complete freedom of the mind, and this recognition is thought then to unleash the extraordinary potential of the healthy body.[27] Note that, as discussed earlier, this definition does not preclude the existence of a multiplicity of modernities.[28]

The Outskirts of Washington, DC – June, 1992

The setting is a stereotypical American yoga class at the local YMCA health club in suburban Maryland. It was the first day of a new session; there were about ten to twelve people, all women except the husband of one. They ranged in age from late twenties to late fifties. When asked what they expected from the class, most referred to "quiet time" or "stress reduction." Some mentioned "flexibility" or "centering." One of the returning students commented that yoga training, especially *pranayama* breathing exercises, had helped her in daily life by allowing her to keep calm at work.

continued

Swami Jayananda, the German-born, green-carded American instructor who had first studied yoga in Rishikesh with Swami Sivananda himself, then asked the class what it meant to be totally physically healthy. The students responded with "to be in condition," "flexible," strong," "have endurance," "have peace of mind." No, Swami Jayananda said – total health is to be unaware of your physical body, a state which could be achieved only by daily practice in using the mind to control bodily responses. Without perseverance in practice, she emphasized, yoga's health benefits could never be realized. I would later see Swami Jayananda and some of her students at a spiritual retreat with Swami Chidananda of the Sivananda Ashram, and in Chicago at the centenary celebration of the 1893 Parliament of the World's Religions.

Sivananda's Yoga: Paths and Practices

At its most general level, evaluation of yoga in an anthropological perspective combines a number of methodological challenges, including how to conduct a multi-site, multilingual ethnographic project, and the integration of experiential with ethnographic, historical, and other textual data. In this book, then, I use many different kinds of data: ethnographic observations and interviews, photography, archival documents, and contemporary media – to move back and forth along the varied pathways which link Rishikesh, India, with assorted other locales around the world. In the following chapters, I examine a variety of evidence for these trans-national flows. Then, using documentation ranging from the publicly available, mass-produced print media representations of yoga in India, Europe and North America (magazines, pocket books, newspapers, etc.) to the privately circulated publications, personal accounts, and websites of the specific yogic tradition of Swami Sivananda and his disciples, I link the specific history of Sivananda in Rishikesh to other presentations of yoga in the twentieth century. Using data collected in India, Europe, and the United States, I explore how the development of Sivananda's yoga has influenced the lives of individuals around the world. Rounding out this analysis of yoga in the public sphere is a discussion of the role personal experience plays in the development of academic representations. The purpose behind presenting this body of data on yoga ideologies and practices from 1893 to 2003 is to demonstrate the relationship between the transnational dissemin-ation of yoga and the changing roles of health and freedom in the ongoing project of modernity. In order to achieve this goal, the book first examines historical relationships through biographical narratives of Vivekananda, Sivananda, and the DLS community, and later moves laterally to explore geographical networks that link the DLS of Rishikesh with other Indian, European, and American yoga practitioners and centers.

In addition to this introduction, the book comprises four main chapters and an afterword. Chapter 2 discusses the mythological and recent history of Rishikesh, India, showing how such a local history has intersected with both the wider history of yoga in this century and the specific life histories of Swamis Vivekananda and Sivananda. Located in the Himalayan foothills, on the banks of the sacred Ganga, Rishikesh's unique geography has made it a popular destination for pilgrims and tourists, as well as saints and scholars. Vivekananda and Sivananda's ideological and organizational legacies are placed in the historical context of Indian nationalism and Independence, World War II, and the rapidly changing global situation since the 1950s.

Chapter 3 focuses on Rishikesh in the early 1990s, examining yoga practice at the original Sivananda Ashram and DLS Headquarters, as well as at a small yoga center run by a former Sivananda Ashram resident and yoga teacher who left the Sivananda Ashram primarily because of a methodological dispute about proper yoga techniques. The yoga methods of another Rishikesh swami, formerly the director of a major ashram run by one of Sivananda's most famous Indian disciples in the West, are also discussed. By assessing the place of yoga practices within their more general pursuit of health and the "good life," I explore the idea that the unified purpose and practice suggested by yoga's textual tradition cannot be assumed. Rather, the Indian and non-Indian practitioners understand and use yoga in different ways. The decision to learn yoga in Rishikesh is for many a decision to engage in a process that transforms the self; although these individuals may return home to a very different local community and environment, the act of participating in the Rishikesh community of yoga practitioners has implications for their practice at home as well. The notion of "oasis regimes" (Strauss 1999) as described below becomes especially important in this context, as does Bourdieu's (1977) notion of habitus as a way of understanding the mutual shaping of self and sociocultural environment through practice.

The detailed ethnographic study of yoga as both practice and ideology offers an opportunity to differentiate between Indian and Western styles of self-development; the personalized meaning attributed to a given individual's *yogabhyas* (yoga practice) can shed light on notions of health, flexibility, and freedom.

Following the network out from its Rishikesh hub, Chapter 4 pursues the trajectories of a few of Sivananda's disciples as they have scattered through India and around the world since the 1950s. The fundamental problematic of this chapter is one of methodology – how to approach the task of conducting a multi-site ethnographic project. I first look out from Rishikesh, following the track of some of Sivananda's disciples to their new or associated institutions in Europe and North America, and then look back to India, where these same disciples have "re-oriented" their institutions. Reversing the flow, I revisit India with several discussants at their homes in Germany to explore the value of a trip to Rishikesh. Several individuals who were interviewed in Rishikesh during 1992 discuss the importance of their trip to India for their yoga practice at home, and compare the approaches and attitudes toward yoga in India and their own neighborhoods.

Chapter 5 moves us from 1993 to 2003. In this chapter, I review how several different mass-media representations of yoga offer ample evidence that "health" and a "healthy lifestyle" are highly valued and culturally variable commodities which are pursued with vigor in India, Germany, and the United States. The media's constitution of yoga as a desirable health practice capitalizes on the promotion of such classic, essentializing dichotomies as body/mind and the spiritual East/material West. However, differential uses of such dichotomies by the Indian, German, and American print media have been driven by specific assumptions about their respective national audiences. I examine how a wide array of print media use the modern concern for personal development of the mind and body to play upon the local, national, and global concerns of their various audiences. I then return to the stories of several individuals whom I had first encountered in the early 1990s, to see how their stories have continued to evolve, building on the networks of people and institutions that grew out from a base in Rishikesh.

Finally, in the afterword, I explore the uses of the World Wide Web in supporting the continued transnational production of Sivananda's yoga.

Yoga, with its origins on the subcontinent, has become a bodily idiom that resonates with the needs and experiences of people across many different cultural and national contexts, and reflect on the methodological shifts necessitated by such a diffuse body of data. Here, I document the ways in which Swami Sivananda of Rishikesh's ideas about yoga have, through the efforts of specific individuals and in association with particular places, developed into a unique, elaborated, and transmissible version of yoga. No longer a set of religious ideologies and ascetic practices belonging only to a relatively small group of specialists on the Indian subcontinent, yoga has also become part of the contemporary repertoire of men and women at all life stages and in many different countries. This modern transformation represents a shift from a regional, specialized religious discourse and practice geared toward liberation of the self from the endless cycle of lives, to a transnational, secular, socially critical ideology and practice aimed at freedom to achieve personal well-being. Sivananda's yoga is here presented as one interesting example, among many that could have been selected, of the historically specific transnational trajectories followed during the last century by a set of ideas and practices from a former European colony, around the world, and back again to the modern nation-state of India.

–2–

Lives and Histories: Rishikesh, Sivananda, and the Divine Life Society

Rishikesh, India – January, 1992

The "deluxe" bus lurched along the Hardwar Road, carrying us from the dry, flat landscape of the Gangetic plain north of Delhi to the abrupt topography of Rishikesh and the lush first reaches of the Himalayan range. We arrived just after dawn. Pink and yellow rays of cool morning sun reflected off the smooth surface of Ganga Ma, the River Ganges, as we climbed down from the bus onto the sandy beach by the river. A few *scooterwalas* stood by their three-wheeled vehicles, and several men milled around a makeshift tea stall, sipping from steaming cups. Gathering up our large collection of luggage, the "needful" for a year of field research in northern India, my husband and I surveyed the scene. Across the river to the east, we noted the long line of brightly painted buildings and temples comprising the Swaragashram district, known for its numerous ashrams and *dharamsalas* (rest houses) catering to both serious religious renunciants and travelers on the way to mountain pilgrimage destinations. Beyond the buildings, forested hills shimmered gray-green in the light breeze. Downstream, in the shallows by the many concrete *ghats* (landing places), men and boys bathed in the sacred water. Others, both male and female, sat or walked along the banks; some were engaged in prayer or meditation, while others dressed or combed their hair. We had spent less than a week in Delhi, but it was a great relief to get out of the city. Walking away from the dieseling buses, the predominant sensation was one of profound peace. Everything I had read or heard about Rishikesh as the "place of saints and sages" suddenly made sense as I breathed deeply of the crisp, clean air, purging the red-black residue of city grit from my body. The peace was short-lived, however, as we began to contemplate how to stuff our bodies and our luggage into one of these tiny, semi-enclosed scooters. Fieldwork had begun.

Locating Rishikesh: Situated Lives, Intersecting Histories

In Chapter 1, I introduced yoga as a transnationally generated and globally recognized set of bodily practices, and suggested that we could use yoga to explore how the values of health and freedom have developed over the past century. Rishikesh is a place where one of the most important streams in the transnational distribution of yoga has its origins. In this chapter, my goal is to situate the yoga practices I recorded and experienced in Rishikesh, and explore how that specific place has itself become entwined in the life histories of particular individuals whose lives and legacies have had a significant impact on the practice of yoga worldwide. I begin with the mythology and history of Rishikesh town and the surrounding districts, detailing something of the physical and cultural geography as well as the sequence of significant events that shaped the region. Following this brief introduction, I present an equally brief overview of the yoga tradition, providing an understanding of how the histories of Rishikesh and yoga practices have grown together. I then show how the lives of Swamis Vivekananda and especially Sivananda came to be woven into the tapestry of yoga practice in Rishikesh and subsequently, exported to the wider world.

The rivers and forests of the Himalayan foothills are home to many of the major figures in Hindu mythology. In particular, the regions known as Garhwal and Kumaun, stretching westward approximately 250 kilometers from the western border of present-day Nepal, have a rich tradition of famous inhabitants. Called Kedarkhand – the abode of the God Siva – in the classical Hindu mythological tradition, the eight hill districts (which until 2000 were a part of the state of Uttar Pradesh) are also referred to as Uttarakhand, the northern abode. These hill districts contained approximately 5 per cent of the Uttar Pradesh (UP) population and 90 per cent of its natural resources (Bisht 1982), leaving the local people in a neo-colonial relationship with their southern neighbors. A separatist movement waxed and waned in the region for decades, calling for economic and political autonomy to rectify extreme resource and population inequities. By 2000, the movement finally reached fruition and the new Indian state of Uttaranchal was born (Figure 3).

In addition to its rich natural features, the region is replete with spiritual wealth: the Ganga and Yamuna rivers, spiritual as well as material resources, originate high in the Himalayan glaciers at the northern borders of Uttarakhand. In this region were said to have lived the great sages Vyasa and Vashistha, as well as the Pandava brothers, heroes of the great Indian epic, the *Mahabharata* (Bisht 1982). Here, too, "came Rama and his brother, to do penance for the death of the demon-king, Ravana,"[1] as described in the other major epic of India, the *Ramayana.* Today, as in the past, when one follows the Ganga up from the plains of Uttar Pradesh toward the Himalaya, the first place at which the transition from flatlands to mountains becomes truly evident is at Rishikesh town, just north of the well-known pilgrimage town of Hardwar, in the Garhwal.

"Without the Ganga, Rishikesh would be just another stinking north Indian town!" The speaker of these words is a middle-aged south Indian swami who lives in a two-star hotel in Rishikesh town, gets up at 4.30 a.m. for meditation and prayer, and loves to watch sports and old movies on TV. Rishikesh is indeed an odd

Figure 3 Map of India, showing Uttaranchal and Rishikesh

place – both a busy regional market town for the rural Garhwal hill villages and a spiritual marketplace for the world. The name Rishikesh has several possible origins: "Hrishikesh" is one of the many names for the great god Vishnu,[2] who was said to have appeared there, but it could also simply refer to the many *rishis* (seers, sages) and yogis who have populated the banks of the Ganga here for so long. Geographically, the region lies at the edge of the Terai, the somewhat wet sector (60 inches average annual rainfall) of the Siwalik hills which was, up until the 1940s or 1950s a breeding ground for malaria and other tropical diseases, as well as for elephant, tiger, and other large animals. This is one of the few places in north India where wild elephants can still be seen regularly, and in fact an elephant migration corridor between Rishikesh and Dehra Dun has been established and protected, with management facilities at the Rajaji National Wildlife Sanctuary, halfway between Rishikesh and Hardwar. At an altitude of 356 meters above sea level, Rishikesh is not quite high enough to qualify as a hill station, one of the summer outposts of the British Raj, where first the British colonists and now the urban Indian elite have come to escape the heat of the plains. Still, the climate is less extreme than either the dry, hot plains below or the snowy mountains above.

The river dominates the town, providing cool breezes even during the hottest days of summer.

Many Hindus make the trip from their village or town to Hardwar, at the edge of the plains, to bring the bones of their fathers for consecration in the Ganga (Gold 1990), to bathe away their sins, or to worship the goddess Ganga Ma at the evening Arati ceremony, a daily tribute to the power of the river goddess. But until the completion of the rail lines in 1930, few except the most hardy pilgrims undertook the perils of a journey 15 miles further to Rishikesh. Still fewer went onwards to points north. Rishikesh was, and continues to be, the embarkation point for the pilgrimage routes to the Char Dham, the four holy places of the Garhwal: Kedarnath, Badrinath, Gangotri (source of the Ganga river) and Yamunotri (source of the Yamuna river). Badrinath, one of the four cardinal holy sites on the spiritual map of India, is a major pilgrimage destination, though until the advent of the motor coach pilgrimage in the early 1980s, it remained an unfulfilled obligation for most. The footpath leading from Hardwar to the high shrines was converted to a passable road beginning in the 1820s, and thereafter, small medical dispensaries were established along the pilgrimage route (Bahadur 1992 [1916]:235).

But as recreational tourism in India increased during the 1970s and 1980s, Rishikesh became more than simply a pilgrimage location. By 1990, according to some sources, over half of all of the tourists visiting India from abroad stopped in Rishikesh (Sangi 1990:488), whether as a primary destination or on the way to the mountains for trekking or whitewater rafting. In 1990, the UP Tourist Office in Rishikesh recorded approximately 7600 visitors, of whom two-thirds were Indian; figures for 1992 at the time of my departure in November looked as if they would be quite comparable. The 1991 figures were much lower, but cannot be compared because the Gulf War created unusual travel circumstances for many people.

Though the geographical region within which Rishikesh lies figures prominently in Hindu literary and religious texts and traditions, little has been written about the recent history of Rishikesh. We know that an assortment of rulers controlled Garhwal from the first millennium BC (Bahadur 1992). Like other parts of north India, the region became Buddhist under the emperor Ashoka in the third century BC, and was then converted back to Hinduism under the influence of the great sage Shankara in the eighth century AD. The Garhwal region was the site of a number of battles with the Kingdom of Nepal throughout the middle centuries of this millennium. From sometime in the thirteenth century, a temple was maintained by priests in the service of the ruler of Tehri, a few dozen kilometers to the north. Still in existence as the Bharat Temple, this shrine was located near the Ganga in what would become central Rishikesh town. It is said that not even the priest would reside there, because of the threat of illness and harm from wild animals (Basnet et al. 1992). The marginalized status of Rishikesh continued until the latter part of the nineteenth century.

Under British rule, from the eighteenth into the twentieth centuries, the region around Rishikesh was divided into three districts: the native state of Tehri-Garhwal, British Garhwal, and Dehra Dun, which was also under British control. Rishikesh as a distinctive location is not indicated in the 1901 version of the Gazetteer of India, although several other towns in the area are detailed. The Ganga at Rishikesh formed the boundary for the three districts, but there were not enough people at that location to identify it as a village – only a few isolated huts and ashrams.[3]

The first direct reference to a place called Rishikesh that I have been able to locate in the administrative or non-religious literature comes in Bahadur's volume, *Garhwal: Ancient and Modern* (1992[1916]:152). Very little data concerning the administration and activities of the town now known as Rishikesh are available until the mid-twentieth century. Religious records and oral traditions, however, yield somewhat more information. By 1880, Kailash Ashram, the first of the large ashrams to be situated in Rishikesh, was said to have been founded (Basnet et al. 1992). Prior to that time, we hear only of the existence of individual seekers and small groups of disciples who congregated on the banks of the Ganga there, and of pilgrims who stopped by at the *dharamsalas* on their way to the high shrines. As mentioned in Chapter 1, the Government of India Tourist Office and the Uttar Pradesh regional offices based their promotion of Rishikesh as "the place to go for yoga" on the image of a beautiful mountain retreat nestled by the banks of the most sacred river in India. The Himalayan mountains of north India were considered from earliest times to be the abode of not just Siva, but all the Hindu gods and goddesses, themselves mere manifestations of the Supreme power of the Universe, and therefore an ideal place to seek realization of oneness with that Universal Self. The mountains, with their cool air and sparse population, provided a stark contrast to the hot, dusty, populous plains. As Bahadur comments,

In the whole length and breadth of India, the land of Garhwal with its manifold beauties alone could appeal to the minds of the earlier Rishis of India that here with such climate, scenery, and solitude, they could develop a very peculiar civilization in which the spiritual and the mental got the upperhand of the physical and which would defy the ravages of time . . . the goal of the Rishis of yore was only to hold communion with the Infinite existence, the transcendental mind, and thus enjoy supreme bliss. From this high level of thought, the present sacred literature of the Hindus was derived and handed down to posterity, i.e., science, poetry, astronomy, physics, history and mythology, etc. All these are detailed in the Mahabharata, composed by Vyas Muni in this land. Thus Garhwal stands a landmark in the history of the spiritual and secular civilization of India, like a giant primeval tree, spreading its branches on all sides to the nooks and corners of India and losing all of its top in the Himalayas, the fairest without a rival. (Bahadur 1992[1916]: 49–50)

We see that Bahadur makes use of the dichotomy between the "spiritual" and the "physical" to highlight the value of the Garhwal region for the entire history of India, a sentiment that echoes throughout the past few centuries. One of the most interesting manifestations of this generally accepted vision of Garhwal relates to the settlement of Rishikesh town following Independence from Great Britain in 1947 and the decision to separate Muslims from Hindus.

When India achieved Independence, one of the major sticking points was the decision regarding borders for the new countries of India (predominantly Hindu) and Pakistan (predominantly Muslim). The repercussions for drawing the lines as they did, with East and West Pakistan separated by the breadth of north India, and Kashmir's largely Muslim population annexed to India because of its Hindu ruler, caused war in 1971 (resulting in the transformation of East Pakistan into the new nation of Bangladesh), and continue to reverberate today. In particular, the Punjab region in the northwestern part of the subcontinent, home to the Sikh religion, was severely affected by what is known within the south Asian context simply as "Partition." Punjab was in essence split down the middle, with members of the same families ending up as citizens of different countries. The Partition of post-Independence India was one of the most significant forced migrations in world history, with at least 10 million people moving from their homes, and at least 200,000 dying over a nine-month period in the resulting communal violence.[4]

According to several of my discussants, some of whose parents were born in the Punjab, at the time of Partition many Hindus living in what would become Pakistan chose to move to Rishikesh precisely because it had such a strong connection to the Hindu religious tradition and would therefore offer a clear starting point for establishing a new life in a free, Hindu, India. One of the tourist guides available in Rishikesh lists the major languages spoken in the town as Hindi, Garhwali, Punjabi and English, and it is certainly the case that the vast majority of business people I met in Rishikesh town were of Punjabi origin. The major castes represented in the region are Brahmans, Rajputs, and Doms (cf. Berreman 1963); there are a few Muslims and a small mosque. Because of its location, Rishikesh draws residents from both the hill villages and the plains; since the early 1990s, there has been a steady stream of urban retirees moving to Rishikesh. Building construction has accelerated rapidly to accommodate these relatively wealthy immigrants to the sacred landscape, who seek both a pleasant view and the religious merit that proximity to the Ganga and Himalaya confers.

Bahadur's portrait of the Garhwal region, like those of the government tourist offices, also draws on many Hindu textual references to the ideal environment for the practice of yoga. Yoga, in earlier times the sole provenience of high-caste men who had renounced life in the world, is traditionally understood to be the most direct path to communion with the Absolute, and thus release from the heavy burden of worldly entanglement. Yoga and meditation could best be practiced in

Figure 4 Rafting on the Ganga River above Rishikesh (author photo)

a place devoid of the influences of "civilization," as many of Sivananda's writings suggest. Many writers, from the German Romantic scholars and the American Transcendentalists of the early nineteenth century on, have thought of these practices as an early example of the "back-to-nature" movement that permitted the best opportunity for becoming "one with the universe." In the 1960s, as yoga gained popularity in the West, Rishikesh itself gained notoriety/fame (depending on your point of view) as the home to the Maharishi Mahesh Yogi's Transcendental Meditation movement and the place where the Beatles (or the "Beatless", as the Uttar Pradesh state government tourist brochure on Rishikesh called them) came to be enlightened.

In addition to its ever-expanding reputation as a center for yoga, Rishikesh's latest tourist gambit is white water rafting on the Ganga. While rafting would seem at first glance to be an activity completely unrelated to yoga, in fact the two have frequently been packaged together for both foreign and domestic tourist consumption all around India. A number of new "adventure travel" agents have opened in Rishikesh since 1990, and it is these businesses, and not the more established religious pilgrimage/tourism agents, who handle the promotion of yoga courses in Rishikesh (Figure 4). River rafting expeditions are marketed to both foreigners and urban Indian elites; Rishikesh is within easy driving range for weekend getaways from Delhi, and so makes an ideal oasis regime for the harried urban professional.

One of the most famous people alleged to have visited the Garhwal region and stayed at the Kailash Ashram in the 1890s is Swami Vivekananda, the foremost disciple of the great mystic-saint Sri Ramakrishna of Kolkata. According to the historians at the Kailash Ashram, Vivekananda and another of Ramakrishna's disciples, Swami Abhedananda, used Kailash Ashram as a model for the development of education and ordination practices in the Ramakrishna Mission (Basnet et al. 1992). In a letter sent back to his fellow disciples in Kolkata from aboard a ship bound for North America, the by-then world-weary Vivekananda wrote, "Do you remember the Ganga at Hrishikesh? That clear bluish water – in which one can count the fins of fish five yards below the surface . . . You remember that love for Ganga water, that glory of the Ganga, the touch of its water that makes the mind dispassionate" (Vivekananda 1989b: 4). Vivekananda developed his ideas about yoga in North America and Europe, and later promoted them in India from his home base in Kolkata. But these other locales did not resonate with the imagined spiritual authority that so imbued Rishikesh, the mythological "Dev-Bhumi," the Land of the Gods. Today, despite significant pollution further downstream, the Ganga at Rishikesh is still quite clean; the bright blue water gives evidence of its glacial origins, telling weary travelers from the plains that they have indeed reached the mountains.[5]

Rishikesh – January, 1992

Although he had acquired a postgraduate university degree, a good job, and a comfortable middle-class lifestyle, at the age of 30 Ram felt stifled by his position as an accountant in Kolkata, and decided that a change of pace was in order. He had always wanted to visit the high shrines of the Himalaya, so he began to plan an extraordinary trip that would take him across the vast expanse of the Gangetic plain to Rishikesh. The traditional means of transportation for making such a pilgrimage is by foot, though this has largely been replaced by bus and train these days. But Ram chose to do things differently: he traveled by bicycle through small villages and along highways for hundreds and hundreds of kilometers. I heard the story of his trip in early 1992, about eight months after Ram had arrived in Rishikesh. He had been supporting himself through freelance accounting and tutoring in English and mathematics, while learning yoga himself. He became my Hindi tutor and research assistant, and as I worked out and translated questions for my interviews with yoga practitioners, he corrected my grammar and answered my questions about what had brought him to Rishikesh, why yoga was important to him, and what all of that had, if anything, to do with health.

Utopian Quests

While nineteenth- and twentieth-century versions of yoga depended heavily on mass distribution of print media representations, training in yoga before then was passed on from master to disciple; the tradition required not only the study of classical texts and the oral teaching of the master, but most importantly, the disciple's continual practice of the specified techniques. The knowledge imparted in words had no value without personal experience. In addition to the proper instruction and practice necessary for succeeding in mastery of yoga, the environment was also considered crucial (Bahadur 1992[1916]). One of the Upanishads calls for practice to be conducted "in auspicious places helpful to the mind and pleasing to the eyes."[6]

Over the past century, the meanings of freedom and health have evolved, and their importance today can be seen in the contemporary concern with health and the process of self-development. Yoga entered the late-nineteenth-century global public arena on the coattails of these key values of modernity. The "therapeutic worldview" (Lears 1981), which gives primacy to the notions of self-help and struggle against alienation through consumption of new (or resurrected) remedies, remains a central concern in the twenty-first century. However, rather than viewing yoga and other health-promoting techniques as antimodern responses to the encroachment of industrial modernity, as does Lears, I see them as thoroughly modern. Vivekananda and Sivananda's versions of yoga do not in any way require the practitioner to abandon life as a middle-class (or any other class) householder; rather, they provide a way to navigate modernity's dangerous waters without succumbing to the undertow of materialist excess. Such a shift from the traditional ascetic practice of withdrawing from society in order to achieve enlightenment to a more participatory norm is made possible by valorization of the status of *jivan-mukhti*, "living liberation".[7]

To give a sense of the period in which Swami Vivekananda's presentations on yoga were received by middle-class American audiences, we turn to a fictional account that had, within five years, generated a political sensation. Writing in the time and place described by Jackson Lears (1981) a century later, Edward Bellamy captures the "contrary pressures" that beset the middle classes in an industrial society. His novel, *Looking Backward* (1888), presents a utopian vision of Boston in the year 2000 from the vantage point of a young doctor born in 1857, who was "rich and also educated, and possessed, therefore, all the elements of happiness enjoyed by the most fortunate in that age" (Bellamy 1995 [1888]: 33). Although represented as a fictional account, Bellamy's vision of the direction America should take resonated with the general public's concerns of the day; the novel was wildly popular, not only in the United States, but around the world. Clubs and political parties designed to foster community and cooperation among all members of society appeared in its wake, but unlike the revolutionary programs of Marx and others, Bellamy's ideals were to be achieved without violence or disruption to the lives of the already fortunate (Lipow 1982). For this reason, it held tremendous appeal for the middle and upper classes. As Bellamy writes in the beginning of the novel, the new order would reward the reliable middle class virtues of work, character, and expertise . . . Here was a society in which technology would be made an ethical force rather than an alien, uncontrolled, and immoral one . . . the Boston of the future demanded no cultural changes. The nuclear family, the private home, and the shopping trip all remained as they had been in the late nineteenth century. (Bellamy 1995:17–18).

In other words, the "achievements" of modernity remained intact, but the negative consequences of industrial capitalism were removed. The fact that the narrator is a physician is not insignificant. In the late nineteenth century, as health became an ever more central concern, the medical establishment began to achieve a position of respectability and authority in Euro-American societies (Starr 1982).

Bellamy's tale, although fictional, serves well to describe the conditions under which Swami Vivekananda arrived in the United States five short years following the initial publication of *Looking Backward*. While his primary purpose was to attend the Parliament of the World's Religions at the Chicago World's Fair,[8] Vivekananda also visited with well-to-do citizens in Boston, Chicago, and Los Angeles. The people into whose homes he came seem, from their descriptions, remarkably similar to members of the 1887 Boston society described in *Looking Backward* (Atulananda 1988; Chattopadhyaya 1993). Such similarities may point to the reason why Vivekananda's American hosts sought alternative visions of the way the world should work, whether from reading Bellamy, listening to Vivekananda and taking up his practices, or following one of the New Thought, Spiritualist,[9] or other emergent movement leaders who offered forms of practice often radically different from the context within which these members of established society grew up. The 1990s, no less than the 1890s, provided the millennial context for an intensification of focus on radical change and new strategies for living the good life, and the great surge in yoga practice that we have seen since the early 1990s reflects this trend.

Kolkata, India – October, 1992

After a long train trip from Delhi, I was finally settled in Kolkata for a couple of weeks of research at the National Library and the Ramakrishna (RK) Mission Center for Education and Culture, which maintains a residence for visiting scholars. The RK Mission is a place of immaculate gardens (and constantly busy gardeners), glowing white walls, and an air of quiet dignity. In the library, rows of heads are bent over many varieties of texts. The cost of the room includes meals, so the visiting scholars and monastics from other RK Missions and Vedanta Centers usually get to know

continued

---

each other over breakfast or dinner, going off during the day to the National Library or one of Kolkata's many museums. One quickly learns that the community of scholars here, as with scholars everywhere, is rather small – at any given meal, someone at the table is sure to have a friend or two in common with one or more of the other diners. The esteem in which the RK Mission is held by the citizens of Kolkata, and indeed by most Indians, whether residents or émigrés, appears uniformly high. When people heard where I was staying and what I was researching, the mere names Ramakrishna and Vivekananda drew exclamations of approval. Pictures of these teachers are everywhere, in homes and in public spaces; the Kolkata middle class are, like Vivekananda, Ramakrishna's children (Chatterjee 1992).

Vivekananda and Yoga

In 1993, many yoga groups in the United States put on meetings and sponsored programs to commemorate "100 years of Yoga in America." The event to which they all look as the first presentation of yoga to American audiences is the 1893 Parliament of the World's Religions. Held in Chicago in conjunction with the World's Fair celebrating the four-hundredth anniversary of Columbus' arrival in the Americas, the Parliament provided a forum for Swami Vivekananda. His charisma and his message of universal brotherhood struck a chord in the hearts of many of the participants and onlookers. Eventually, the stories reported in numerous Western periodicals were carried back to the press in India, and Vivekananda's fame, both at home and abroad, was assured. Vivekananda spent four years in North America and Europe between 1893 and 1897, becoming enormously popular because of his facility in English, pleasant demeanor, and universalist message. He returned to the West once more, in 1900, following his establishment of the Ramakrishna Mission in Kolkata. By the time of his death in 1902 at the age of 39, Vivekananda had traveled around the world twice and seen the early success of the organizations he founded to honor his master, the Ramakrishna Mission and Vedanta Societies of India and the West. The RK Missions, as they are known in India, are a central component of middle-class Hindu life. They are extremely well respected for their scholarship, sponsorship of art and cultural events, and programs for schoolchildren. The institutional format upon which these two institutions were based derived from Vivekananda's experience of Rishikesh's first institution, the Kailash Ashram. Completing the link back from Kolkata and the mouth of the Ganga to Rishikesh and its headwaters, we see that Sivananda used the RK Missions and the Vedanta Societies as models for his own Divine Life Society.

Although Vivekananda's physical life was short, the volume of writings that he left behind (in English and Bengali, with translations to many other Indian and western languages) has allowed his words to live on in the minds of readers around the world. Vivekananda was one of the most influential thinkers of the "Hindu Renaissance" of the nineteenth century (Halbfass 1988; Kopf 1979; Schwab 1984). He remains one of the most venerated figures of twentieth-century India, although compared with the tremendous number of scholarly works that discuss his teacher Ramakrishna, relatively few publications centered on his life and work have emerged. Within the larger context of his writings on the Hindu tradition, Vivekananda's work on yoga stands out. His categorization of yoga into four divisions, *Karma, Bhakti, Raja* and *Jnana*, presented a simplified classificatory scheme of yoga ideology and practice specifically for consumption by middle-class, English-speaking audiences that is still very much evident in the contemporary context. This schema was developed first for the West and only later conveyed to Indian audiences, also drawn largely from the emergent middle class, especially in Bengal.

A great deal has been written about the local elite of Kolkata and colonial Bengal (see, for example, Kripal 1995; Raychaudhuri 1989; Sarkar 1992; Shils 1961). Now often referred to as the *bhadralok*, they had previously been labeled the "new middle class," "literati," "intelligentsia," and "petit bourgoisie" (Chatterjee 1993:35).[10] Vivekananda was the perfect mediator for these people caught in the middle. As upper-caste elites, this group of people had relatively high status under the British rule. They were not self-governing, but were nonetheless in positions of power with respect to the rest of the Indian population, and were valued by the British. Vivekananda was one of their own, yet he was also heir to the mantle of Ramakrishna. Second, like his beloved master, he was an extremely charismatic individual, but unlike Ramakrishna, he was also a chameleon, comfortable in settings ranging from a rural south Indian village to the international cities of New York or London. In addition, he spoke to the need for the Hindu middle class to reclaim their birthright, not simply in the religious sense that Ramakrishna had addressed, but in economic and political arenas as well. Vivekananda repeatedly presented a strong nationalist message, telling the people of Bengal, and of India at large, that they possessed the capacity to stand up for themselves and take charge of their destiny: "Stand up, be bold, be strong. Take the whole responsibility on your own shoulders, and know that you are the creator of your own destiny. All the strength and succor you want is within yourselves. Therefore, make your own future" (Vivekananda 1977 (II):225). He suggested that the leaders of such a revolution would come from the new middle class, the *bhadralok*, and that the end of British rule was within sight. Vivekananda's valorization of the middle classes is clear in this comment from his book, *Raja Yoga*: "In human society . . . too much wealth or too much poverty is a great impediment to the higher development of the soul. It is from the middle classes that the great ones of the world come. Here the forces are very equally adjusted and balanced" (Vivekananda 1990b:27).

Vivekananda's presentation of yoga and the Hindu spiritual tradition depended heavily on essentializing India as "spiritually wealthy," in contrast to the "material wealth" of the West. Without that opposition, he felt he had nothing with which to barter; his stated goal of going to Chicago to lobby Western people for money to help poor India required the offering of something else of value. That something was universal spirituality, cast in terms of yoga. In its capacity as an essential metonym for Hindu spirituality, yoga appears as a monolith whose authenticity can be attributed to its more than 2000-year-old historic tradition; it is often assumed (by Indians and foreigners alike) that somewhere, underneath all of the apparent diversity of contemporary yoga, there exists a single core of yoga philosophy and practice. In many contemporary treatments of the subject, this core appears as Vivekananda's four-fold set of *bhakti* yoga, *karma* yoga, *raja* yoga and *jnana* yoga. The various other names and forms of yoga – *kundalini, mantra, hatha, laya,* and so on – are thought to be somehow less central or authentic than these four (see, for example, http://www.real-yoga.com/9.yoga). Vivekananda's characterization of yoga has become so entrenched that people today often assume that it represents the "original" or "true" backbone of yoga, out of which all of the other paths of yoga emerged. While these four terms, and all of the others, existed prior to Vivekananda's lectures, the emphasis on love, work, self-control, and know-ledge (corresponding to the four) was part of an overall reorientation of yoga that fit into Vivekananda's nationalist agenda and organizational plans.

Swami Vivekananda produced a modern interpretation of the Hindu Yoga tradition for consumption by middle-class American and European audiences. His ability to frame yoga and the philosophy of *Advaita Vedanta* (non-dualism) in English, the language of his Indian middle class, was the prerequisite for generating worldwide interest in and recognition of these ideas and practices. Without a common language, the market for yoga could not develop. In the following pages, we will see that Sivananda's use of this same strategy yielded similar success. As the first Indian to present yoga and vedanta to mass audiences in the West (Eck 1995), Vivekananda's quest to reconcile various Hindu philosophic traditions with modern science to create a universal religion was a case of translating Hindu thought into European language,[11] and Rolland (1988 [1931]: 83) notes that the "problem was how to harmonize everything without renouncing anything." Vivekananda asked his disciples to make two vows: self-improvement and the service of others.[12]

Vivekananda's vision of yoga was universal, spiritual, rational, and practical. Rather than making a claim for the superiority of Hindu thought as an exclusive tradition, Vivekananda's rhetoric, taken up by Hindu nationalists throughout the twentieth century, was inescapably universalist and inclusive: Hindu ideas were universally applicable, because, using the doctrine of *maya* (the illusory nature of the lived world), everything could be defined as consistent with Hinduism. His uses of yoga emphasized the spiritual in direct opposition to the materiality of Western values, not as a way to require poverty, but as a way to claim the moral high ground. As for the rational, Vivekananda took great pains to reconcile his own extensive knowledge of western scientific and philosophical traditions (see Chatterjee 1993; Raychaudhuri 1989) with the certainty of religious experience; he asks if religion is

> to justify itself by the discoveries of reason, through which every other science justifies itself? Are the same methods of investigation, which we apply to sciences and knowledge outside, to be applied to the science of religion? In my opinion, this must be so, and I am also of the opinion that the sooner it is done, the better. (Vivekananda 1977(I):367)

To demonstrate the rationality of spiritual belief, Vivekananda encouraged his followers to judge his recommendations for spiritual enlightenment for themselves, something they could do only through practice. He felt that the only way to bring skeptics (of the sort he himself had been) to the realization of universal unity was through experiential knowledge; yoga provided a technique which all could learn. "Practice is absolutely necessary. You may sit down and listen to me by the hour every day, but if you do not practice, you will not get one step further . . . We never understand these things unless we experience them. We will have to see and feel them for ourselves" (Vivekananda 1977(I):139).[13] As we shall see, emphasis on experiential knowledge also anchored Sivananda's Divine Life Society; he implored seekers to practice yoga, as well as to "Be Good and Do Good," rather than simply reading the classical texts.

Sivananda and Rishikesh

How did a wealthy south Indian physician come to be one of north India's most internationally recognized religious figures? Swami Sivananda (Figure 5) was born Kuppuswami Iyer to a distinguished Brahmin family in Tamil Nadu, in the year 1887.[14] After completing his Western-style medical training, Dr. Kuppuswami worked in a pharmacy for a time, and spent a few years practicing in Trichinopoly, where he also started to publish in English a "high-class medical monthly" called *The Ambrosia* (DLS 1985a). The journal continued for four years, until the young doctor decided to take a new job at a hospital in Malaysia. There, according to his official biographies (Ananthanarayanan 1987; DLS 1985a) he lived a prosperous life for ten years, always wearing fine clothes and ornaments. In 1992, I heard one rumor around the ashram in Rishikesh that Sivananda had married and had children there, leaving after they died in an epidemic. Another asserted that his one

Figure 5 Swami Sivananda Commemorative Postage Stamp

remaining son visits the DLS ashram regularly. Neither of these stories is confirmed by official records.

Dr. Kuppuswami gradually became dissatisfied with his life abroad and began to read what he could of Hindu philosophy, including the works of Swami Vivekananda. He tried to practice yoga on his own and to meet with itinerant swamis who came to town. Finally he made the decision to return to India. From Madras, he made his way northward, stopping in the holy city of Benares. Speaking no Hindi, he eventually managed to learn that the Himalaya he sought were still several hundred miles further north. By a circuitous route which took him through Pune, many hundreds of miles southwest of Benares, he eventually ended up with a train ticket to Hardwar in 1924. He walked from there to Rishikesh, where he took vows to renounce worldly life, conducting his own death ceremony and becoming a *sannyasin* (monk/renouncer); the *sannyasin* who directed the ceremony gave him the name Sivananda.[15] He settled into a life of meditation and service on the banks of the Ganga, taking his food with the other ascetics at one of the many *dharamsalas*, and giving medical care to pilgrims and *sannyasins*.

In between his medical service and his own spiritual practice, continues the officially sanctioned narrative of the master, Sivananda began sending jottings of advice and philosophy home to friends and family in Madras; these notes were then distributed locally, generating a stream of aspirants headed north to Rishikesh beginning in the mid-1920s. Since Sivananda spoke little Hindi, and the language of his own education had been English, he continued to produce his scores of pamphlets and instructions on how to practice yoga and live the "divine life" in English.

When Sivananda arrived in Rishikesh in 1924, the town was very small; only a few other institutions had been established there, most notably the Kailash Ashram, visited by Vivekananda over twenty years before. According to his many biographies (e.g. Ananthanarayanan 1987; see also David Miller 1989), Swami Sivananda took his meals at the well-known stopover on the Himalayan pilgrimage rout, the Kali Kambli Wala *dharamsala* ("resthouse of the black-blanketed one"), and spent most of his time in meditation by the banks of the Ganga (DLS 1987b). He also took charge of seeing to the health of the other wandering and resident ascetics, providing medicines and food from his own savings. Sivananda's reputation gradually became known further afield, in part because of his facility with the English language. Students came, wanting to learn from him, and by the late 1920s he had a permanent group of disciples, with whom he built a small community on the eastern banks of the Ganga. In 1929, thanks to contacts from his earlier life, Sivananda's first book of teachings about yoga was published in Madras.

The strength of Sivananda's personality and the sincerity of his practice – not to mention his fluency in English – brought a number of disciples to his door. During the latter part of 1930 Mircea Eliade, a young Romanian working on his PhD in the philosophy of religion, desired practical training in yoga and sought out Sivananda. Eliade had spent the previous two years reading the classical yoga texts with the famous philosopher DasGupta of Kolkata as part of his requirements for a doctorate from the University of Bucharest. He had been directed to Sivananda by acquaintances in Delhi who had heard of the English-speaking swami in Rishikesh. Eliade came to Rishikesh in search of authentic yoga practice to complete his education, though another more personal motivation was to escape the aftermath of an ill-fated relationship with DasGupta's daughter, Maitreyi. While Eliade clearly had an extensive interest in yoga to begin with, his desire to practice yoga was also linked to his desire for this unattainable young woman. He thought that the practice of yoga would in some way make him "more Indian" and therefore more acceptable to Maitreyi and her family, though at the same time, Eliade thought that these practices might help him to suppress his feelings for a woman he could not marry.[16]

Eliade's choice of yoga teacher and site for immersion in the life of a Hindu ascetic are a significant indicator of the influence and impact of Sivananda and

Rishikesh on the development of a transnational community of yoga practitioners, since Eliade went on to become one of the most influential scholars of comparative religion of the twentieth century, and was for decades the primary academic authority on the subject of yoga. Sivananda's name is mentioned only briefly in Eliade's extensive autobiographical and academic works, but Eliade's experiences in Rishikesh with the Swami do figure more prominently in his various fictional works, including *The Secret of Dr. Honigberger* and *Maitreyi*. The veràcity of these descriptions is perhaps open to question, located as they are in works of the imagination. Yet Eliade's works tended to reflect his life, and we can see this clearly by comparing a fictional description of Sivananda, which appears after a mention of "visiting Rishi Kesh in the Himalayas" in the story of *The Secret of Dr. Honigberger*:

> This Swami Shivananda was . . . a most remarkable man in every respect. He had been a doctor in Singapore, he had been married and he had two children, and one fine day he left everything and set off to seek salvation, as he put it, in a monastery in the Himalayas. Some day, perhaps, I shall write the truly amazing life of this ascetic doctor, who had traveled all over India on foot, had taken part in all the religious ceremonies of all the sects and had studied all their philosophies in search of peace for his soul. And he had found this peace in a hut on the bank of the Ganges, at Rishi Kesh, where he had decided to settle some seven years before my arrival there. (Eliade 1970: 53)

As the story continues, Sivananda shows the protagonist (Dr. H.) the illusory nature of the world, demonstrating the control of *maya* that only the true yogi can perform. Certainly, many of the known facts about Sivananda tally with this account: the timing of his arrival in Rishikesh, against that of Eliade; the medical practice abroad; the attainment of *samadhi*, the highest meditative state achieved through yoga practice, in a hut called Ananda Kutir (Hut of Peace) on the banks of the Ganga. In fact, the only piece of information given here that is not corroborated by official DLS accounts is his marriage and resulting children, a point for which there exists other evidence.

We can compare the passage from *Dr. Honigsberger* with an entry from his non-fiction essay collection *L'Inde*, published originally in 1934 and again in 1988. *L'Inde*, a collection of periodical articles and radio talks published by Eliade during the period between 1929 and 1933 (Ricketts 1988:337), presents a great deal of information about his first meeting with Swami Sivananda:

> I go down to Swarag-Ashram in search of a swami of whom I heard tell since Delhi: Swami Shivananda [*sic*], who had been in this retreat for seven years. We find Shivananda in his kutir, on the banks of the Ganges,in the company of an imposing man with lively eyes – he reminded me somewhat of Rudolf Steiner – this is Swami Advaitananda. The latter, a doctor of law in London, had traveled throughout Europe, was well read,

and had occupied an enviable social position when he had abandoned everything for consecrating the rest of his life to meditating in the Himalayan solitude. Swami Sivananda, man of the south, is tall, broad of shoulder, very brown, and as happy as a Franciscan. He practices Vedantic sadhana and laughs a lot; he has gained the friendship of notable Europeans in Singapore, where he had practiced medicine for ten years. He was 35 years old when he lost his wife and one child – because of this, he had abandoned everything and left Singapore on foot, headed toward the Himalayas. (Eliade 1988:165–167; my translation from the French)

Though one is fact and the other ostensibly fiction, the individual described clearly shares a number of similar traits.[17] We can see that Sivananda's cosmopolitanism, fluency in English, and congenial attitude brought him wide recognition. Swami Advaitananda, apparently quite learned in Western as well as Hindu philosophy, was among the first of many well-educated and often international disciples and companions to surround Sivananda in Rishikesh.

The official history of the DLS that was prepared for the Sivananda birth centenary in 1987 discusses the "Stones, Bricks, and Mortar," those "exceptionally talented, rare and evolved souls . . . who were drawn towards the Master, like iron filings towards a magnet" (DLS 1987b:210), and who helped Sivananda build his ashram. By the mid-1930s, the number of followers had increased to the point that Sivananda decided to organize his small ashram into an official group. In 1936, he founded the Divine Life Society. The DLS history begins in 1932 with Swami Swaroopananda, "a very learned man . . . well-read in English, Hindi, and Sanskrit" (DLS 1987b:210). Advaitananda is not mentioned, nor is Eliade, though both had in fact been with Sivananda three years before. In fact, none of the Western disciples, even those who stayed for long periods, receive mention in the 1987 DLS volume – a revisionist history indeed.

Eliade spent six months with Sivananda on the banks of the Ganga; during that period, Sivananda told the student that he, Eliade, would be the "next Vivekananda," spreading the message of yoga and vedanta throughout the West. Commenting on this suggestion, Eliade remarked that he thought this was a terrible idea, that he found Vivekananda's writings quite superficial and he had no desire to carry on in that tradition – had he been hailed as another Ramakrishna, he would have been happier, as the Great Swan (Ramakrishna's nickname among his disciples) seemed to Eliade the more genuine of the two (Eliade 1990:190).

In fact Sivananda's prophecy came true, in a way: Eliade returned to the West and in 1933 received his doctorate for the monograph that would become *Yoga: Immortality and Freedom*, still considered a classic analysis of yoga in the history of academic religious studies, and now even more widely available at esoteric bookshops and yoga websites. We can see that Eliade – just as much as his mentor Sivananda and his mentor's own inspiration, Vivekananda – contributed to the production of an "imagined community" in Anderson's (1983) sense – a global community of people who, though they are rarely acquainted in the face-to-face sense, nevertheless feel themselves connected through their shared interest in and practice of yoga. This imagined community, as Anderson described in his seminal work on the emergence of nationalism, depends on the broad circulation of print media to provide the shared knowledge and practice base necessary for not only national, but also transnational community development. As with other imagined communities whose solidarity rests on the success of print capitalism, the basis for the camaraderie seen in the yoga world has as its anchor a vast array of print (and now electronic) media, from specially created texts to pamphlets and handbills, but it is also supported and promoted through intervals of face-to-face association at conferences, seminars, and retreats. It can indeed be said that Eliade's interpretations of yoga, developed through his association with DasGupta and Sivananda, have been among the most influential in determining how the wider world has come to understand the meaning of yoga.

Independence: The DLS and the New Nation

With this general overview of the origins of the Divine Life Society in mind, I want to focus now on the evolution of this institution during the period surrounding Indian Independence, a "critical juncture" in the history of India as well as the DLS. The pre-Independence (before 1947) period saw an increase in the activities of the DLS, with ever more disciples and lay members from many countries joining Sivananda's community. During this time, the DLS produced many books and pamphlets through its press, the Sivananda Publication League, and Sivananda's reputation continued to spread. With the expansion of the DLS, a tension arose between Sivananda's broad goal of global spiritual unity, and his attention, however muted, to the politics of Indian nationalism. The events surrounding World War II, particularly the development of nuclear weapons technology, provided a rationale for many people, in India and elsewhere, to take up the practice of yoga. In the aftermath of the war, Sivananda's message of universal unity and brotherhood became still more appealing. The development of nuclear weapons created a world in which it was no longer possible to imagine completely detachable nations, able to remain unaffected by events on the other side of the globe (Omkarananda 1960: 94). Peace and security, wherever and however they could be found, were top priorities for many of the people who sought Sivananda's advice, whether in person or through his standing offer of a "postal" discipleship.

Word of Sivananda's teachings reached many foreigners through the availability of his English-medium pamphlets. In the 1940s, a German man named Boris Sacharow became a "disciple-by-mail." He never visited Rishikesh, but nevertheless, Sivananda bestowed on him the honorary title of *yogiraj* (Fuchs 1990), or master of yoga, in 1947. Sacharow began the first yoga school in Germany and is today considered one of the main forces in the development of professional yoga instruction in Europe, though in the mid-1990s, his successor, Feuerabend, had a major falling out with the BDY, the dominant professional yoga organization in Germany.[18] One of the cornerstones of his instruction was the so-called Rishikesh *Reihe* (German, meaning "sequence") of postures, which he learned from Sivananda, and which was often cited when I asked German yoga students in 1992 their reasons for coming to Rishikesh to study.

The increasing number of disciples and correspondents from the West in the post-war years supplemented the growing popularity of the DLS in India (DLS 1985a). In 1945, Sivananda announced the creation of an "All-World Religions' Federation" and in 1948, the Yoga-Vedanta Forest Academy at DLS headquarters in Rishikesh. Both were designed to accommodate the "systematic spiritual training" (DLS 1987b:24) of residents and visitors alike. India's Independence on August 15, 1947 created further opportunities for reflection on questions of religious freedom, political alignment and the new United Nations, as well as the importance of bringing India up to speed in the modern world. India's position as a leader of the non-aligned movement (A. Gupta 1992) meshed well with the frequently heard assertion that India had a universal spiritual message to share.

The Diamond Jubilee Commemoration Volume of Sri Swami Sivananda was published on September 8, 1947, and contained many references to India's new-found Independence, while retaining the organization's universalist message. Prefatory pages included two songs written by Sivananda, "The Universal Anthem" and "Mother India: A National Anthem." In the first, Sivananda extols

Glory to Thee, O fair Mother Earth, common Parent of all . . . Though conduct, actions and behaviour appear as diverse, One alone is the power that works in the Universe. Though words and languages differ in Peking or in Rome, One alone is the Primal Sound, the Root Vibration OM . . . As one Sun illumines the whole Earth outside, the One Spirit Universal in Man doth reside . . . A Golden Cord Spiritual, the whole world to bind, in bonds of Love and Brotherhood and Unity Eternal. (DLS 1947: xxx)

But on the next page, he strikes a different chord:

May God bless Mother India, our sacred glorious Hind, The land of Rishis, Yogis, Sages of high spiritual culture. India is the only land where God-realization is the goal; India is the only land where Rishis, yogis abound . . . It is a land of Dharma, where people practice Yama and Niyama, It is a sacred land, where holy Ganges, Jumna, Sindhu flow; It is a peaceful land of broad tolerance, where all religionists dwell, Glory to India, glory to Hind...May India's fame extend fully all over the world! (DLS 1947: xxxi)

In the space of two pages, Sivananda demonstrates the two cornerstones of the DLS: universal unity, expressed in English as a transnational medium, and a national identity for India based on the first two steps in Patanjali's classical eight-fold path of *raja* yoga. These steps are *yama* and *niyama*, roughly translated as moral observances and self-discipline. Sivananda's message, as we have discussed already, strongly echoes that of Vivekananda, who also asserted the value of yoga as a universal science and emphasize service in the world (or *karma* yoga) as a way to transcendence of it. In addition, the tension between the universalist and the Hindu nationalist positions which appears in Vivekananda's writings is also present in Sivananda's work. The DLS projects an image of universal tolerance to the global community, while simultaneously catering to the agenda of wealthy Hindu nationalists.[19]

A few years after Independence, Sivananda undertook his first and only major tour of India, establishing new local and regional branches of the DLS and making contacts in urban and rural areas alike. His 1950 All-India tour took Sivananda from Rishikesh east across Uttar Pradesh, through the cities of Lucknow and Banaras, through Bihar to Kolkata; south to Madras and then Cape Cormorin, the southernmost point in India; north up the center of the subcontinent through Bangalore and Mysore, west across to Pune and Bombay; and finally through Baroda and Ahmedabad to Delhi before returning home to Rishikesh – a total of over 7500 miles (DLS 1951:xi–xxiv).

Before setting out from Rishikesh, Sivananda and his associates participated in a farewell banquet at the railway station, to which all the "important personages of Rishikesh" were invited, including the station master, the postmaster, the police officer, the bank manager, some businessmen, a representative of the Tehri royal family, and many senior sannyasins. The official account states that the "service and the layout were in European style; but the spirit was thoroughly Indian, as also the dishes" (DLS 1951:3). As Sivananda made ready to depart from the Rishikesh railway station with his entourage, he spoke to the gathered crowd, saying "If you want to enjoy peace and happiness, practice this simple Sadhana. Adapt, Adjust, and Accommodate. Lack of this divine quality of adaptability is the cause for disharmony, quarrels, riots and wars" (DLS 1951:5). What a clear picture of the DLS this gives: the structure and material goods are European, but the substance, the spirit and the food, are Indian – a truly transnational blend! Here we see no signs of radical nationalism. Instead, we have the essence of middle-class conformity, the perfect colonial/national subject/citizen, who never makes a fuss and expects that if one simply "adjusts, adapts and accommodates," everything will be fine.

The official purpose of undertaking this 1950 tour of India was to preach tolerance, love, understanding and harmony, in order to counteract the religious intolerance that had swept the world. Certainly, the rift between Hindus and Muslims on the subcontinent that had driven Partition and ripped apart the lives of millions was a pressing concern at the time the All-India Tour was planned. Sivananda's intention was "to spread the Gospel of spiritual evolution and universal peace and love . . . never was the need for peace and good-will among nations so great or so urgent as [then]. If the world [was] to save itself from the physical devastation, the moral degradation and the other calamitous consequences of a third world war, there [was] only one way" (DLS 1951:xxi). His approach to solving the world's problems, as well as India's, was grounded in personal reform, both physical and spiritual, and the notion that if each individual made him or herself into a better person, the world would indeed be a better place. Two days after starting out, Sivananda spoke to two young boys who had come into his train compartment, telling them to "[s]erve, love, give, purify, meditate, realize – these few words give you the essence of Yoga and Vedanta. Be good, do good, be kind, be compassionate. This is what all the scriptures teach! If you do these simple things, the whole world will love you" (DLS 1951: 7).

For Sivananda, this philosophy was expressed in his later writings, presented as the goal of *jivanmukhti*, or living liberation. *Jivanmukhti* entails achieving self-realization while still participating in worldly social life. While freedom from the bonds of colonial rule had been one of Vivekananda's rallying cries at the turn of the century, Sivananda was much more personal than political in his arguments. He focused first on personal health and then on the freedom generated by self-realization. Rarely did he suggest that spiritual seekers give up their school or job and renounce worldly life; instead, he exhorted them to continue as productive citizens, support their community and country, and take brief visits to Rishikesh for rejuvenation of the spirit:

> Yoga is primarily a way of life, not something which is divorced from life. Yoga is not forsaking an action, but is efficient performance in the right spirit. Yoga is not running away from home and human habitation, but a process of molding one's attitude to home and society with a new understanding. (Sivananda 1979:vii–viii)

Indeed, Sivananda was instrumental in helping erode the distinction between religious pilgrimage and secular tourism (a distinction which has always existed in India – see van der Veer 1994:108) by encouraging the path of *jivanmukhti*. *Moksha* or *mukhti* are synonyms for liberation from the endless cycle of birth and death is a primary goal in the Hindu tradition. *Jivanmukhti*, or attaining absolute freedom while still living, has received a great deal of attention since the classical Hindu thinkers like Sankara (cf. Fort and Mumme 1996), but its emphasis in neo-Hindu revival of the past century reflects the fact that this ideal was well suited to the lives and goals of the emergent middle classes in India and the West.[20] It did not require them to give up the basic structures and activities of everyday life, but only to reformulate their attitudes and concepts of self and others through the addition of yogic practices. As Halbfass notes, the freedom accorded the *jivan-mukhta* does not release him from the bonds of social obligation, because he must still "behave in accordance with his human nature as well as his caste membership" (Halbfass 1991:385). This constraint fits well with the programs of the neo-Hindu nationalists, who sought to develop good, law-abiding citizens who would work to support a free Indian nation, not independent free thinkers who wanted to sit in isolated prayer or dance wildly in the streets. Entwined with this conception of liberation was the Western ideal of freedom. By translating *moksha* (or *mukhti*) as freedom, Vivekananda laid the groundwork for the conflation of Western ideas of individual freedom with Hindu notions of spiritual liberation. The further elabora-tion of the concept of the *jivanmukhta* then provided a middle way. Neither Vivekananda's nor Sivananda's version of yoga required the practitioner to aban-don life as a middle-class (or any other class) householder; rather, they provided a way to navigate modernity's dangerous waters without succumbing to the undertow of materialist excess. By emphasizing that traditional *advaita* Hindu goals could be achieved while continuing to participate in worldly life, using yoga as the vehicle, Vivekenanda and his successors offered, quite literally, the best of all possible worlds to their followers.

The ideal of *jivanmukhti* offers a chance to shift from the traditional ascetic practice of withdrawing from society to achieve enlightenment to a more socially engaged norm. In this way, Sivananda encouraged his disciples to partake in what I have called "oasis regimes," using the DLS ashram in Rishikesh (and later, other properties purchased by the ashram or its affiliates) to engage in an ascetic lifestyle for a short while, in order to improve not only their own hectic lives but also the world around them, when they go back home (discussed further in Chapters 3 and 4).

The popularization and name recognition of Rishikesh has more than a little to do with Sivananda. Like Vivekananda, he relied heavily on the use of inexpensive printed pamphlets and books for the dissemination of his message. Distribution of print media is relatively inexpensive and allows broad coverage, but it often requires a catalyst of some sort to achieve the kind of authority that assures continuing attention. Sivananda's solution was to promote the "export guru" as an authentic Indian product (Narayan 1993). The traditional mode of knowledge transfer for yoga is the *guru–shishya* (master–disciple) pair, which provides for direct one-on-one instruction, but does not reach mass audiences easily. The books capitalized on this tradition, by using informal language clearly directed at the individual seeking to better him/herself. Sivananda encouraged his reading public to write to him for advice on their spiritual progress, enhancing the sense of one-on-one contact. But by the late 1950s, the volume of mail must have gotten quite enormous. Sivananda had spent twenty years cultivating a crop of disciples capable of spreading his message. In the decade before his death in 1963, he began to send his young swamis on missions to other parts of India and the world. Although he rarely left Rishikesh himself, Sivananda developed an international clientele through extensive distribution of print and audio media. In addition to sending material on request to individuals interested in yoga or Hinduism, Sivananda regularly mailed literature to people or institutions he thought important. For example, upon arriving in London for archival research in 1993, I was surprised to find pamphlets inscribed "To the British Museum" and signed by Sivananda among the extensive collection of Sivanandiana housed there. Similarly, libraries at many American universities, including Stanford and the University of Colorado, have inscribed copies of Sivananda literature in their collections.

We can see how, in the period from the 1930s to the 1960s, but especially in the 1950s, Sivananda promoted the development of a community of practitioners as a subset of (or precursor to) a broader global community by examining one of his more popular books. This volume, published for a wider public by D.B. Taraporevala Sons & Co., Bombay, is entitled *Yogic Home Exercises: Easy Course of Physical Culture for Modern Men and Women*; it shows how Sivananda linked the concepts of personal health with global security. Although originally published in 1959, it has been reprinted several times, most recently in 1983. This volume is "[d]edicated to the men and women of East and West who desire to possess wonderful health charming and powerful personality, longevity, abundant energy, muscular strength, and nerve-vigour through the practice of Yogic Exercises" (Sivananda 1983 [1959]: iv). The first chapter of this treatise is called "Health and Freedom," and it asks "what is that precious thing that makes life worth living? It is health" (xiv). Sivananda extends the answer to this question by quoting the author of the *Caraka Samhita*, a well-known Ayurvedic medical text: "Health is the best cause of virtue, wealth, desire and emancipation and is the blessedness of life" (ibid.). In this introductory chapter explaining the value of yoga for the "modern men and women" of the book's title, Sivananda makes it clear that the practice of yoga is important not only for the physical and spiritual health of individuals, but also for the nation, and indeed the entire planet:

Sattwic ahara or good wholesome food rich in vitamins, or a well-balanced diet, systematic practice of Asan and Pranayam, right and simple living and right thinking are the important prerequisites for the preservation of health and the attainment of a high standard of vigour and vitality. These are the sublime principles on which the Rishis and Yogins of yore lived a long peaceful life. These are the important methods on which they based the system of Yoga to achieve perfection in health of body and mind. These are the supports on which the sinking nation must fall back if it wishes to regain her lost glory and splendour.

Sivananda continues, saying that

> India, the land which produced Bhishma, Bhima, Arjuna, Drona, Aswattama, Kripa, Parashuram and countless other chivalrous warriors . . . now abounds with effeminate impotent weaklings . . . The laws of health are ignored and neglected. The nation is suffering and dying. The world requires numberless brave, moral, Adhyatmic soldiers who are equipped with the five virtues [of yoga]. *Those who possess health and strength . . . those who have knowledge of the Self, they alone can secure real freedom for the world.* (Sivananda 1983 [1959] xiii–xiv; emphasis added)

The thread running through all of these statements is that the realization of the oneness of the Self with all other selves, or in other words, the affirmation of universal brotherhood, is the key to individual bliss as well as world peace and the freedom deriving from these.

Sivananda, like his predecessor Vivekananda, promoted the notion of combining the bliss of self-realization with the ability to continue living life in this world (usually at a fairly high standard). Overlaid on this conception of liberation was the Western ideal of freedom. By translating *moksha/mukhti* as freedom in his English-language publications, Vivekananda laid the groundwork for the conflation of Western ideas of individual freedom with Hindu notions of spiritual liberation, and Sivananda continued along this path. The further elaboration of the concept of the *jivanmukhta* then provided a middle way. Vivekenanda and his successors emphasized that traditional *advaita* (monist) Hindu goals could be achieved while continuing to participate in worldly life, using yoga as the vehicle. Mircea Eliade found this notion quite attractive, and used it as a key example of *coincidentia oppositorum* – the "coinciding of opposites" (Rennie 1996) such as life and death, or social bonds and absolute freedom – that constituted one of his main contributions to the comparative study of religious traditions.

Creating a Transnational Community

While certainly central to the propagation of DLS ideology and yoga practices, the availability of yoga publications worldwide has only whetted the spiritual appetites of the reading public for "the real thing." Authenticity in traditional Hindu spirituality and particularly in the practice of yoga depends on the physical presence of a teacher (Eliade 1973 [1958]; Juergensmeyer 1991), so books, tapes, and photographs remain only supplements. Though Sivananda did have many "disciples by mail," the ideal situation was for them to visit the ashram at some point. Sivananda's trained students were sent out from Rishikesh both for lecture tours and for the purpose of establishing DLS branches or, in some cases, their own organizations. While many of the more experienced disciples like Chidananda and

Vishnudevananda were sent out by their master in the late 1950s and early 1960s, others were sent or left of their own accord after Sivananda's passing. The period after Sivananda "left his body" in 1963, achieving the state of *mahasamadhi* (understood by the devout Hindu as attainment of highest consciousness, but recognized simply as death by others), was a quiet one in terms of public activities, but chaotic for members of the DLS community. Until the power structure at the DLS became settled, there were few organized tours. Chidananda was designated the president of the DLS and successor to Sivananda, while his *gurubhai* (spiritual brother) Krishnananda became the general secretary of the organization. In this way, a balance of power between two very different personalities, both with large personal followings in the community, was constructed. Chidananda was invested with the greater spiritual power in the organization, but Krishnananda, while also maintaining his place as one of the primary spiritual advisors, acquired at least equal secular power in terms of institutional structure and the ability to control ashram visits.

The sense of empire-building is difficult to escape. On one hand, more and more foreigners had been visiting Rishikesh since Indian Independence, and they asked Sivananda and his younger associates for help in continuing their education at home. On the other hand, Vivekananda's example as an ambassador of Hindu spirituality, and the related facts of increased availability of radio and mass media, as well as less expensive and faster travel, made short trips abroad a more feasible option. In addition, since Independence there were ever increasing numbers of expatriate Indians abroad, for whom the presence of Sivananda's emissaries might be comforting. Other branches of the DLS were founded in Europe, notably Germany and the Netherlands, and in the United States.

Separate organizations were also created, and of those, several are still quite visible today. Swami Jyotirmayananda left the ashram in 1962, after an invitation from some students in Puerto Rico. He later moved to Florida, where he continues to run a yoga school and research foundation, advertisements for which can be found in many "New Age" magazines (DLS 1987b:246). Swami Shivaprema-nanda, one of the mainstays of the editorial staff at the DLS, was sent in 1961 to Milwaukee at the request of an America devotee. He ran the Sivananda Yoga-Vedanta Center there for three years, then moved to New York City to found another branch. After 1970, he moved south to Buenos Aires, developing Siva-nanda Yoga Vedanta Centres in Argentina, Uruguay, and Chile (DLS 1987b: 225). South Africa had long been a DLS branch location, first under the direction of Swami Sahajananda, and later, in 1961, under Swami Venkatesananda, who used that venue as a base for opening DLS centers in Madagascar, Mauritius, and Australia. Another major DLS affiliate appeared in Malaysia in 1956, under the direction of Swami Sadananda, a former professor of History at Presidency College, Madras, who was extremely active in the Yoga-Vedanta Forest Academy, as well as the Sivananda Publication League (DLS 1987b: 228–9). Sivananda carefully covered all of the continents in his effort to create a universal community of yoga practitioners.

From the late 1960s through the 1980s, the DLS experienced quiet growth stimulated by the exploding counterculture movement in the West. The Beatles visited Rishikesh in 1968 (Saltzman 2000) to see their guru, the Maharishi Mahesh Yogi, a visit that increased the international visibility of the DLS along with all of the other Rishikesh ashrams. At the same time, the growth of the second generation of DLS "offspring" – notably Vishnudevananda's Sivananda Yoga Vedanta Center in Quebec (among other North American locations), Satchidananda's Integral Yoga centers and Yogaville ashram in Virginia, and several other branches and affiliated ashrams in India and around the world, as noted previously, boosted the numbers of individuals trained in the philosophy and practice of Sivananda's style of yoga. A crucial form of dissemination of Sivananda's yoga came in 1972, when Lilias Folan's television yoga class hit the public television airwaves.

Carterton, Maryland – June, 1992

As we drive along, the scenery shifts from rural farmland to suburban freeway, and then to urban jungle. I listen to a story of modern life, a story of connections and of movement. The winding drive mirrors the meandering paths that Swami Jayananda has taken in her life, leaving her birthplace in Germany to travel far, first to India and back, and then, in the late 1950s, to North America. In the mid-1950s, when she was only 17 and an art student in Freiburg, her landlord (who was also one of her art teachers) was a disciple of Paul Brunton, author of *A Search in Secret India*, and himself a disciple of the well-known saint, Ramana Maharshi, who had been the subject of a large article by *National Geographic* magazine in 1949. Swami Jayananda had read the *Bhagavad Gita* before arriving in Freiburg to begin her program, but had not really pursued the study of things Indian until she came to know this teacher and his wife. Things were not going so well at art school, and one day, she found an Austrian yoga magazine that included an interview with Swami Sivananda of Rishikesh. The article made Sivananda and his ashram sound wonderful. Swami Jayananda, a tall and well-developed woman, said that what really caught her attention was the photograph of Sivananda: he was a large, robust, healthy-looking man with a smile to match, not a small, thin, withdrawn ascetic. So, in her best "schoolgirl English," she wrote to him; he wrote back with an invitation to visit the ashram in Rishikesh. Through a number of fortuitous encounters and events, Swami Jayananda eventually arrived, and spent four months with Sivananda learning yoga in 1958.

continued

Upon returning to Germany, she found that her brother was about to immigrate to Canada. Since Canada was a Commonwealth country, she figured that it would make a good staging point for future trips to India, and decided to accompany her brother on his journey. Swami Jayananda's arrival in Montreal nearly coincided with the arrival in North America of another one of Swami Sivananda's disciples, Swami Vishnudevananda, who had been teaching in New York City. Jayananda, then known as Sita, met up in Montreal with another young German woman, Sylvia, who had been at the DLS a year before her with Sylvia Hellmann (yet another German woman, the first Sylvia's ballet teacher, and soon to become Swami Sivananda-Radha, founder of the Yasodhara Ashram in British Columbia). The three of them opened their own yoga studio and became the center of DLS-related activities in Montreal. They invited Vishnudevananda to visit from New York, and soon he took over the facility, founding his first yoga school and the basis for a now global network known as the Sivananda Yoga Vedanta Centers and Ashrams. Although Swami Jayananda declined to acknowledge Vishnudevananda as her guru, she did continue to work at the center and take yoga classes with him for awhile. By the early 1960s, however, she and her new husband, another European immigrant, moved south to became the managers and yoga teachers for the Ananda Ashram in Monroe, NY, run by Dr. Mishra (another medical doctor, later known as Swami Brahmananda). Ananda Ashram was a major stopping place for the leaders of the counterculture, including Timothy Leary and many others, and Sita and her husband soon found that the atmosphere was not conducive to raising their young family. With the help of many supporters, they moved to a nearby town and started their own yoga school, continuing to sponsor visits from Chidananda and other swamis from Rishikesh, and becoming the touchpoint for North Americans who wanted to be part of the global Divine Life Society community.

Transnational Flows: The DLS and Worldwide Yoga

During the course of researching this project, I visited several tourist offices in the north of India, and a number of Government of India information offices in Europe and North America. In each, I asked where to find the best place for learning yoga. With rare exceptions, the response has been, "the Sivananda Ashram in Rishikesh." This advice has been given to foreigners asking about yoga since at least the time of Eliade's visit. The other disciples during that early period were primarily well-educated Brahmans (DLS 1987b) from southern India. By the 1950s, however, foreigners like the German women who would become Swamis Jayananda and Sivananda-Radha became a more expected sight around the ashram. There are now perhaps a dozen non-Indian permanent residents of the ashram, as well as a regular cast of visiting disciples from various countries. Kailash Ashram, already mentioned as the first ashram in Rishikesh, is considered to be the most "traditional" of the Rishikesh ashrams; teaching is conducted only in Hindi and Sanskrit, so very few foreigners, or even south Indians, are part of its community. In contrast, the Sivananda Ashram is run primarily by south Indians and operates largely in English; there, one can find very few native north Indians, except those who hail from cities like Delhi, Kolkata, or Mumbai (Bombay), and whose education was in English even if their mother tongue was another Indian language. There are, of course, many other ashrams in Rishikesh, numbering perhaps in the hundreds. Here, however, our focus remains on the DLS and the teachers who were trained there.

Many scholarly discussions of transnational flows of ideas, practices or products deal with the process of flows from the center or "core" and their differential uptake in the various corners of the "periphery." Yoga is unusual because it represents one of the few examples of an export from what has been assumed to be the "periphery" of economic and political power to the "center." Viewed in light of a political-economic model of core and peripheral nations (Wallerstein 1974), the phenomenon of yoga traveling from its origins on the Indian subcontinent to the West provides an excellent example of what Hannerz (1992) calls a "counter-current" in the larger body of transnational cultural flows. If we begin with an idea of centers and peripheries which emphasizes not political-economic power differentials, but rather philosophical-religious traditions, then the notion of an Eastern center and a Western periphery appears much more commonsensical. Over the centuries, the notion of a spiritual East and a material West has been propagated by people on both sides of this celebrated divide. The wisdom and spirituality of the ancient East has rarely been disputed, and in fact has been glorified by the American Transcendentalists, German and English Romantic poets and scholars, environmental activists worldwide, and of course the many representatives of Indian nationalism. Vivekananda himself justified the trip to Chicago as his opportunity to bring the spiritual wealth of India to the West, and to acquire some of the material wealth of the West to enrich the poor of India. With this background in mind, we can begin to understand how charismatic figures like Vivekananda and Sivananda have influenced how yoga is practiced and understood today, both in India and elsewhere around the world.

–3–

Balancing Acts: Doing Yoga in Rishikesh

Rishikesh – January, 1992

The *scooterwala* dropped us off at the junction of the Railway Road and the Hardwar Road, and there we stood, again surrounded by luggage. Three hotels were visible. My task was to find a temporary place to stay while beginning fieldwork, because I had not decided whether to look for a permanent room with a family, a place in an ashram, or some arrangement or combination as yet unimagined. After checking in at the closest hotel, my husband Carrick and I set out to explore. I was very glad for Carrick's presence and assistance as I settled in for fieldwork in Rishikesh. He left after two weeks to go back to his job in Switzerland, and did not return to India until the final three weeks of my research year.

Here, on the Hardwar Road in the heart of Rishikesh town, we were surrounded by the everyday clatter and bustle of streets lined with busy people, vegetable carts and popcorn vendors, travel agents and tour guides, hotels and restaurants and shops with textiles and cookware, flowers, incense, and party supplies for *pujas* (acts of spiritual devotion) and weddings, punctuated by the occasional doctor's office, motor parts shop, or pharmacy. The cloistered ashrams and peaceful Ganga of Lakshman Jhula (the northernmost section of "greater Rishikesh"), where we had been deposited by the bus upon arrival from Delhi, seemed impossibly far away. This very workaday "downtown" area also stood in contrast to what we had seen at Swaragashram on the east bank of the river, where blaring loudspeakers chanting prayers and brightly colored temples demanding to be noticed were the norm. The people strolling along the street and in the shops were a mixed bag: there were small clusters of orange-robed *sannyasins* (Figure 6); occasional white-clad Jains with long dusters to brush the bugs away lest they be trod upon and killed (violating their vow of non-violence toward all creatures); mountain villagers in colorful saris come down to town for supplies; uniformed schoolchildren; housewives whose critical eyes scoured the vegetable tables; and businessmen on their way to the local Rotary meeting at one of the fancier hotels. We encountered scattered pockets of well-dressed families on deluxe bus tour/pilgrimages from the cities, as well as the odd foreigner, often dressed in orange or disciple's white, or bearing the standard backpack and searching look. The town itself seemed to be growing at a phenomenal rate, with new construction springing up everywhere. Many of the new residences were for retirees from the cities; rather than renouncing worldly life, these older people were just bringing it up here to the banks of the Ganga.

Figure 6 *Sannyasins* at Tea Stall, Rishikesh (author photo)

Sivananda's Rishikesh: The Place to Go for Yoga

So far, we have reviewed some of the ways yoga has become a widespread set of ideas and practices both inside and outside of India, and how Sivananda's Divine Life Society, among other institutions, contributed to this process. Yoga became a technique promoted both for personal development and for nation-building over the course of the past century; it was even offered as a solution to broader global problems. We have seen how a particular place, Rishikesh, has served as one of the hubs for such a transnational cultural flow (Appadurai 1990). In this chapter, we take a closer look at the town of Rishikesh in the 1990s, with particular emphasis on the development of a translocal community of practice based on the yoga teachings of Sivananda. I suggest that the attraction of yoga practice, especially in Rishikesh, demonstrates the value of an "oasis regime" for reconciling the difficulties of satisfying the competing demands of life under conditions of modernity.

Rishikesh, at the crossroads between the mountains and the plains, between the sacred goals of pilgrims and the secular needs of local people and visiting travelers, serves as a point of departure for an examination of yoga as a set of ideologies and practices which originated on the Indian subcontinent, but which has, over the past century, been transformed through its transnational dissemination and re-presentation in India. In a country that has sought and received special recognition for its high degree of spirituality, the town of Rishikesh has had a particularly strong claim to fame. Rishikesh occupies a space that has been linked to the Gods because of its proximity to both the Ganga and the Himalaya, a place where "spiritual vibrations" are said to be highly concentrated, and where those who devote themselves to disciplined practice believe they will have a good chance of achieving liberation. As with any ethnographic description, my version of Rishikesh will not be identical with the Rishikesh experienced by others, but it will surely be recognizable. Rather than considering the full range of yoga instruction available in Rishikesh, my goal here is simply to discuss the DLS and two other Rishikesh yoga centers with affiliations to Sivananda's teachings, as they are seen by Rishikesh residents, yoga students, and visitors. In Chapter 4, I will follow the network out from Rishikesh to Delhi and beyond.

While the study of yoga is not the only reason that people come to Rishikesh, it is certainly one of the more visible activities once one arrives; signs offering yoga instruction are posted at regular intervals along the main roads of the town. Locals are well aware of the yoga business, and many practice yoga themselves. Visitors often give it a try, "just to see what it's all about." The reasons for doing yoga are quite varied, but fall into three primary though non-exclusive categories: spiritual advancement, stress relief, and physical fitness. In one of his earliest publications, *Fourteen Lessons on Raja Yoga*, Sivananda defines yoga as

> complete life. It is a method which overhauls all aspects of the human personality . . . Yoga shows you the marvellous method of rising from evil to good, and from goodness to holiness and then to divine splendour. Yoga is the art of right living. The yogi who has learned the art of right living is happy, harmonious, peaceful, and free from tension . . . It is an exact science, a perfect, practical system of self-culture. (Sivananda 1979 [1932]:vii).

In this chapter, the relationship between yoga practice and life goals receives detailed attention. How do individuals from very different sociocultural traditions perceive the value of yoga for their everyday lives? In what ways are yogic practices associated with the values of health and freedom and the emergence of specific new forms of community?

Rishikesh – February, 1992

From time to time, Swamiji would regale us with stories of his earlier life. He had earned a college degree in engineering, and by the mid-1970s had a job as an electrical engineer in the high-tech city of Bangalore, often referred to as India's

continued

Silicon Valley – a city where modern life intersects with colonial remnants such as authentic English pubs. Swamiji left it all behind to become a monk. His brother lived in Houston, Texas, and he had himself been offered a job in Germany, but he didn't want to leave India. His choice to renounce his former life and become an ascetic, living simply and without worldly attachments, came about in an unusual way.

Swamiji, then known as A.J., had gone with some friends to a lecture given by the internationally known Swami Vishnudevananda, whose organization was based in Canada. Swami Vishnu dared the Indian members of the audience to take *sannyas* (the ritual process of renouncing worldly social ties), as many of the Westerners there had already vowed to do. According to Swamiji, it was a matter of pride – he couldn't let the Westerners be more Hindu than he, a born Brahman, the highest caste in the Hindu religious and social order. So he took the dare, and began the process of detaching himself from the life of a modern engineer. Coming from a religious family, Swamiji had already felt a lack of spiritual depth in his own life, and had been considering the possibility of taking this step, but the senior Swami's challenge certainly sped up the process.

To become a *sannyasin*, one who has taken the vows of *sannyas*, is no small matter. Swamiji had to perform his own death rituals, the religious ceremony that his family would have done for him had he actually died. By engaging in this symbolic act, he announced to the world that he was leaving his old life and family behind. He would now go forward alone, intent only on his spiritual development. Having taken his vow in 1977, Swamiji became one of the primary leaders of Vishnudevananda's large ashram in southwestern India by the mid-1980s. But after ten years of watching the ashram's increasing commercialization, he quit. For Swamiji, money and spirituality did not belong together. He hated being obligated to recruit others into yoga classes, and to ask them for payment. The quest for a spiritual life, he felt, was something that could not be fulfilled under those conditions. He moved to Rishikesh to improve the quality of his own spiritual life, and if others chose to seek him out as part of their own quests, well, he would do what he could to help.

Swamiji viewed the practice of yoga and other meditative techniques as the old Hindu texts described them – methods for achieving a high level of spiritual awareness and liberation. He spurned the popular view, so common in the West, of yoga as merely a health and fitness routine. On the other hand, he touted the physical health benefits of yoga, because a person should take care of his body, at least long enough to reach a state of advanced spiritual awareness. With the everlasting power of the Ganga and the Himalayas, Rishikesh was, in Swamiji's eyes, the perfect place to practice yoga and to attain his goals.

Yoga in Rishikesh

In 1992, I spent eleven months in Rishikesh, practicing yoga at the Sivananda Ashram, as well as with several other yoga teachers who were associated in one way or another with the DLS and with Sivananda's living disciples. I conducted multiple and extended interviews with thirty six individuals with whom I had, for the most part, developed extensive relationships during my stay, as well as many less formal interviews with a wide range of other people both in Rishikesh and elsewhere. Later, I had the chance to pursue follow-up interviews with several of the German and American yoga practitioners who had left India to return home. All but four of the people I interviewed were between 25 and 50; of the Indians, most were male, while the majority of the non-Indians were female (I will return to the question of gender later in this chapter). All of the people interviewed shared lifestyle concerns that reflected a common dilemma articulated by many middle-class people around the world: how to balance goals of personal health, well-being, and *"Bildung"* in the Romantic sense of self-development, and growth against obligations felt to family and society (cf. English-Lueck 2003).

Styles of travel in Rishikesh have shifted from the traditional pedestrian religious pilgrimage to the intermediary tour-bus pilgrimage to the current fashions of health and eco-tourism, reflecting a transformation from the modern to the late modern (or even postmodern). John Urry (1995:145) points out the importance of reflexivity in modernity; the reflexive health tourist looks both outward (to the "experts") and inward (to the self) for the answers to health problems, and to prevention rather than cure. In this view, health is a coping strategy, which can be purchased, but only indirectly. The practice of yoga has become one such strategy, transformed from a method to achieve spiritual release to a method for managing stress and promoting health. The intention of such "oasis regimes," as introduced in Chapter 1, was to use yoga practice to both improve quality of life as well as increase workplace efficiency in the taxing human services occupations (medicine, social services) which engaged most of the yoga practitioners I met in Rishikesh. Transnational or translocal travel allowed these individuals to restructure their bodies and lives through displacement and replacement. Once an oasis regime has been established, it can be recalled and implemented at home, to much the same effect as had originally been accomplished through travel.

Oasis Regimes: Seeking Freedom through Health

A quick look at the home page for the Government of India's Tourism Office for Europe (*http://www.india-tourism.com/de_home.0.html*), or at any of a number of other tourism websites from India (see *http://www.geographicdestination.com/ inbound_packages/inbound_packages.htm* and *http://www.vihari.com/package tours/indiatourism.htm*) will show that one of the main topic headings is Wellness. The Wellness trend represents a shift in the perception of what it means to be healthy. The WHO UNICEF (1978) definition of health, "a complete state of physical, mental and social well-being, and not merely the absence of disease or infirmity," is a fundamentally unattainable state. For many Europeans and Americans, and increasing numbers of middle-class members of other societies around the world, health has become a prerequisite for freedom to succeed in a capitalist system. The term "wellness," coined by Halbert Dunn in a 1959 article in the *American Journal of Public Health,* was defined as the combination of well-being and fitness. Competition in the capitalist sphere, as Emily Martin (1994) has reminded us, requires flexibility, one of the hallmarks of the fit person. Schetter (1998:20) combines this definition with the WHO ideas of multiple levels of health and the "New Age" concepts of self-responsibility and conscious living. Where health had previously been defined as the absence of disease, definitions in the 1990s became increasingly synonymous with wellness:

> [Health is] the ability to identify and to realize aspirations, to satisfy needs, and to change or cope with the environment. Health is therefore a resource for everyday life, not the objective of living. Health is a positive concept emphasizing social and personal resources, as well as physical capacities.
>
> (from *www.hsd.uvic.ca/HIS/programs/s97cours/h270/wtegart/hconcept.htm*)

The trend toward wellness tourism requires flexibility and personal initiative. For example, consider yoga practitioners/tourists in Rishikesh, whether they came there from Germany, the United States, or another part of India. Few could be considered purists, seeking to renounce worldly life completely by spending seven years in Himalayan caves under a vow of silence – though I did meet a few who had done just that. Rather, most people that I met were working to develop a personal (and generally eclectic) routine of yoga practice that they could continue when they returned home. Instead of focusing on their personal spiritual growth by realizing the separation of physical body from self, and the unification of "little" self (*Atman*) with the universal self (*Brahman*), as traditional yoga practice would require, the primary goal of many of the Rishikesh yoga practitioners that I met was to have the opportunity to learn yoga without the distractions of their everyday hectic lives. They hoped to be able to develop a discipline that they could take home with them, a strategy that would help them get through their stressful work weeks in a less frenetic way. The practice of yoga was a way to create a separate space, both temporally and emotionally, but not geographically. It was, quite literally, a way to take a time out.

The health tourist's quest is not for authentic others, but for an authentic Self – a self which is at ease, relaxed, able to express itself without being buffeted about by external pressures. That Self is one thing that cannot be bought, cannot be mechanically reproduced, cannot be commodified. However, the time and place to locate that Self can indeed be bought, and through the development of an oasis regime, a set of self-building practices cobbled together in another zone (whether temporal or geographic) an individual can learn to take that "time out of time" back home. The authentic Self is healthy, in every sense of the word. It is another manifestation of high modernity's "reflexive project of the self" (Giddens 1991:5). Unlike the Romantic early modern self-development quests (*Bildungen*), the new goal is not for a youth to develop into a fully formed and productive adult member of society, but rather a sense of continual self-making, with no end in sight. Authenticity in this new kind of Self refers to an ongoing process of managing the various aspects of everyday life, from the most physical to the most philosophical, and trying to bring them into a dynamic balance. Wellness has become a metaphor for living in this perpetual balancing act.

Rishikesh – January, 1992

The first task I set for myself was to find a Hindi tutor, so that I could brush up on language skills. Walking down the main street in Rishikesh, I saw an advertisement for Hindi classes outside of the Omkarananda Bhavan, a multistory cement-block structure which houses a primary school and hosts evening programs for adults. The young man at the front desk was Ram, the Bengali bicyclist I mentioned in Chapter 2. Although he was in fact working part-time as an accountant at the Omkarananda Bhavan, and was not their "official" Hindi teacher, the administrator in charge there agreed that he could tutor me, since it seemed that their other courses, geared primarily for literacy training, would not be appropriate for my needs. We arranged to meet the next day at the Yoga Center where he took classes; it turned out to be one of the places I had read about in a German travel book before leaving for India. At that time, Ram was the house manager of Yoga Bhavan, a private house that had been donated to the Yoga Center as a hostel for visiting students. At the Yoga Bhavan, I met Canadians, Americans, Israelis, and Germans who had all come to Rishikesh to study yoga. Ram seemed to be the perfect tutor/assistant for this project – well-educated, easygoing, and an ardent yoga practitioner. We planned to review grammar using my textbooks for a month or two, and then move on to the problem of developing and translating my interview questions.

My reading of Ram proved true – he was a good friend and helpful assistant for the entire year. At the beginning of 1992, he considered himself only a student of yoga; by mid-year, after over a year of twice-a-day yoga instruction at the Yoga Center, he became the primary instructor at the Omkarananda Ganga Sadhan, a brand-new facility on the banks of the Ganga catering to visiting yoga students, and run by a Swiss woman, Mataji. Because he was a very sociable person, Ram had met a wide circle of interesting people in the short time he had been living in Rishikesh, and kindly introduced me to many of them.

Yoga Practice in Rishikesh

One methodological issue that I confronted on a nearly daily basis in Rishikesh was that of participation: participant-observation is one of anthropology's primary research strategies, but it was more than that for me. Participation in yoga classes was absolutely essential, not only to gaining credibility in the eyes of the community, but also to the personal bodily understanding of the transformations these practices make possible. Sivananda's oft-repeated formula for yogic life is "Be Good, Do Good"; "doing" and "being" are in this context at least as important as "knowing," if not more so. I have made an effort in the following pages to discuss my own experiential knowledge of yoga, gained through the course of these two years of research, in terms of the explanations and representations collected from interviews and the media.

As Sivananda told his reading public in an appendix to his first book, Rishikesh is an ideal place to meditate or do yoga. There, "[c]harm and spiritual influence are simply marvellous. You can put up your cottage . . . there is ample space for erection of new cottages" (Sivananda 1929:112). In the many years since this was written, thousands of people have taken his advice to heart. After considering many options, I decided to make one of the tourist hotels into my permanent home base. Though a bit unusual, this choice suited my research needs quite well: I was able to leave my books and computer equipment locked in my room, and go off to stay at an ashram for two or three weeks at a time, or travel to Delhi or Calcutta for library research. Interviews could be conducted in a quiet area of public space at the hotel, and I could come back from the ashram during the day to work on fieldnotes. Once my husband left India to return to his job in Switzerland, I was alone, and it was easier for me to eat at the hotel restaurant than to try to cook for myself or worry about managing domestic help. But the key deciding factor for choosing a hotel as my primary residence was Swamiji, the hotel swami, who had at that time been living at the hotel for about two years. He had become friends with the owner of the hotel more than a decade before, when he had made travel arrangements for Swami Vishnudevananda. Vishnudevananda's entourage had always stayed at this hotel on their way up to the high mountain shrine at Gangotri every year, and so "Swamiji" (as he was called, "-ji" being the honorific term attached to the name of any respected older person) had had ample opportunity to become acquainted with the hotel staff. According to Swamiji, the increasing commercialization of Vishnudevananda's organization had made him less and less interested in staying with the group; instead, he had made plans to go up to Gangotri, the source of the sacred Ganga, and live there by himself. But on the way up to the mountains, he again stopped in Rishikesh, and was persuaded to stay on at the hotel. Whether the hotel owner viewed this offer as a way to win spiritual merit, or a marketing ploy to display authenticity by virtue of having a resident *sannyasin* is not clear. Perhaps it was a little of both, as the arrangement seemed to work out well for everyone. In the lobby of the hotel stood a large sign proclaiming the availability of free yoga lessons daily, and it was this advertisement that sparked the idea of making the hotel my permanent residence. Where else could I find such a convenient yoga teacher? Swamiji turned out to be an extremely pleasant, articulate, and talkative person, and the opportunity to observe him in action for the year proved fruitful (Figure 7).

Rishikesh, India–February, 1992

Sunrise in the rooftop garden of the hotel provided a beautiful and calm setting for Swamiji's yoga classes. One morning, at 5.30 a.m., another hotel guest and I sat on our thin foam mats, hands to our faces, alternately closing one nostril and then the other, breathing deeply of the crisp morning air. According to Swamiji, this type of breathing created a balance in our respiration, leading to inner calm and reduced fatigue. Swamiji's yoga classes were held on an individual basis, whenever anyone wished one. In between instruction in the classical yoga postures, or *asanas*, Swamiji doled out advice for living a healthy and productive life.

Swamiji's yoga sessions were all exactly the same, starting with alternate nostril breathing and a few prayers, then moving on to a specific sequence of postures. His pace was slow and easy. Many of my friends who normally attended classes at another yoga center in town enjoyed coming to Swamiji's classes from time to time, just to have a break from their teacher's more militaristic style. In between the poses, Swamiji often told stories about his life and the people he had known, frequently punctuating his narrative with loud peals of laughter. Many stories poked fun at various yoga establishments; he once said that if he were to give anyone *sannyas*, he would name the person Swami Hypocrit-ananda just to be up front about what he saw as a pervasive problem, people choosing to become monks without having true spiritual motivation. He said that he hated going out to walk around in town, because he invariably saw some of his fellow swamis, and all they wanted to do was gossip about secular concerns.

I remember especially the story he told to illustrate the powerful vibrations that could be generated by the proper execution of yoga poses. He had come to the end of one of his classes at the ashram in south India. While his students were lying down in the relaxation pose of *shavasan* (the "corpse"), Swamiji saw a poisonous snake slither into the room. Watching the snake, Swamiji wondered what it would do; he didn't want to alarm everyone or risk danger by having them all jump up to get away from it. As it got closer to the meditating students, the snake's movements got slower and slower, until finally it curled up and went to sleep. The students, having completed their session, filed out without even noticing the snake. It was still sleeping when Swamiji took it and returned it to the forest: such is the power of yoga, or so he told me.

continued

Figure 7 Swamiji (author photo)

The style of yoga that Swamiji taught us is one that is very commonly practiced today; he learned it through Swami Vishnudevananda, one of the best known of Swami Sivananda's disciples. The poses and sequences of poses that Sivananda, and therefore Vishnudevananda, taught are considered by many to be a more authentic style of yoga than others available in the West, in part because they were so strongly associated in people's minds with the holy city of Rishikesh. But Sivananda's yoga tradition is only one of many developed in India over the centuries, and is no more or less "authentic" than the others. It is, however, more popular than many; today, one can find a Sivananda-style yoga class offered in major cities on nearly every continent.

Swamiji teaches yoga using a sequence of postures that includes the shoulder-stand (*sarvangasana*), and continues through plow (*halasana*), fish (*matsyasana*), forward bend (*pashchimottanasana*), cobra (*bhujangasana*), locust (*shalabhasana*), bow (*dhanurasana*), spinal twist (*ardha-matsyendrasana*), and finally headstand (*sirsasana*). The sequence begins and ends with an inverted posture, and the poses in the middle alternate between bending the spine forwards and backwards, and then to the side, which allows for the body to be stretched in all possible directions. This specific string of poses, Swamiji told us, produces balance. Failing to move the body equally in all directions will throw a person "out of whack," making him or her imbalanced in every aspect of life. While these positions and stretches were obviously good for physical health, Swamiji told us that with continued practice we would achieve a sense of balance throughout our lives.

Circles and Centers of Practice

During the course of my fieldwork in Rishikesh, I alternated staying at the DLS, at a small ashram close to Sumit's Yoga Center (YC), and at the hotel where Swamiji was based. These settings are quite different, but each represents a particular variant of what we can call the "Sivananda style" of yoga that forms the basis of an oasis regime. If we think of yoga as comprising several different families of practice, each of which can be understood as a language with its own structure and vocabulary, we can then view the yoga practices of Swamiji as a slight dialectical variation on the Sivananda tradition, and those of Sumit as a pidgin that mixed Iyengar-style practices with Sivananda-style presentation and framing. There were many other yoga centers and ashrams in Rishikesh, each professing to teach its own "brand" of yoga practice. My selection of these three teachers in no way represents the full range of "yoga in Rishikesh," much less that of India or the world. It does, however, clearly demonstrate the family of yoga instructors associated with Sivananda's Divine Life Society.

The definitional Sivananda-style regime is found at the DLS (Figures 8 and 9), where daily activities are stringently prescribed. To gain permission to stay there and participate in the DLS program, one must either write ahead – a strategy which rarely works, as the letter is invariably "lost" – or go for *darsan* of the general secretary of the DLS (who at that time was the legendary Swami Krishnananda) during his daily visitor audience, and ask permission directly. The tactic of having prospective visitors ask Krishnanandaji was a good one, in the sense that only those who truly want to stay would go through with approaching this Swami, widely known for his gruff manner and harsh-seeming words to many of the aspirants (cf. McKean 1996:193–204). For those individuals who passed this ordeal, Krishnananda's assistant would send to the front office a chit indicating acceptance of the visitor, who is then assigned a room. The quality and location of the assigned room depends on the identity of the aspirant, including family and business relations as well as national origin and how much she is expected to contribute (see McKean 1996), though of course the link between monetary donations and material conditions is never made openly. There is no charge for staying at the ashram and taking meals there, but a donation on the last day is customary. The DLS staff will not suggest an appropriate or typical amount to donate, however, even if asked.

Along with the room assignment comes a schedule of daily activities. When I was living in Rishikesh in 1992, a typical day at the Sivananda Ashram began with an hour of group meditation at 5 a.m. in the Satsang Hall, followed by a 90-minute *hatha* yoga class, then breakfast at last! The published schedule did not indicate, however, that there are usually one or two swamis giving lectures in English on the

Figure 8 Dancing Siva at the DLS, a.k.a. Sivananda Ashram (author photo)

Figure 9 DLS from Ram Jhula (author photo)

Gita or other texts after breakfast – one had to find out about such "informal" classes by word of mouth, and they were usually filled to capacity. After lunch there were again some informal classes. The second of the daily scheduled yoga classes began at 4.30 p.m., followed by dinner and *satsang* (community program including prayer, chanting, and featured lecture or guest presenter) until 9.30 or 10 in the evening. A glance at the website for the DLS branch in Germany shows that the 2003 daily schedule at the ashram in Rishikesh has changed, most notably adding the post-breakfast lecture classes, and separating male (a.m.) and female (p.m.) yoga classes (*http://www.divya-jyoti.de/Reiseinformationen/text_Ashram_Programm.htm*).

I spent several weeks at the DLS during the course of the year, and found that the position of *hatha* yoga instructor was not well honored. Each time I attended classes, I found a different young man in charge, and learned that since 1989, they had had difficulty keeping good yoga teachers interested in staying on. Therefore, the job fell to whichever young *brahmacharin* (student) was available, even if he knew nothing of *hatha* yoga technique. Consequently, the efforts made to teach a good class were minimal; this is of course in stark contrast with the fact that all of the Government of India's tourist offices sent visitors interested in yoga to the DLS, and many urban Indians whom I asked saw the DLS as one of the best places to go if one had an interest in learning *hatha* yoga. The question then arises regarding why the DLS retains its reputation as an excellent place for yoga instruction. One part of the answer lies in the simple fact of reputation; as has been demonstrated, word of Sivananda and his ashram has been circulated in English-speaking communities and centers (and this includes all Indian tourism bureaus) since the late 1920s, and that is not an easy thing to reverse.

Second, Sivananda's disciples in other parts of India and the world generally do provide comprehensive instruction in *hatha* yoga, and many of their students come to Rishikesh to gain an authentic link to their own swami's master. In these cases, the students may be somewhat disappointed by the instruction available in yoga, but they are generally rather pleased by the other components of the DLS headquarters experience. Finally, the mythological reputation of Rishikesh as a place of great spiritual power completely supercedes most concerns with the quality of instruction; as many people have told me, you can feel the spiritual vibrations of previous generations of meditators, including Sivananda himself, and so the practice of yoga and meditation is inestimably enhanced in this location.

Sumit and his Yoga Center

Sumit's Yoga Center offers a substantially different kind of program. Sumit, formerly a disciple of Swami Krishnananda, the general secretary at the DLS, had reportedly left the DLS because of a disagreement about how yoga should be taught. Sumit became a follower of B.K.S. Iyengar in 1981, during one of Iyengar's regular visits to the DLS ashram. Iyengar, another south Indian related by his sister's marriage to T. Krishnamacharya (father of T.K.V. Desikachar and uncle of Pattabhi Jois – all well-known yoga teachers in their own rights, with now global followings), is perhaps the most famous yoga teacher in the world today. Iyengar studied yoga with Krishnamacharya as a youth, and then began to develop his own style at an early age. He married young as well, having six children in quick succession. Iyengar was well settled as a yoga instructor when he met Sivananda in 1950, during the All-India Tour described in Chapter 2. The story Sumit told me, confirmed by other DLS residents, was that in 1950, Sivananda was impressed by Iyengar's proficiency at yoga, and asked him to come back to live in Rishikesh and be part of the DLS. Iyengar declined, saying that he had his family and did not want to renounce his householder lifestyle; however, after that meeting, Iyengar began to make regular visits to Rishikesh, first for *darshan* of Sivananda, and later for the opportunity to sit with Krishnananda and the other senior DLS swamis. I was somewhat surprised to hear that Iyengar engaged in this kind of regular spiritual fellowship, as might others who have heard of or experienced the very rigorous, physically strenuous, and almost militaristic style of an Iyengar yoga class. For those who have studied extensively in Pune with Iyengar, or who have read his bestselling books carefully, however, the spiritual aspect of Iyengar's insistence on physical exactness is affirmed.

After his initial meeting with Iyengar in Rishikesh, Sumit traveled to Pune to study more extensively with him, and now returns to Pune every other year for a few weeks of training. Sumit's Iyengar-influenced methods were apparently considered quite unorthodox by the DLS management, or at least by Swami Chidananda, though not by Krishnananda. Although Sumit himself declined to comment in detail on the reason for his departure from the DLS, one long-time resident told me that Chidananda had come into the yoga studio one day to find Sumit with an older woman visitor suspended by rope upside down on the wall – a common enough use of "yoga props" (see Figure 1) as developed by Iyengar. Horrified, he asked Sumit to stop teaching yoga classes; this may also have affected the pool of replacement yoga teachers, for it was from this time on that the DLS had difficulty finding appropriately trained students to teach for them. Word around town and the DLS had it that Sumit was caught in the ever-present, but rarely acknowledged, internal battle between the disciples of Chidananda and those of Krishnananda, which some people at the ashram suggested even extended to fights between the children of servants of the two.

In any event, Sumit had his supporters. With the help of a few wealthy backers, he started the Yoga Center, a large concrete barn-like structure on the banks of the Ganga, about three miles south of the DLS. There, he held regular morning and afternoon classes throughout the year, at 5 a.m. and 4 p.m.; he also conducted four "yoga intensives" of three weeks each in April, August, October and January. In addition to regular classes, I attended two of Sumit's intensive courses, which entail two 2-3 hour *hatha* yoga classes each day, one at 5 in the morning, and one in the late afternoon hours, as well as lectures, demonstrations, and assorted special activities throughout the day. Sumit had lived at the DLS for nine years and so had a very good relationship with many of the residents. He taught his yoga classes at his own center, but brought his students to the DLS for *darshan* of various senior swamis (including Krishnananda, but never Chidananda), or for special *pujas* (ceremonies) on holidays. Every morning he said prayers before his shrine, which included not only the gods Siva and Krishna, but also Sivananda and Chidananda as his successor (the power of the guru–student relationship demands that the lineage be honored, regardless of personal opinion); every evening, he conducted his own Ganga *Arati* (ceremony to honor the goddess Ganga Ma) for his students. Sumit's classes provided sharp relief against the half-hearted efforts of the DLS instructors I observed; his dedication to the practice of yoga was evident.

At the YC, everything operates at a rapid pace, with a fierce precision. Sumit, like his mentor Iyengar, barks orders and grabs arms and legs to shove them into proper yoga position. The studio contains many "props" for helping students achieve the most difficult positions: ropes, chairs, blankets, bolsters, blocks of wood. Sumit demonstrates from his place on a beautiful carpet atop a platform at the front of the room, with the Ganga flowing along past the window behind him (see Figure 2).

The students who participate in the regular daily classes are mostly Indians who are residents of Rishikesh, though not necessarily from Rishikesh by birth; for example, Ram attended these classes, as did several of the white water rafting guides. In contrast, the "intensives" draw a large number of foreigners. Again, tuition is not charged, but donations are expected. The foreign students usually stay at the Yoga Bhavan, a house high on the hillside above town, donated to the YC by another benefactor, or they stay at a small ashram on the Ganga. Though it is called an ashram, that facility is really more of a hostel. It is run by a woman from Delhi whose husband decided to renounce worldly life, bought this property on the Ganga, installed his wife there, and promptly took off to wander the Himalaya. The wife is not a particularly religious person, but at least having this hostel in such a well-visited town as Rishikesh keeps her fed and clothed, so she maintains her image while awaiting her husband's return.

The third yoga program that I joined was that of Swamiji, the hotel swami, who had been introduced to Sivananda's style of yoga through one of the earliest DLS "export gurus," Swami Vishnudevanada. In contrast with the other two institutions, Swamiji's classes were held on an individual basis, whenever anyone asked. Usually, he taught on the hotel roof for an hour in the morning, at around 7 a.m.; evening classes were possible, but didn't occur as frequently. Swamiji's classes followed a very similar sequence to that found at the other Vishnudevananda-affiliated centers, with a few additions and minor variations. Again, no fees were charged, and in Swamiji's case, no donations were expected – all of his needs were taken care of by the hotelier's family.[1] Since he lived in the hotel, out of the domains of the other monastics, Swamji had complete freedom to set up his own schedule of classes and activities. In addition to these three primary yoga training sites, I also made a point to visit yoga classes wherever I went in India. In Delhi, I attended many classes at the Sivananda Yoga Vedanta Center. After my Hindi tutor, Ram, became the official yoga teacher at the Omkarananda Yoga Sadhan Center in Rishikesh in July, 1992, I frequently attended classes there as well.

Health and Freedom through Yoga

The related questions of who practices yoga, and why, are addressed in the remainder of this chapter. Yoga, as utilized by the Rishikesh-based community of practitioners that I interviewed, appears to serve primarily as a component of an effort to "correct" modernity, rather than abandon it in a fit of Romantic dissent. As I discussed in Chapter 1, my working definition of modernity is as an ongoing process of interaction in the world which assumes that unlimited progress is both possible and desirable. Note that this definition, leaving open the meaning of "progress" as it does, is open to interpretation, and therefore to many alternate modernities. The members of the community of yoga practitioners that I became a part of during the course of my research understand "health" as another one of their human rights, without which a truly good life cannot be achieved; another way of understanding health is to invoke the metaphor of balance. They speak of the association between health and being "balanced," another positive value, sometimes in terms of such medical traditions as Ayurveda or other forms of humoral medicine, or of ecologically grounded metaphors of harmony and carefully counterbalanced biophysical systems. Many of those I interviewed saw yoga as a universal spiritual system for both health and morality maintenance, and thus a useful tool in the quest for a good life. Such an association between health and morality is of course not new. Harvey Green (1986), Haley (1978), and Lears (1981) point out that in both Europe and North America, the nineteenth century was characterized by a resurgence in health reform as a strategy for achieving broader social reforms. Conrad (1994: 388) has explored the degree to which "the pursuit of fitness and wellness has become a path of individual and moral action" among Americans.

In India, traditional medical practice does not mark out health and morality as separate domains. As Zimmerman (1987: 73) demonstrates, Ayurvedic medicine and religion are usually "mutually supportive . . . regions and things [that are] (physically) unhealthy are generally also (morally) impure." In terms of nineteenth- and early-twentieth-century Indian nationalist rhetoric, as we have seen in Chapter 2, the healthy body was a prerequisite for the development of a healthy nation (for further discussion of this theme, see Alter 1992, 1997). The quest for health has preoccupied the minds of both Indians and Euro-Americans for the past few centuries, carrying the weight of moral virtue along with the physical benefits of simply feeling good. In this context, Freedom – first that of the individual and then of the nation – has been valued above all. As we have already seen, one of the concepts that figured prominently in the nineteenth-century neo-Hindu revival was that of *jivanmukhti*, "living liberation."

The concept that links health and freedom is flexibility, sometimes described as the ability to adapt to new situations. One goal I heard voiced repeatedly was the desire to become flexible: people sought the ability to change as circumstances dictated, without losing their health, their freedom, or the monetary income that facilitated both. The techniques of yoga, whether postures, breathing, meditation or mantras, are tools to maintain control and stay balanced, thus achieving "peace of mind." My discussants suggest that self-control – discipline – and flexibility, are the keys to a successful modern life. Understood in this way, flexibility becomes a prerequisite for "fitness" in the evolutionary sense – that is, the capacity to survive and reproduce, whether one is speaking of biological reproduction or the ability to have one's ideas reproduced, as is so important in the "information age." The value placed on flexibility can therefore be understood as part of the quest for unlimited progress, characteristic of modern mindsets. Progress (defined as forward motion) can be achieved only if one is capable of adapting to accommodate "changing times."

Discussing Yoga in Rishikesh

I would like now to introduce some individuals from India, the United States, and Germany who practice yoga to varying extents, and who have at least as much in common with each other as they do with members of their "own" culture. The vignettes of yoga practitioners that appear in this chapter derive from lengthy, semi-structured interviews conducted in Rishikesh in 1992. Here, I show the ways that ideas of health and freedom, as discussed above, are incorporated into the everyday lives of people who do yoga. Practitioners' responses to selected open-ended questions about yoga, health, and the "good life" are presented through the telling of several stories, which though certainly unique, represent themes common to the entire group of those interviewed. These stories are linked by analytical segues which incorporate the experiences of other discussants. I have tried to summarize key points from both the interviews and also from my less formal knowledge of these people's lives, gleaned from many hours of casual conversation and shared practice. Although they demonstrate many common values, they also demonstrate various local or national histories. Clearly, the people who would travel to Rishikesh to learn yoga do not represent the majority of yoga practitioners around the world; there is another, larger, population of yoga practitioners and interested onlookers that has chosen to practice yoga, either exclusively or in addition to other available physical practices, but who have not had sufficient interest or funds to pursue these practices to their origins in India.

Here, then, are the stories of eight yoga practitioners I met in Rishikesh in 1992.

Trudi, in her early forties, works in a medical research laboratory in central Germany. She is blonde, in reasonable but not extremely good physical condition. Trudi had at one time been enrolled in medical school, but had to drop out because of health problems. She and her husband, a university professor, have visited Rishikesh two or three times before; the last two trips had also included a few weeks in south India, at the Kerala ashram of former Sivananda disciple Swami Vishnudevananda. Health is a subject of concern for Trudi, about which she has done a great deal of thinking. "Mind, Body, and Spirit: when these three things meet, when they are in equilibrium, then I feel healthy," she said in an interview. She had a lot of trouble earlier in her life, with her parents and in general:

> [I] looked for a lighter, simpler life . . . I wanted to do what I liked, to look and see what was in me. I wasn't centered, I wanted to journey inside and see . . . I had traveled a lot and seen other things, but . . . I was trying to find a kind of harmony . . . [now, through yoga, I] can live with conflict, I'm clearer in my head, more centered. I have no great wishes or desires anymore; to develop inside, yes, but . . . I'm really satisfied.

For Trudi, yoga was and continues to be "the possibility of freedom." Despite having always traveled, having no children, and generally creating a lifestyle as independent of others as she could, she felt she had never achieved freedom before doing yoga. For Trudi, the quest to be free begins with the biological question of having children, but extends into every other aspect of her life. She told me that she had put off having children for so long that she was no longer sure whether it would be possible. She said that she had delayed having children because she couldn't bear the thought of being "tied down," of giving up her perceived freedom for the sake of a child. But now, she had begun to see her freedom in a different way, not as solely the physical ability to take off for a new place at a moment's notice, and this reconception of freedom has made her reconsider the issue of childrearing. Trudi hopes that her work in medical research helps others, but her primary concern seems to be staying at peace with herself after what she describes as a hard life.

Like Trudi, other discussants also often linked ideas of health, balance, and moderation to notions of freedom; even the self-defined "traditional Brahman wives" mentioned independence and self-reliance as desired attributes. A typical definition of health among these yoga practitioners used the following logic: To be healthy means to be balanced, to have equal parts of physical, mental, spiritual, and social well-being. Moderation in all things is the best way to achieve this balance. Without health, one lacks the basic equipment required for self-reliance; one cannot make choices independent of the desires and abilities of others. So, to be healthy is to be free to pursue one's own ends. To be unhealthy is to be dependent on others.

To this end, self-control is highly valued, since regulation of one's own condition at every level – the avoidance of excess, the pursuit of moderation – is seen as conducive to achieving a good (that is, modern, independent, healthy, free) life. Yoga, as a system of self-management that embodies the values of flexibility and control, offers one way of addressing these concerns. But such a perspective on social interdependence is also clearly at odds with many traditional Hindu concepts, and these competing visions are certainly a source of difficulty for many of the Indian yoga practitioners I interviewed (see Ajay, below).

John, an American medical doctor in his early thirties, spent a year traveling in Asia before ending up in Rishikesh. Bearded and intense, with the look of a lifelong athlete and outdoorsman, John and his wife **Patricia** *(also a physician) were taking a sabbatical following the completion of their medical training. John describes an axis that runs between the poles of constraint/rigidity and freedom/flexibility, along which he feels that he has directed his life's choices. For him, physical well-being, one part of the physical/mental/spiritual/social quartet which constitutes good health, is being "well-rested, well-stretched, and well-breathed," in addition to following a diet of "variety and moderation." The high value placed on flexibility extends from direct bodily sensation to financial freedom; John sees yoga as a "code of living" which satisfies his need to have a flexible structure around which he can organize his life. Flexibility also means the capacity to make choices, or to have options. Yoga provides a non-religious set of values, or rather, values which he sees as not religious "in any rigidly defined way."*

John seems to agree with Sivananda's assertion that the "Science of Raja Yoga is universal, it is applicable to all. Here indeed is shown the way to live a full and happy life to one's own personal advantage and usefulness to others" (Sivananda 1979: vi). Though "some can get enlightenment by darsan" (visual contact with a manifestation of god), yoga is good because it offers people like John – "skeptical, constrained, rigid" – the possibility of experiencing enlightenment through direct practice. John described how he kept his interest in yoga "in the closet" for a long time, because he didn't want to appear "flaky" to his all-American college fraternity brothers; he sensed that yoga appeared to threaten mainstream American materialist middle-class values, though he himself didn't feel a great conflict.

John and Patricia provided perhaps the most direct mirror for my own situation. Although they were a few years older than my husband and me, we had gone to the same universities (though we had not known them at the time), had some friends in common, and shared many of the same aspirations for our lives and our children-to-be. For Patricia and John, as for many other discussants who worked in the field of health or social services, the ability to function competently and caringly depended on the maintenance of their own health, framed in spiritual as well as physical terms. As Brown (1994) points out, many middle-class workers in the service or symbolic analysis sectors are involved in the business of shaping or producing certain feelings which are intimately bound to the image demanded by their jobs. Maintaining cheerful, calm, competent appearances can be extremely stressful, and so a need to develop stress-reducing strategies becomes critical, not only for optimal enjoyment of life, but simply to keep one's job.

---

*Rather than worrying about the opinions of his friends and family, like John, **Ajay** is torn between his desire to explore new places, ideas, and practices, and the more traditional framework his parents would like for him. A Rishikesh native whose father had come down from the hills of nearby Pauri Garhwal after Partition, Ajay had just turned 30 at the time of our discussion. He had completed a BS in chemistry at the local Degree College. After working for a time as an organic chemist in a nearby research and development laboratory, Ajay decided that this profession was not satisfying; "if you want to be happy, you have to be close to nature," he told me at one point. To seek a better life, Ajay took a job as a trekking leader for a leading Delhi travel agency, and then pursued a Master's degree in tourism at Garhwal University. He opened his own adventure travel firm in Rishikesh in 1990. Ajay, like John, was visibly fit and clearly enjoyed an active lifestyle. He tended to dress in Western-style sports clothing – warm-up suits and track shoes – and moved energetically from place to place.*

Though he grew up in a Brahman family in Rishikesh, Ajay's interest in yoga arose only after two or three non-Indians who were staying at his guesthouse (part of his travel business) told him about the various paths of yoga, and encouraged him to practice. He describes himself as "nothing special, I'm as common as other people, exploring this world's different styles, working hard, trying to achieve what is good in this world – good books, good music, good countries, trying to achieve that. Exploring myself and exploring this world are the most important – I'm trying to do that." Ajay's greatest dilemma is deciding how to follow his own dreams and still be a good son to his traditional Hindu parents:

> *In India things are very different [from the West], you are so attached, you don't do what you want, but you do what people want. If you don't do, then you are in a problem. That is for sure . . . For me, I haven't come to the conclusion yet, whether I have to do the things*

continued

> *my parents want or what I want . . . I'm trying to make a balanced thing, what they want and what I want . . ."*
>
> Ajay contrasts the Western appetite for yoga with his perception of a lack of interest on the part of Indians, saying
>
> *It's very human . . . it's with you, it's with me, it's with East, it's with West – whatever you have, you don't realize that. I mean, I see Ganga everyday, but I don't remember when I last went there for a dip . . . I know the day I want, I can go there. And then life goes on, and you don't go there. Right now, the people of India, I mean domestic clients [of my travel business] who come to Rishikesh, for them buying a Mercedes, buying the latest model of National or Sony VCR or VCP is more important than doing yoga. Going to Europe, have fun there, and come back. It's more fun going to Dubai and buying things and come back – it's more fun. But the West, they have everything, they have these things. But it's very simple, the grass on the other side, it's always greener, you always try to go there.*
>
> Yet for Ajay himself, yoga, too, is a means for exploration: "it's a way to explore yourself, explore your body, make your senses stronger, feel how your body is." Since the foreigners introduced him to yoga, it has been part of his health mainte-nance routine. Health, Ajay says, "is the most important thing," because "life is to explore the world, to explore yourself, without [health] you can't do anything, then the meaning of life is nothing."

In John's case, his American parents had provided all of the freedom and support to "find himself" and choose a path that would be most satisfying to him; for him, the choice to practice yoga was made to help order to a life that he felt was too open-ended and lacking in structure. Ajay's family, however, offered a great deal of structure, and yoga for him is a path to freedom, a way out of that rigidity that provides the opportunity for self-exploration without straying too far from the bounds of cultural acceptability. In describing the consumer orientation necessary to contemporary middle-classness in urban Nepal, Mark Liechty (2003) points out that youth in Kathmandu see the "practice" of fashion – not just the clothes and accoutrements themselves, but the identity-building acts of choosing and wearing fashions – as a path to freedom from traditional structures, both social and material. Because yoga practice invites accrual of two kinds of social capital simultaneously, as a set of practices both unassailably "Indian" and also of value to a cosmopolitan transnational elite, it is an ideal way for young adults in India to achieve a modi-cum of freedom within the constraints of social obligation. Yoga practitioners acquire a social identity that is by definition independent of family ties, and, taken to the extremes currently observed in the United States, also a material identity in the form of specially marketed yoga clothes and equipment, including personal "props" and bags. Clearly, this is a transformation from the original type of "freedom" – *mukhti* – described by the ancient texts and valorized by Eliade (1973[1958]), and from the use of special saffron or white clothing for renunciants.

Ajay's story illustrates a common difference found between the Indian and non-Indian discussants in my sample. Nearly everyone was concerned with reducing "stress," but the origin of the stress varied. Non-Indians tended to see the stress as emanating from their jobs, or from an excess of personal freedom, from too many available choices, while Indians tended to see family conflict, and the split between personal and social expectations, as a significant source of stress in their lives.

Beate, *a Berlin-based Bavarian social worker in her early thirties, spent approximately eighteen months in India, alternating residential stays in yoga ashrams with treks in the Himalayas. Like Ajay, Beate sees exploration of other lifeways as essential. Yoga provides good training for such exploration, but for Ajay, this training is matter of freedom, of widening horizons first internally and then externally. For Beate, yoga provides direct experience of limiting options, of structuring and balancing her responses so that she can maintain control. She defined health as feeling "comfortable in my body, that I have a balanced mind, that I have time to relax and am not all the time busy inside or outside...that I have enough food to eat and a top over my head if it's raining...that I'm able to be happy about things." She emphasizes the importance of good social relationships, and the ways that good relations provide energy, while bad ones drain energy. For her, relationships extend beyond the human to the environment, and she said that "being in nature gives me a lot of health," as opposed to being in the city. "A good life," she said, "is a natural life."*

One of Beate's greatest concerns was the ability to control her emotional responses to things: "I would like to have more control over my mind . . . for me, yoga has a balanced effect – my personality is quite unbalanced, it's not good, yoga is to balance my mind, my emotions, to get control of my mind, to keep my body strong." The values she would like to pass on to her children, should she have any, are similar to those her parents gave her – "as far as possible, a free life . . . to find a connection to nature." But her parents never had the opportunity to travel as she has, and she hopes to give her children knowledge of "other countries, other philosophies, other people, to help them get a real open mind for the world" The decision to have children or not is, for Beate, as for Trudi and many other non-Indian women, a question of being free. She speaks of her internal struggle: "One side wants freedom, the other side wants children."

The search for emancipation continues at many levels in Beate's life. Ajay and his wife, engaged in the same kind of struggle, have also put off starting a family – a decision which does not go unremarked upon in Rishikesh town as well as in their families. Several people told me that Ajay's parents are very upset with Ajay's wife because she has not borne any children yet, but my interviews with Ajay and his wife revealed quite clearly that the choice not to have children lay primarily with Ajay. Although none of the people who are profiled in this chapter have children, there is a good reason for this apparent skewing of the sample. Travel to India is not an easy undertaking, and so most of the non-resident people whom I met in Rishikesh were childless. There were, however, at least three Swiss families with children whom I interviewed; John and Patricia now live in Alaska and have two children as well. Additionally, the practice of yoga is most often undertaken in a serious way by those who have the time to spend on themselves; within the context of the classical Hindu life cycle, with its stages for students, householders, forest-dwellers, and renouncers, those who are participating in the second stage are rarely intensively engaged in yoga practice (unless the entire family is so involved in practice, as with one family I met in Rishikesh).

---

*Being closer to nature and learning to control emotional responses are central concerns for Beate as well as for **Michael**, a wiry, intense 30-year-old Christian whose parents were from the state of Kerala, though he was brought up in Assam, educated in Mysore, and currently working out of Delhi as a trekking and safari guide. Michael was enticed to come to Rishikesh by another trekking guide, who told him that it was the best way to reduce stress. After completing a month-long course, he agreed, saying that yoga allowed one to "better control one's mind and be stress free." At first, when he didn't know anything about yoga, he "thought it was exercise that somehow promotes good health," but now, he said, it's "a mental effect, you learn to relieve stress . . . I'm prone to being very excited about things, this will help me be cooler about things. Dealing with everyday life in India has become very stressful, especially with inflation."*

For Michael, nothing is more important than independence, being "totally self-reliant." The second most important aspect of a good life was "to be doing something for wildlife, and for others. To run my own company, to take care of people, not to exploit them, but to educate them, people from rural areas. Out in the country there are really good people." What he most hopes for any children he might have is that they "do something of their own, something creative which gives satisfaction and also enough to take care of themselves, that they live closer to nature," or at least "have a base away in nature." His own father wanted him to be an engineer, or at least work at home in the family business, but Michael couldn't convince himself of the value in following either of these professions. For his own children, he says, "I wouldn't like them to get embroiled in the competition of this present day modern life."

Michael, unmarried, has dealt with what both he and Ajay see as a pan-Indian problem of parental aspirations by making a stark break with his family; he had only recently resumed contact with them when our conversation took place. Michael's story was in many ways more like those of the non-Indians than those of the Indians I interviewed, and his Christian background may have played a part in this. However, I think that his sentiments more likely reflected the extreme cosmopolitanism gleaned from his intense exposure to wealthy Indians and foreigners for whom he led safaris.

Dr. Arjun Kalwar and his wife, *Dr. Gita Kalwar,* provide an interesting counterpoint to the stories of the young Indian men told previously. At 50, Arjun was one of the older people I interviewed in Rishikesh; his wife was 47. He practiced general medicine in Rishikesh, and she had a PhD in Geography from the Delhi School of Economics, and had published some scholarly articles. Their sons attended the prestigious Doon School in nearby Dehra Dun. Arjun had high hopes for his sons to continue the family medical tradition. They were married in 1972, and Gita moved to Rishikesh from Delhi; she was Punjabi, but had lived all over the country because her father was in the military. Arjun's family came from the Punjab just before Partition, because his aunt had a house in Rishikesh, and because his father, also a physician, said "there are a lot of Brahmans there." Neither felt that their own desires for their children differed greatly from those of their parents. In response to my question about his description of himself, Arjun said, "I am a satisfied person and I consider serving one's parents to be the most important thing and I believe more in joint family system and I am a pious person with great faith in God."

However, one point of difference stood out – both Arjun and Gita wanted their sons to have "international careers," and have the opportunity to travel, and more importantly, be known by others outside of India. Gita's self-description consisted of the words "cultured, educated, truthful, obedient, humility." They had both practiced yoga at varying points in their lives, and felt that it both improved their physical health and also gave them peace of mind. One point that Gita made, with which Arjun concurred, was that knowledge of yoga, at least in rudimentary form, was something that "every Hindu person learns at home."

As we saw in the first page of Chapter 1, the Bombay businessmen I encountered on the Rajdhani Express train, though upper-caste Hindus, were not of the same mind as Arjun. Yet for those Hindus who do have some experience with the practice of yoga, and even many who only know the name, there is certainly a sense of proprietary domain, that these practices, because they are indigenous to the subcontinent, are therefore more psychologically and physically suitable for Indians to engage in than, for example, aerobics or, prior to Independence, British-style militaristic physical training.

When asked about the scarcity of Indian women in yoga classes in Rishikesh, Gita's response echoed that of other Rishikesh women I interviewed (who were all wives of local businessmen, but generally about twenty years younger than Gita). She said that it was very difficult for women in Rishikesh to practice yoga outside their homes. In Delhi, or other urban areas, she said, it would be less of a problem. There had been a woman teaching yoga at her own home in Rishikesh for several years in the late 1980s, and almost all of Gita's friends had taken classes with her, but then the teacher left to pursue a degree in chemistry, and since then, there have been no classes in Rishikesh specifically geared for women. One of the younger wives had taken some classes with Sumit, because her husband also attended classes at the Yoga Center, but she stopped after her in-laws became upset by such public activity; it was not the practice of yoga, per se, that constituted the problem. Rather, the breach of upper-caste Hindu norms of modesty generated by interaction with unknown men in a public place was the primary concern. The yoga classes I attended at the Vishnudevananda's Delhi yoga center comprised of as many Indian women, of all ages, married and single, as men; this is the difference between an urban, cosmopolitan population and a rural, conservative one. All of the Rishikesh women, whether practicing at home or taking classes, felt that yoga was primarily beneficial as a way of losing weight or staying fit, but with the added benefit of relaxing the mind, and being slower and gentler than some of the all-women aerobics classes available. The spiritual component was less important to them, perhaps because all of the Indian women with whom I spoke were Hindus involved with many other kinds of religious practices and for them yoga filled a different, though complementary, purpose.

In contrast, most of the Rishikesh men, as well as the visiting men (both Indian and non-Indian), did see yoga as a religious activity, in addition to its utility for physical fitness. The non-resident women whom I met in Rishikesh, whether Indian or not, generally expressed attitudes more similar to the men, both resident and visiting, Indian or not. These differences between resident Rishikesh women and everyone else can be explained by the fact that all of the resident women were from high-caste families and married, thus subject to varying degrees of the seclusion that is typical of rural north Indian society (Jacobson and Wadley 1986; Jeffery et al. 1989). I met only two visiting women at the various yoga centers who were Indian. One was widowed and the other highly educated, never married, and from an urban area. Based on the yoga self-help literature available, both those works produced by the DLS and the myriad of others, there was certainly no indication that women should not practice yoga. Indeed, many publications explicitly discuss the benefits of yoga for women practitioners.

But what about the extremely high proportion of Western women involved in yoga, as compared with men? From the beginning, Vivekananda had more female disciples than male. One of the reasons that his message might have appealed so much to Western women is its nationalist subtext. As noted previously, it was designed to help Indian men strengthen their bodies and minds in preparation for serving a strong and independent Indian nation. The process of decolonizing a geographical territory requires a commensurate decolonization of the body, as Nandy (1988) has argued. In a speech, entitled "The Future of India," Vivekananda (1990a:230) likens the men of India to a nation of women, and his tone is not complementary. Such self-damnation on the part of Indians calls to mind Memmi's seminal analysis of the impact of colonialism: the first response is to emulate the oppressor, suppressing all of his traditional life, and the second is to "reconquer all the dimensions which colonization tore away from him" (Memmi 1965:120). As Nandy (1988) also suggests, the feminization of the colonial subject in relation to the masculinized oppressor was one opposition Vivekananda attempted to use in his reform effort. However, when Gandhi appeared, he took the feminization of the colonial subject and turned it into a positive emblem of opposition. Luhrmann (1994) has likewise noted the impact of postcolonial nationbuilding on selected segments of the Indian population. She studied Jains in Mumbai, finding that the dominant discourse among prominent Jain families who had been quite powerful under the Raj, but who were no longer so influential under the new government, concerned the effeteness of their sons.

As for the contemporary situation, the 1997 *Yoga Journal* survey reported just over 80 per cent female readership, and the statistics collected by Fuchs (1990) for Germany were comparable, as were my own observations of Western practitioners in India. By 2003, the *Yoga Journal* advertising demographics figure shifted to 89 per cent female (*http://www.yogajournal.com/advertise.cfm*)! Similarly, the German Yoga Teacher's Association (BDY) reports 4 million yoga practitioners in Germany (13 million estimated for the United States), 15,000 yoga teachers, 800 yoga schools, and an 80 per cent female ratio for practitioners (*www2.yoga.de*). One of the most obvious interpretations of this phenomenon concerns the meaning of yoga practice itself. Yoga is a method for re-forming the body; physical practices are used to modify the self. As in the case of the women's movement and most of the other new social movements, efforts to change society begin with a reformation at the level of the person. We can then see a strong parallel between the arguments made for the practice of yoga in India as part of a reclaiming of control over colonized male Indian bodies, as discussed above, and the situation for Western women seeking equal rights. Many Western women have engaged in bodily practices that emphasize the importance of control as a way of gaining power in other arenas of their lives; the strategy is one of connection rather than domination. On the other hand, for Western men, that very sense of connection may pose a threat to their perceived need for autonomy. In Chapter 5, I return to this theme through an exploration of contemporary print and web-based media representations of yoga in India, Germany, and the United States.

West Bengal – October, 1992

The train ride out of Kolkata plunged us into a lush green landscape, away from the noise and smell of the city and into a place of oxcarts and handplows. Ram's parents lived about an hour away, in a village known for its high numbers of learned Brahmans. Ram's directions were explicit, and we informed the pony-cart driver of our destination when my friend, another Fulbright scholar who was fluent in Bengali, and I disembarked from the train. The driver took us to the village, and from there asked directions to the home of Ram's father. After a small comedy of errors involving identical names, we arrived at the proper house. The entire extended family, from 4-year-old to aged grandmother, along with some of Ram's friends, were there to greet us. We were ushered in, and the eating began. Seven different kinds of sweets! In between mouthfuls, I gave news of Ram and explained how I had come to be his emissary. After the meal was over, we sat down to watch the video I had brought of Ram in Rishikesh.

Representing a Good Life in Rishikesh

The last case I want to present is both unusual and also strikingly similar to the stories already told. **Ram**, my friend, teacher, and discussant throughout the year I was in Rishikesh, held many of the same values already discussed here. In many ways, he offered a "textbook" case of a young Brahman brahmacharin, yet his background, education, and reflective approach to his life put a distinctive twist on the stereotype. During two interviews over the course of my fieldwork in Rishikesh, Ram gave the following definitions of a good life:

> A good life means, "Be Good and Do Good." This is the teaching of Sivanandji, and I believe it, that this is a good life.
>
> An ideal life is one in which I am happy and along with me, society is happy. When will I get it? What is the standard for this, what is the target? [My father] led a very ideal life . . . I would like to reach the standard of my father . . . [But] why should I not be like Swami Vivekanand? But that is very far. First I should be like my father.

The first interview occurred early in the year, at my request. He initiated the second late in the year. Over the year, he had spent a great deal of time thinking about this and other questions we had discussed. In his early thirties when we met, Ram had completed a Master's degree in Commerce at Calcutta University. In 1991, he left his

continued

job as an accountant in Calcutta, intent on circumnavigating India by bicycle; as *he described it, "my cycle tour is not to go here and there and see, that is not my purpose . . . it is a quest, it is a search . . . I want to seek something that is not available in my place."* He arrived in Rishikesh several months later; it was to be a brief stop on the way to the high Himalaya and the source of the river Ganga. But in Rishikesh, he found a yoga teacher, and began to study techniques he had only read about. After spending fifteen months intensively practicing yoga, Ram defined yoga in this way:

> *Yoga means a balance. Balanced life in eating, in talking, in working, in sleeping, in company, and day-to-day life . . . everything balance, that is called yoga . . . If you are able to balance yourself then all the universe will be balanced in front of you . . . yoga means control the mind through your controlled body and that leads to disciplined life and you'll be happy, and day by day you'll be spiritually developed, and finally, enlightenment.*

Ram's goal in life now is to teach yoga to the youth of India, to help them gain discipline and avoid the bad influences of the Kaliyuga (the last, destructive age of humankind, which occurs before the rebirth of the world), which makes everything happen too fast, so that life rages out of control. To achieve this goal, he plans to follow Vivekananda's lead and go West, teaching yoga and performing traditional music in Europe and North America to raise enough money to open a gymnasium/ yoga center in Rishikesh. When I left India, he was teaching yoga in one of the local schools; a year later, he wrote me that he had left Rishikesh altogether, and gone to Delhi to teach yoga classes at the All-India Medical center, one of the premiere medical facilities in India. Though he is certain that the path he is taking is right for him, he still exerts a great deal of energy trying to explain this to his family, who think that he should have married and settled down by now.

Several months after I first interviewed him, Ram decided to make a video of his life in Rishikesh for his parents in Calcutta. His rationale for producing this tape derived in part from the imploring letters he had been receiving from his father:

> *The purpose [of this video], it is multipurpose. Main point is that it is to record the yoga practice and my life around here, and you see, save a memorable thing. I want to record so that in old age I can see. Other purpose is, I left home nearly three years ago. So it's a long time, my close friends, my relatives, they are not finding me . . . it is a long interval. So some days ago, a little thinking has come in my mind. How can I express to them. Several times a letter is coming from my father, that "Your grandmother is very old now . . ." But how can I go there, this is a very important time in my life and Rishikesh is the best place for what I am doing. But I can't move in the near future. So I think, what is my daily life? They'll be happy to see – but another point I want to make, maybe somebody will misunderstand, this is not my manifestation, this is not a manifestation of Ram.*

continued

> The videotape was designed to show his middle-class Bengali Brahman family that he was indeed living a good life, even though he was not following his profession (accounting) and had not married. He was very concerned that others should not misunderstand his purpose, that no one think that this production was an egocentric activity. He wanted to be sure that we recognized that this video was "not a manifestation of Ram," meaning "Ram's ego," or the showing off of his talents. Rather, he hoped that the video would offer proof, a testimonial, to his family that his life was not being wasted, and partly as a result of these reflections, had decided to make a videotape of his life in Rishikesh for his family in Kolkata. Additionally, he wanted to have something to look back upon when he grew old, suggesting that he ultimately expected to leave Rishikesh and the ascetic lifestyle of the yoga student/teacher there.

Ram asked me to interview him about his life and goals on tape, and to play-act a student in his yoga class. Both of these roles replicated our "real-life" relationships. I posed questions from a script he gave me, based on his memory of my previous research interview. The video also included footage of Ram performing yoga *asanas* on the roof of one of the ashrams, with Indian music he had performed himself playing in the background. The sequential presentation of *asanas* was similar to the catalog of yoga poses found in many standard yoga books by Sivananda and his affiliates, and so represented a "moving" twist on what has become a standard genre for yoga texts, or, in this case, a life in yoga presented as a text to Ram's family and friends. I offered to pay for the video production costs as a way of thanking him for his help, and also requested my own copy of the finished tape for both personal and research purposes. He agreed, and as I would be traveling to Kolkata to use the National Library, I was designated the courier – in effect, representing Ram's case to his family, as his proxy.

As we spent the afternoon with Ram's family, my sense of frustration grew. Although my friend spoke Bengali and I spoke Hindi, very little English or Hindi was understood by the older members of the family for whom Ram had specifically created this message. Ram's father had received the letter explaining my visit, so everyone was on hand to welcome me and have direct word of Ram's health and life. They all marveled at his abilities in yoga and music as demonstrated on the tape. Unfortunately, power surges and failures made clear viewing of the three-hour video nearly impossible. Between language barriers and technological difficulties, very little of the carefully constructed explanations of Ram's life and goals actually came through. This technological problem didn't seem to bother anyone, however: the mere sight of Ram seemed sufficient. For them, the practice of yoga had a certain meaning – the ascetic's quest for *moksha* – and Ram's personal life goals of improving the nation by teaching yoga to children were irrelevant. He had told them of these goals in letters already, anyway, so the combination of a visual record and an educated Western courier only served to reinforce and validate what Ram had told them previously. Since almost no one there spoke English, which Ram certainly knew, it seems curious that he would choose this language for conveying such important information, and not at least use Hindi, which I could also speak, so more of his family and friends would understand. Before beginning to shoot the video, I had in fact asked him about the language question, since our first interview had been in Hindi – but he insisted that English would be better. Why? Perhaps the answer lay in the image; Sivananda and Vivekananda both wrote in English, and the 1992 equivalent was surely a video in English, with a musical soundtrack.

Ram's story highlights the difference between old and new middle-class values in one modern Bengali family. Ram's apparent "return to tradition" by living a life based on yoga causes his "traditional" Hindu family consternation. They wondered why they had sent him to university, why he left his "good job" as an accountant in Kolkata. Though they felt that living in such a holy place as Rishikesh and practicing yoga are auspicious activities, deserving of their support, they also thought that a son should stay near home, contribute to the family economy, marry and have children – not indulge in a restless quest by bicycle clear across India.

Did the video in fact ever convey Ram's message as he had explained it to me? For his family, visual proof of his health and accomplishments of the previous year and a half was a welcome sight, but I think they still wondered when he would stop this nonsense and come home. Ram's notion of yoga is that of a disciplinary corrective to the evils of the *Kaliyuga*, the fourth and most decadent era in the traditional Hindu cycle of the ages of Man.[2] But it is important to understand that this does not make him anti-modern in any way. Rather, just as the *Kaliyuga* is inevitable, so too are the changes wrought by modernity, and if one seeks a good life, it must be worked out within the framework available.

Ram was torn between feelings of obligation to his family, who clearly wanted him to become a householder before he decided to renounce social relationships and his own deeply felt need to pursue the path of yoga, though not necessarily by remaining isolated behind ashram walls. Instead of pursuing the promising career in the business world made possible by his MSc in Commerce, Ram wanted to obtain knowledge of yoga to help himself both "be good" and "do good" in the world. He held up the examples of Vivekananda and Sivananda as models for serving society by first developing the self. As one of the swamis at the DLS told a packed classroom of aspirants, "You don't try to cover the whole forest with leather, instead you get a pair of shoes." This sentiment has been repeated in many ways by many people, but the basic process involves each person first taking charge of him/herself, and then trying to help others.

Helping Others, Seeking Health

The high percentage of yoga practitioners in the "helping professions," as seen in both my study and the *Yoga Journal* survey cited earlier, can be interpreted as an effort by these individuals to resist domination by technocrats and other organizational specialists of modernity. Kriesi (1989) points out that the majority of supporters for most of the so-called New Social Movements (peace, environment, women, etc.) are employed as "social and cultural specialists," a group within which he locates "semiprofessionals and professionals in medical services, teaching, social work, arts, and journalism" (Kriesi 1989:1082). These professions may appeal to certain individuals precisely because the fact of providing service seems to overshadow their complicity with market forces, thus allowing their practitioners to feel as if they are escaping "direct implication in capitalist economic relations" (Kriesi 1989:1084). These helping professions then provide a rationale for living in the world while attempting to transcend its desires. They are another "middle way" between the horns of a dilemma, a sustainable choice which seeks a compromise between physical comfort and spiritual satisfaction. Ram's video project, though ostensibly for his family, provided a way for him to reflexively construct his own idea of the good life, and so mediate (literally) among the lifestyle choices available to a middle-class Bengali Brahman in the 1990s. Because he had consciously patterned his thinking after the writings of Vivekananda, Sivananda, Iyengar, and other yoga teachers whose audiences were drawn primarily from the educated classes of India and equally well-educated foreigners, his vision of his life could best be told using a similar medium.

Vivekananda's motto, echoed in the second of my interviews with Ram, was *Bano, Banao*. Literally translated, this motto would be "Become Something, Make Something." As Ram said, *"Bano-Banao*, Be and Make, that is my mantra – to make yourself, and to cause someone else to make [him/herself]." Swami Sivananda's version of this motto, also cited by Ram and visible in block letters around the ashram and on every publication of the Divine Life Society, is "Be Good, Do Good." With these words, the call for self-development and selfless service continues to resonate within the ranks of the transnational middle class. Ram's family, like many Bengalis, had pictures of Ramakrishna and Vivekananda around the house. Ram held both Vivekananda and Sivananda as role models and inspiration for his own life choices. Both leaders promoted the idea of an experientially based spiritual tradition that was at once thoroughly Indian – by which they meant spiritual in a predominately Hindu way – as well as compatible with Western rationality. They tried to solve the classic dilemma of choosing between science and religion by "going between the horns." In their quests for the good life, Ram and other members of the transnational community of yoga practitioners have also sought a space in the middle of many pairs. I argue that this community has constituted itself in part through its efforts to find a happy medium; they come mostly from the "middle" class not only by virtue of their socioeconomic status, and self-descriptions, but also by their mediating strategies. The search for balance dominates the lives of all of the people I have described here. Almost without exception, they see yoga as a strategy for helping them cope with the stress of being pulled between the poles of personal happiness and family or other societal responsibility. Most work in service occupations, where the welfare of others is in their hands; they have chosen to practice yoga primarily because they find that it gives them a way to foster the internal strength necessary to continue helping people around them.

By practicing yoga, non-Indians seem to be seeking a way of centering themselves, quite literally, so that they are not cut loose entirely. The metaphor of connectivity is quite prevalent in discourses on yoga practice in the West, but what most of the non-Indians hope to connect with is primarily a global community, and not a local or national one. One frequently heard assertion in the interviews with non-Indians was that "visiting Rishikesh/India is like coming home." In part, such a statement reflects the search for grounding in a sea of limitless possibility (Appadurai 1996:44), yet the majority did not interpret that statement as exclusive (i.e., that an individual could have only one home) – rather, they simply asserted that the presence of like-minded people mattered more than place or history. I certainly met several non-Indians for whom India felt more comfortable than their birthplaces as a place to live, while for a few other discussants, India itself was seen as a difficult or unpleasant place to live, but the ideas they associated with India, specifically yoga philosophy, transcended the unpleasantness they found in the material conditions. Indian yoga practitioners are also concerned about the need for an antidote to the stressful rootless, pace of modern life, but their vision of yoga in this process makes the added claim of birthright, validated now by the claims of Vivekananda, Sivananda, Kuvalayananda and the like, to conform with the tenets of modern science.

From these stories, it becomes clear that one difference between the Indian and non-Indian yoga practitioners is the way that yoga practice is situated; especially for Hindu Indians (but also, to a degree, for non-Hindu Indians), yoga practices are embedded in a sense of familial or national belonging. Whether the individual has much actual experience with yoga practice matters less to them than the identification with yoga as a tool that derives from their own pasts, nostalgically imagined or actual. In this way, for the Hindu Indians (and many non-resident Indians, but not for non-Indians) I spoke with, to belong to a community of practice based on yoga means to stay anchored in tradition. It does not matter whether that "tradition" has been reformulated as a secular or public strategy for health maintenance and freedom from stress, or is seen as a religious practice for the attainment of release from suffering in the world. But for non-Indians, especially those of Euro-

American descent, the practice of yoga provides something else. It is not a way to regain lost heritage, or family tradition, but rather to "find oneself," to anchor the self in a cosmopolitan society which is rapidly deterritorializing.

In this chapter, we encountered several individuals who had done intensive yoga practice in Rishikesh, many of whom first learned of yoga when they were living far from India. In the next chapter, we will move out from Rishikesh to explore the ways that Sivananda's message has been presented in other parts of India and the world. While Sivananda himself traveled little after he founded the DLS, his words in print and on tape have had a significant impact on the shape of yoga in the contemporary world.

—4—

Moving Out: Yoga for a Transnational Community of Practice

Hannover, Germany – November, 1993

After an evening's rest at the youth hostel in Rheine, I arrived in Hannover. Stella met me at the busy, modern, dreary train station. The functional post-war edifice was filled with bored and somewhat dangerous looking youth, public bathrooms with a purple cast from the bacteriacidal ultraviolet lights, and police on patrol. Everyone seemed to be circling warily for one reason or another, and the feeling of urban, industrial decay was inescapable. We left quickly for her flat, a few kilometers away. Stella was about 65 years old, and quite slight. Her graying hair was pulled back into a bun, revealing strong, sharp features. As a professional ballet dancer, she had traveled from her native Hungary to live all around Europe for many years. Though she had once married – her daughter was now 40 – she had been separated for over twenty five years. While Stella was working as an itinerant dancer in Bern, Switzerland, she first saw a German translation of Vivekananda's *Lectures from the 1000 Islands*, as well as other books that discussed the practice of yoga. In Switzerland, Stella met the well-known yoga teacher Selvarajan Yesudian, who had lived for a number of years in Hungary after leaving India. From these books and Yesudian's classes, Stella became interested in the practice of yoga. She moved to another dance company in Hannover, and eventually retired to start her own ballet school there. In the 1960s, she met a woman who had been to Rishikesh, met Sivananda, and brought back his books and ideas to Germany. That woman in turn introduced Stella to Swami Chidananda on one of his visits to the Divine Life Society of Cologne, Germany. Although she has had at least two dozen yoga teachers over her thirty years of practice, she considers Chidananda to be her guru. Our paths initially crossed at the DLS Spiritual Retreat held in Maryland before the 1993 Centenary of the Parliament of the World's Religions, where I helped translate English instructions and comments for her. Stella retired from her ballet school in 1989 in order to pursue her training in yoga. She completed the German Yoga Teachers' Association's full three-year intensive teacher training program, and, as she put it, "failed to achieve enlightenment." Stella had visited the DLS in Rishikesh once before, and wanted to return for a longer stay. When I met her, she had begun a course in Sanskrit at the university, and hoped to be able to read the ancient texts in the original – perhaps that way, she thought, enlightenment would finally come. When I asked her what goals she had for her daughter, a professor of classics at an institution a few hours south, she answered "Happiness and Peace of Mind." "That," she said, "is yoga. That is a good life."

Shifting Terrain: Multi-local Ethnography in Practice

Following my initial period of fieldwork based in Rishikesh, I pursued multi-local ethnographic research in Germany, Switzerland, and the United States for another fifteen months, making short research trips from my home base in Zurich, where my husband worked. The fieldwork conducted during the course of studying Sivananda's Divine Life Society, in both India and elsewhere, was both cosmopolitan, as discussed in Chapter 1, and also multi-local. In an overview titled "Ethnography in/of the World System," George Marcus describes multi-local ethnography in terms of movement "out from the single site and local situations of conventional ethnographic research designs to examine the circulation of cultural meanings, objects, and identities in diffuse time-space" (Marcus 1995:96). In this book, I have taken that charge seriously, and have developed a framework for conducting and describing the circulation of cultural meanings and activities in multilocal context, using the building blocks of vector and matrix presented in Chapter 1.

Marcus's (1995) review article elaborates upon one of his essays of a decade earlier, in which he had set up the question of how we can understand the anthropological project of holism as both research and representational strategy "once the line between the local worlds of subjects and the global world of systems becomes radically blurred" (Marcus 1986:171). At that time, Marcus suggested two possible ways of addressing this question ethnographically:

> First, by sequential narrative and the effect of simultaneity, the ethnographer might try in a single text to represent multiple, blindly interdependent locales, each explored ethnographically and mutually linked by the intended and unintended consequences of activities within them . . . While there are texts like this in fiction, I know of none in the literature of ethnography . . . In the second, much more manageable mode, the ethnographer constructs the text around a strategically selected locale, treating the system as background, albeit without losing sight of the fact that it is integrally constitutive of cultural life within the bounded subject matter. The rhetorical and self-conscious emphasis on the strategic and purposeful situating of ethnography is an important move in such works, linking it to broader issues of political economy. The fact is that the situating of most anthropological ethnography – why this group rather than another, why this locale rather than another – has not been acknowledged as a major problem . . . Instead, it has often been dictated by opportunity. (Marcus 1986:171–172)

My fieldwork in India exemplified the opportunistic mode of site selection at the outset, though the direction it took upon arrival made strategic use of that locale. I had done preliminary research in a town about 150 kilometers from Rishikesh, but was later told that a visa for research in that region would be hard to come by because of certain political problems in adjacent districts. A far less politically sensitive fieldsite, the director of the American Institute of Indian Studies told me, would be the tourist town of Rishikesh. Following his advice, I applied for and received permission to carry out research in Rishikesh town on the subject of health, images, and yoga. At that time, I fully expected to engage in a "traditional" single-site ethnographic project, to be carried out *not* "behind mud walls" but behind the colorful concrete walls of Swami Sivananda's DLS Ashram.[1]

In the usual manner of these things, it took a few weeks for work to get under-way at the ashram, and in that time, I realized that such a fixed local ethnography would be insufficient to describe what was going on in Rishikesh, especially in terms of yoga. Rishikesh is a pilgrimage town, and at any given time, one can find residents of any state in India, as well as a wide variety of international visitors, with residents of Western Europe, North America, Japan and Australia dominating that population. The primary impression I received upon first wandering the streets of Rishikesh town was heterogeneity. As I have mentioned, throughout the year I found that I was using nearly as much German, and far more English, than Hindi in my interviews and interactions with the yoga practitioners, ashramites, and townspeople who helped me learn about this complex locale. Marcus (1995:101) points out the methodological difficulties of multi-site fieldwork, saying that "[i]t is perhaps no accident that exemplars thus far of multi-sited fieldwork have been developed in monolingual (largely Anglo-American) contexts." As serendipity would have it, I had studied German for several years in high school and college before taking up French, and later, specifically for fieldwork, Hindi. In another twist of fate, a job caused my husband and me to take up residence in German-speaking Switzerland several months prior to beginning research in Rishikesh.

Both of these circumstances made it possible for me to follow through on a multi-site project in a way that would otherwise have been linguistically and financially untenable, since first fieldwork funding for research in Europe was at that time nearly impossible to obtain, especially for someone who, like me, was considered to be a "South Asianist" by training. Marcus's observation that if translocal "ethnography is to flourish in arenas that anthropology has defined as emblematic interests, it will soon have to *become* as multilingual as it is multi-sited" (Marcus 1995:101; emphasis added) demonstrates his own Anglo-American bias; for anthropologists from many other parts of the world (with Switzerland and India certainly providing fine examples), operating in a multilingual environment is nothing remarkable at all.

Another bit of kismet which helped shift my research orientation from the local to the global – or, rather, from one locale to a global web of interrelated locales – was a family health emergency which required me to leave India in the middle of the year. Despite my fears, this proved disastrous neither on the personal nor on the professional front. Once the cause of my leave of absence from India was resolved, I was able to follow through on a number of leads in both the United States and

Europe which provided new insights on the very institutions, people, practices and ideas I had begun to sort out in Rishikesh. In fact, I saw a number of the same people in at least two different locales and experienced most of the same practices in several different contexts both inside and outside of India. Ever-present at all of the sites were the ubiquitous pamphlets, tapes and images that are the main stock-in-trade of both Sivananda's Divine Life Society and Vivekananda's Ramakrishna Mission/Vedanta Society. While the range of sites in which I conducted fieldwork was uneven, in the sense that I spent different amounts of time in the various locations, continuity of purpose was maintained through direct human and print-media links back to Rishikesh.

Oasis Regimes: Creating a Community of Practice

To illustrate what I mean by a shared community of practice, we need to make an excursion from Rishikesh town to Switzerland, and from there to the east coast of the United States, and the event at which Stella and I met, a yoga retreat in Maryland. This excursion has as its basis a set of specific practices developed by Swami Sivananda. Sivananda created a set of Twenty Instructions for Spiritual Success that one can find in a number of different contexts around the DLS ashram: in books, pamphlets, signs, and a singular obelisk in the middle of a central plaza near the library and the main temple, as well as on the official DLS website (*http:// www.divinelifesociety.org/teachings/20instructions.html*).

These instructions begin as follows:

1. Get up at 4 a.m. daily. Do Japa and Meditation.
2. Sit on Padma or Siddhasana for Japa and Dhyana.
3. Take Sattvic food. Do not overload the stomach.
4. Do charity one-tenth of your income or one anna per rupee.

and progress to

11. Reduce your wants. Lead a happy, contented life . . .
14. Do not depend on servants. Have self-reliance....
17. Adhere to the motto "Simple living and high thinking" . . .
20. Keep a daily spiritual diary. Stick to your routine.

At the bottom of the pillar, the reader is admonished that "[t]hese 20 spiritual instructions contain the essence of yoga and vedanta. Follow them all strictly. Do not be lenient to your mind. You will attain supreme happiness." Those who stay overnight at the ashram receive a printed handbill with the daily schedule on it.

These instructions, and the pattern of daily life encoded in them, are reproduced in nearly every place that Sivananda's presence is found. Together they provide Sivananda's prescription for a divine life through yoga.

In order to become a member of the community of practice, then, it is useful at least to be familiar with these instructions, even if one is not entirely successful at fulfilling all of them. At the DLS ashram in Rishikesh, for example, no one will make a visitor wake up at 4 a.m. and participate in the program, but most of the non-residents I met during my visits made sincere efforts at least to try. I saw the same basic program in place at most of the Sivananda-affiliated institutions or programs outside of Rishikesh, and many individuals who claim discipleship with someone of the Sivananda lineage also use this framework to help structure their personal lives. By placing these instructions prominently on the DLS website as well, the DLS ensures access for global community of Sivananda's disciples.

And so our journey begins in Rishikesh, where I observed how these instructions fit into everyday life of DLS-affiliated yoga practitioners. When I asked if there were any foreigners who visited the DLS headquarters frequently, one of the North American residents of the DLS ashram suggested that I speak with Becki, a Swiss woman who had been visiting regularly for twenty years. Upon returning home to Zurich, I had the opportunity to visit Becki at her apartment. She was extremely excited to have contact with another person who had recently been physically present at the DLS ashram and who would understand her lifestyle, home decor, and practices. When I arrived, I saw images of Sivananda and the current DLS president, Chidananda, on the walls, and was shown Becki's shrine and meditation room, just as prescribed in Sivananda's instruction list. She told me that she did indeed get up early every day to meditate before work, maintained a vegetarian diet, and generally tried to follow Sivananda's rules. While showing me around, she repeatedly commented on how glad she was to have a visit from someone who "really understands" her, because she felt that no one in her local neighborhood, a typical middle-class Swiss suburb, could understand her practices since they had not experienced such things themselves.

As it happens, although there are a number of yoga schools and practitioners in the Zurich region, most of the Swiss who are affiliated with Sivananda or one of his disciples live in the western part of the country, around Geneva and Lausanne. Becki knew those people well, but saw them only rarely. Her feeling that my experiences with participating in a yogic lifestyle gave me greater insight into her personal situation was typical. Like Becki, many yoga practitioners whom I interviewed were reluctant to discuss their practices in great detail with someone who has had no experiential knowledge of these practices herself. An Indologist friend confirmed the importance of shared practice when he told me about his experiences in researching yoga in India. He said that the practitioners he consulted with commented favorably on his Sanskrit skills and ability to read the original texts, but would not discuss their own practices because they felt he could not properly comprehend them (Peter Schreiner, personal communication).

Becki's experience demonstrates a shift from the traditional geographically based community – Tönnies' (1957[1887] *Gemeinschaft*), still an extremely strong component of Swiss identity (Niederer 1996) – to deterritorialized, ideologically and praxis-centered communities. This type of shift in identity often leaves individuals caught in the middle, feeling neither fully a part of their local surroundings, nor yet capable of consistently accessing members of the dispersed community in order to reduce their sense of alienation. Many forms of "instant" communication, including telephone, fax, and computer network – the infrastructure for any kind of virtual community – do of course exist (more on these in Chapter 5), but whether they will prove up to the task of replacing everyday, localized, grounded communities remains an open question.

Over the next few months, Becki and I spoke occasionally on the telephone; then she left for one of her nearly annual trips to Rishikesh and the DLS Ashram. The next time I saw her was in the United States, late in the summer of 1993. Swami Chidananda, Becki, and several other people associated with the DLS had gathered in rural Maryland for the previously described spiritual retreat which preceded the centenary celebration of the Parliament of the World's Religions in Chicago. Sponsored by the DLS of Maryland, this retreat provided an opportunity for seeing many old friends whom I had already interviewed in Europe or India and meeting others whom, like Stella, I would later interview at their homes on other continents.

The schedule for the retreat closely followed that experienced by visitors and residents at the Rishikesh DLS Ashram, with meditation and *hatha* yoga early in the morning, followed by breakfast and lecture/*darshan* (seeing and being seen) by the swami-in-residence. The yoga classes were led by various well-known followers of the Sivananda tradition, including Lilias Folan, whose public television series on yoga, launched in 1972 and still syndicated, is perhaps the best known representation of yoga practice found in the United States today. Lilias, in the preface to one of her many books, has also supported my presentation of yoga as generative of a "community of practice," and referred to her television and reading audience as a "scattered brotherhood" (Folan 1981: ix), suggesting a network of known and unknown participants in a shared project. The uncovering of this network provided the basis for my multi-site ethnography of yoga. We will hear more about Lilias's experience with the DLS and her subsequent transmission of these teachings to the American public in Chapter 5.

Follow the Yellow Brick Road

Marcus (1995) points out that multi-site ethnography "is designed around chains, paths, threads, conjunctions, or juxtapositions of locations in which the ethno-grapher establishes some form of literal, physical presence, with an explicit, posited logic of association or connection among sites that in fact defines the argument of the ethnography" (Marcus 1995:105). He suggests several possible ways to construct these chains of locations, including following people, things, metaphors, plots/stories, lives, and conflicts. To this list I would add one more: follow the practice. While I did indeed follow some individual *people* from site to site, my effort to understand yoga in its transnational context has largely been a process of following the history and social life of a set of *practices*, like the Rishikesh Reihe, conveyed sometimes by people, sometimes by books, pamphlets or other printed texts, and sometimes by moving images like video or television. Understanding how yoga practices fit into the lives of people (sometimes the same and sometimes different ones) in disparate locales allows us, as Appadurai (1988a) suggests, to blur the boundaries between places and see the family resemblances as well as the distinctive features which cross-cut cultures. In this way, we can begin to see how multi-local ethnography can help anthropology avoid binding particular cultural forms to particular peoples and places. Rather than seeing Rishikesh as "the place for yoga",[2] we see people involved with practices that together comprise their lived experience (Ots 1994) in particular places; when the people move to different places, their practices may change, or they may not; if they stay in one locale, the same may be true. By highlighting the effects of translocally constituted practices on people living in disparate geographical spaces, we gain new insights on how to observe and understand peoples and cultures as fluid manifestations of specific historical configurations which may span not only temporal, but also spatial dimensions. Seen in this light, it becomes increasingly difficult to relegate people to the status of incarcerated natives bound to "their" places by the authenticity of local cultural forms.

San Francisco, California – December, 1992

The Sivananda Yoga Vedanta (SYV) Center of San Francisco, a converted apartment building turned ashram, is located near the campus of University of California, San Francisco (UCSF), at the edge of the Haight-Ashbury district that was made famous by the flower children of the 1960s. I was visiting the center on my way back to my temporary home in Switzerland, after having spent most of the previous year in India.

continued

The event that was taking place on this particular day was an Open House, a typical promotional strategy used by all of the SYV centers worldwide to attract new customers. Free food, videos, and yoga demonstration classes are the mainstays of these programs. Books and tapes may also be purchased, and payment of registration fees for classes arranged. The swami in charge at the San Francisco center is a Vietnamese-French woman with a very aggressive personal style. During my first visit to the San Francisco center, in 1990, I had seen no South Asian faces among the many Open House visitors, and had inquired if Indians, who represent a substantial portion of the San Francisco Bay area population, ever participated in their programs. The swami on duty answered that there were only rarely Indian participants, and offered the explanation (ethnocentric, and certainly not representative of the tolerance put forward in the DLS literature) that "they just weren't interested in this kind of hard work!" A few years later, at the time of my second visit, the center was still advertising their programs in the "Yoga and Health" section of *India Currents*, the local magazine of the Bay area South Asian community, and there were still very few Indians involved in the SYV center programs.

Exporting Yoga: Indian and Western Audiences

A different perspective on why Hindu Indians in San Francisco might be less interested in taking *hatha* yoga classes than Westerners, offered by a number of my discussants in Rishikesh but echoing the sentiments of Vivekananda 100 years before, is based on temperament. Several comments made by Indians during interviews, as well as a number of others that cropped up in casual conversations, related to the type of yoga that would attract different kinds of people. People said that Europeans and Americans were more attracted to *hatha* yoga than Indians because they had more *rajasic* temperments, while they viewed Indians as having more *tamasic* natures. This comment refers to the theory of the *gunas*, or qualities of matter, which comprise all substances including humans. The three *gunas* are *tamas* (heaviness, inertia, obstruction), *rajas* (energy, intenseness, movement), and *sattva* (intelligence, lucidity, calmness).[3] All matter is comprised of the *gunas* in varying degrees, and health is in part a function of balancing out the three *gunas* through appropriate food consumption. This is the rationale given by many people, from Dr. Kalwar, to the manager of the hotel where I lived in Rishikesh, to the swami in charge of the dining hall at the DLS, for the minimal use of spices in much Rishikesh restaurant and ashram cooking, because spices, as well as certain foods like onion, are not considered *sattvic*, that is, not conducive to becoming a balanced, spiritually pure individual.

The theory of the *gunas* figures prominently in ideas about appropriate yoga practice. The rationale assumed by the individuals I spoke with concerning Westerners' attraction to *hatha* yoga practice was that they were too hyperactive and nervous, and needed the physical calming effects of *hatha* yoga to use up their excess energy and allow their minds to become still, a reference to the second aphorism of Patanjali's *Yoga Sutras*: "Yoga is the cessation of the turnings of thought." The people who said that this was the reason that so many Westerners were attracted to the practice of *hatha* yoga used the same reasoning to suggest why it seemed to them that fewer Indians were interested in the practice of *hatha* yoga: because they were already slow-moving and didn't need that kind of calming, but rather they needed to rally and become more active. A parallel here can be found in Vivekananda's motivational speeches in India, upon his return from the West. Speaking to young audiences, he asked,

> What did I learn in the West . . . ? There, I saw that inside the national hearts of both Europe and America, resides the tremendous power of men's faith in themselves. An English boy will tell you – "I am an Englishman, and I can do anything." The American boy will tell you the same thing, and so will any European boy. Can our boys say the same thing here? No, nor even the boys' fathers. We have lost faith in ourselves . . . it is necessary to rouse up the hearts of men, to show them the glory of their souls. (Vivekananda 1990c:41)

As more and more expatriate Indians have become aware of the availability of organizations like the DLS and the Sivananda Yoga Vedanta centers in the West, however, and more and more Indian citizens travel abroad, the mixing between "native" and "foreign" visitors has increased. One of the visitors I spent time with in Rishikesh was a university student named Ramesh, who had grown up in Geneva, Switzerland, and only in the past few years started to read about yoga and try to develop his own practice. He came to India looking for what he termed "authentic" yoga and felt strongly that the DLS ashram provided this commodity.

Moving Out from the Center

As we have seen, Rishikesh draws an international clientele that defies description as one particular bounded cultural tradition. First a pilgrimage center and now also a hub for Himalayan adventure travel, Rishikesh defines itself in terms of both its mythology – as an essential Hindu locale – as well as its economy. Rishikesh is a market town that draws in local buyers for household goods and cosmopolitans from elsewhere in India and around the globe who want to share in its proclaimed natural and spiritual splendor. Although many people visit this town, most eventually return home. One effect that the DLS has had on the dynamics of India's interactions with the rest of the world derives from its near-missionary zeal in sending young yoga teachers out from Rishikesh to colonize the West. This globalizing process is important for understanding the ever-increasing market for yoga in both India and elsewhere. The DLS disciples who traveled out of India and set up yoga schools in Europe and North America (as well as Africa, Australia, and other parts of Asia, though these are beyond the scope of this research) were bringing what might be called "authentic" (local, situated, non-mechanically reproducible) yoga to new audiences. But this authentic product was, as we have seen in Chapter 2, itself developed out of the transnational flows of people and ideas that began with Vivekananda in the late nineteenth century. In keeping with Hannerz's (1992) notion of cultural creolization, I see yoga's transformation as a process of mutual interactive practice: we can take a snapshot of the transmission of yoga practices at any time, but the motion never ceases. More importantly, the perception of that process differs depending on the observer. This might be old hat in terms of theory, but it is important to remember when trying to explain the concrete fact that a specific set of ideas and practices called yoga has been constructed anew in a transnational context, becoming prevalent in parts of the world quite far from where it started, as well as experiencing a renaissance in India.

In its global manifestations, we can view yoga in a variety of ways: as ideology, practice, lifestyle, metaphor, commodity, and generator of a Turnerian emotive *communitas* which has come to substitute for the sort of physically grounded communal co-presence now available only sporadically, filling in the interstices of modern cosmopolitan lives. The quest for *communitas*, a sense of oneness without regard for socially imposed structural difference (V. Turner 1987[1969]), while certainly a universal spiritual ideal that is in many cases "contradicted by easily observable empirical facts" (van der Veer 1989b:60), can be viewed at a number of different levels in relation to other kinds of more material globalizing processes measured by consumption patterns and the like.

Most of the non-Indian visitors to Rishikesh with whom I spoke had learned about this particular place (and about yoga more generally), through both the written word, in travel guides and through the writings of Sivananda and others, as well as by word of mouth. For most of the Indian visitors, Rishikesh's fame as a pilgrimage destination derived explicitly from its culturally validated status as a place of great spiritual power, and therefore an ideal place to learn yoga. Despite the antiquity of its mythical referents, however, tourism and settlement in Rishikesh are both quite recent phenomena, as was discussed in Chapter 2.

Exporting Gurus: Satchidananda and Vishnudevananda

Two of Swami Sivananda's best known disciples from the early period of "export guru" dissemination are Swamis Vishnudevananda and Satchidananda. Swami Satchidananda (1914-2002) initially went to Sri Lanka in the 1950s at the bidding of Sivananda, in order to start a new branch of the DLS. He later visited the United States in 1966, eventually founding an ashram community in Virginia. This ashram, now called Yogaville, was based on his interpretation of Sivananda's yoga, renamed by Satchidananda to the trademarked "Integral Yoga™".[4] After his death in 2002 during a trip back to his native Tamil Nadu, Satchidananda's body was returned to Yogaville for final rites. The centerpiece of the Buckingham, Virginia, ashram is the LOTUS (Light Of Truth Universal Shrine) temple. Satchidananda's most visible disciple in recent years has been Dr. Dean Ornish, a California cardiologist whose clinical studies of the effects of vegetarian diet and yoga techniques on cardiovascular disease have spawned a number of popular books as well as a reasonable measure of professional credibility.

Ornish provides an excellent example of the "mainstreaming" of yoga in American life. He began his efforts to document the health benefits of yoga in the mid-1970s, when he was a medical student. He did not receive a great deal of support initially (Rachelle Doody, personal communication, 1994), and took great pains to remove any reference to yoga or vegetarianism (or anything else that could be considered marginal or "cult-like" by the medical establishment) when he wrote up his research. After the initial results proved favorable, Ornish gradually began to change his vocabulary and his audience. The transformation from marginal to mainstream culminated in the publication of a major New York Times bestseller, *Dr. Dean Ornish's Program for Reversing Heart Disease* (1990). As a tenured member of the UCSF Medical School faculty, he can finally speak openly about the health benefits of yoga. His rise to fame, along with the popularization of other alternative therapies based on Asian diets and bodily practices by individuals like Jon Kabat-Zinn and Deepak Chopra, have been accompanied by the creation of a new section at the National Institutes of Health, the Office of Alternative Medicine (OAM).[5]

Of all Sivananda's disciples, Swami Vishnudevananda best exemplifies the commodification of yoga, Indian spirituality and the guru in the world market. Vishnudevananda was one of the first of Sivananda's disciples to emigrate to the West. In addition to his main ashram in Val Morin, Quebec, he set up centers in the Bahamas and several locations across North America and Europe, in both cities and mountain/retreat areas, before moving back into the Indian sphere. He is perhaps the first of the "export gurus" to have developed the concept of the "yoga vacation," an idea that essentially reproduces the European spa experience – another classic "oasis regime" – with, quite literally, a new twist. For Vishnudevananda, the establishment of the Indian sites was, at least in part, a way to provide an "authentic" base for Western students and disciples to visit, a place with that aura of originality and intensity, described by many disciples as "spiritual vibrations," that cannot be replicated (Benjamin 1968[1955]), no matter how carefully schedules or activities are reproduced, as at the DLS retreat in Maryland. Though often staffed by local people, they initially catered to the needs of foreigners.

Swami Vishnudevananda, who had been known in Rishikesh primarily for his skills in *hatha* yoga, also arrived in New York in the 1950s. He was the first designated "professor" of *hatha* yoga at the DLS Yoga-Vedanta Forest Academy/ University and was invited by visiting students in 1957 to travel abroad and teach classes. With the permission of Sivananda, he left the ashram and by the end of the 1950s had set up a base in Montreal, working with Sita (Swami Jayananda) and Sylvia Hellman (Swami Sivnananda-Radha) to make a good start into what eventually would become a major international career. His story is extremely important for understanding the worldwide dissemination of yoga, and also for interpreting the stories of several of my discussants, most notably those of Swami Jayananda and the Rishikesh hotel Swami.

I learned of Vishnudevananda's death in 1993 while visiting Beate, one of the German discussants, at her home in Berlin, and although she did not consider herself to be a disciple, she was nevertheless quite saddened by his loss; reflecting on Vishnudevananda's death, she commented that it made her feel more strongly her ties to the global Sivananda yoga community, mourning his loss for them as well as herself. In his first book, originally published in 1960, Vishnudevananda stated that

> Yoga philosophy holds not only the answer to all man's problems, but also offers a scientific way to transcend his problems and suffering. Moreover, Yoga philosophy does not quarrel with any religion or faith, and can be practiced by anyone who is sincere and willing to search for the truth. There is no vague doctrine involved. (Vishnudevananda 1988[1960]: 11).

This statement provides some insight into the appeal generated by many of Sivananda's young emissaries. How could anyone find fault in such a system? As with Vivekananda's presentation of the yogic tradition, the DLS version offered "scientific" answers to the difficulties of human existence, without contradicting any particular religion, and without requiring the learning of abstract doctrine. Instead, sincerity and willingness to participate in a specific set of bodily practices were all that were required. Over the years, as Vishnudevananda's organization grew, his message became more and more distilled. In the 1988 preface to the same volume, he states that

> By closely observing the life-style and needs of the modern men and women of this planet I have synthesized the ancient wisdom of Yoga into five basic principles, which can be easily incorporated into everyone's own pattern of life. These principles are: (1) proper exercise; (2) proper breathing; (3) proper relaxation; (4) proper diet; and (5) positive thinking. (Vishudevananda 1988 [1960]: xi).

Following these principles, he says, will provide "strength and balance to face this decisive world era . . . If you can heal your own body and mind, you will be capable of healing and taking care of the planet" (xiv). Vishnudevananda was quite a showman, and many of his more flamboyant efforts were carried out in the name of global problems. In the late 1960s, he became known as the "flying swami" because he hired a pilot to fly him across the Berlin Wall, so that he could drop flowers and leaflets with prayers for world peace; he also flew over Northern Ireland with Peter Sellers, and over various places in the Middle East. He called his efforts the TWO, or "True World Order." In 1992, Swami Vishnu (as he was often known) took out ads in major newspapers that included a photo of Sivananda and a plea for mass participation in chanting and writing "*Om Namo Narayanaya*" (the name of the god Narayan) "to turn the tide of inevitable doom" and have the "whole world attain peace and harmony." McKean (1996: 237–239) notes that, as part of the Sivananda Birth Centenary activities in 1987, Swami Vishnu also took out full page ads for the TWO, quite similar to those described above, but with an added dimension of concern for invasion by UFOs (unidentified flying objects). The appeal for world unity in the face of extraterrestrial attack is rather extreme, but not inconsistent with his basic universalist position.

Swami Jayananda, described in earlier chapters as the head of the DLS in Maryland, had met Vishnudevananda first at the Sivananda Ashram, and then encountered him once more in Montreal, when they were both new to North America. She took some yoga classes with him, and found him to be very good at *hatha* yoga, but his approach was not her own, and she thought him to be overly concerned with making a name for himself and requiring allegiance of students. When Jayananda found another teacher, Swami Brahmananda (previously Dr. Mishra, physician and founder of Ananda Ashram), whom she felt could better explain the philosophy of yoga in addition to the postures, she stopped attending Vishnudevananda's classes. Swamiji, the Rishikesh hotel swami, was quite engaged by Vishnudevananda's style at first, and was one of his primary assistants in India (in fact, he was the director of Swami Vishnu's main Indian ashram in Trivandrum at the time of the Sivananda Centenary in 1987), but as time went by, he, like Jayananda, became disillusioned by the extreme market orientation of Vishnude-vananda's organization.

At least twenty-six different centers in thirteen countries are run under the auspices of the main Sivananda Yoga Vedanta Centre in Val Morin, Canada. Some are ashrams in beautiful settings, with comprehensive facilities for holding teacher's training courses, while others are storefront operations in urban areas, often near universities, with small yoga studios, boutiques selling incense, books, and clothing, and a few resident disciples to manage the activities. All the centers teach the same basic yoga class, which follows a sequence of postures based on, but not identical to, the familiar Rishikesh Reihe of Sivananda. Swami Vishnu's version differs in that he puts the headstand first (instead of last), and then proceeds through the rest of the sequence, adding three new postures, crow (*kakasana*), standing toe touch (*pada hasthasana*), and triangle (*trikonasana*) at the end. Though different teachers give partial rationales for this sequence, generally in terms of complementary motions (forward bends, backward bends), the main concern seems to be that everyone know what the trademark sequence of postures is, so that they will be able to join in classes at any one of the centers worldwide, without feeling that they are outsiders.

One of the Rishikesh hotel Swamiji's former students from his teaching days at the Kerala ashram began to direct Vishnudevananda's yoga center in New Delhi in 1992. The student is a British man, married to a British woman of Indian descent; they teach yoga practice and philosophy to upper-middle-class Indians. When the center opened, also in 1992, only a few people attended each class, but interest grew rapidly. During my visits to Delhi, I usually stayed in the relatively wealthy neighborhood called East of Kailash; the family I stayed with lived conveniently down the street from this same Sivananda Yoga Vedanta Center (SYVC) of Delhi. Attending yoga classes there was quite interesting – in many ways very similar to my experiences at other SYVCs in San Francisco and Geneva. The Delhi SYVC, which shares space with a school of classical Indian dance, attracts mostly older professional people, both male and female, who want to lose weight, get in shape, relieve stress, or become more aware of their own heritage. The center operates entirely in English. This is perfectly agreeable to the clientele, who, though mostly competent in Hindi, often hail from other linguistic regions of India, and share fluency in English. Some of these clients arrange to go to Rishikesh to visit the DLS, or down to Vishnudevananda's Neyyar Dam ashram in Kerala. The yoga practitioners whom I met in Delhi, like those in Rishikesh, were part of an affluent, highly educated, cosmopolitan set; they represented the vanguard of yoga's renaissance in India. Like yoga's surge in popularity in the United States and Europe since the early 1990s across wide sectors of the population – now expanded from the middle classes to the homeless (see http://www.streetyoga.org) – yoga in India has also seen a greatly expanded practitioner base.

The Politics of Yoga

As McKean (1996: 268) argues, "spirituality, with its privileging of transcendental values, is used by specific groups to simultaneously advance and mask their own interests." She demonstrates how, for the Divine Life Society and other "main-stream" spiritual organizations, "[t]he ideology of spirituality and charity camouflages the political and economic activities of religious and charitable organizations, activities which serve to reproduce exploitative social relations of production and exchange" (McKean 1996: 265). It is certainly the case that many of the institutions, including Vishnudevananda's and others associated with the DLS, have done little beyond the superficial to improve the situations of anyone beside themselves. I have no quarrel with McKean's basic argument, and agree that the power wielded by these organizations, though used to some extent to support charitable endeavors, is, nonetheless, primarily self-serving.

However, I want to be careful not to make light of the sincerity of individuals who may participate in the activities of such organizations. It is an oversimplification to assume that people are only participating in these groups as part of a "feel good" effort that requires only monetary donations and spiritual lip service. As Richard Fox (1989: 74) suggests, the relationship between individual actors and sociocultural institutions and systems is not simple; neither determines the other, but they are both constantly "in the making." The yoga practitioners whom I encountered were, for the most part, involved in yoga as one part of a lifestyle which entailed substantial service to others, as well as an effort to live a less resource-intensive life than many others with a similar level of education and cultural capital tend to enjoy. They are certainly not saints, but their individual actions do tend to demonstrate a greater sensitivity to existing socioeconomic and political imbalances than would be assumed using McKean's more institutional analysis of the membership of the DLS community. It is perhaps true that those individuals who have restructured their lives to include intensive bodily practices like yoga are in fact also more likely to make other tangible changes toward increasingly sustainable lifestyles and provision of services to those less fortunate, with an eye to shifting the existing balance of power. In a study of the motivating factors for "environmentally friendly behavior," a group from the Geographical Institute at the Swiss Federal Institute of Technology used a cartoon depicting one of their interviews as a cover image. The cartoon showed an interviewer holding out a microphone to a man in the headstand position. On the walls of the room were Greenpeace posters and artifacts of Hindu spirituality. Though humorous, the cartoon reiterates the study's findings that behavioral changes to more sustainable patterns of resource use are closely linked to both personal beliefs and social structural constraints and opportunities (Zierhofer and Ernste 1994).

Like Beate in Berlin, or John and Patricia in California, or Ram in Rishikesh, the majority of the Sivananda-affiliated yoga practitioners that I met on three continents felt strongly about two things: the importance of their own personal practice, which followed the Sivananda model presented in his "Twenty Instructions" to a greater or lesser degree, and the relevance of that practice for extending a sense of well-being to others in their communities through positive environmental and/or social action.

Winterthur, Switzerland – July, 1992

The trip to Winterthur from our home near Zurich was short; in forty-five minutes, we were walking across the tracks, away from the Winterthur station, past the industrial buildings and up the hill to a peaceful residential street. At the top of the hill we could not fail to notice our destination: a collection of houses painted electric blue – the Divine Light Zentrum, now the Swami Omkarananda Ashram International. They are ordinary houses, but of a startling color. We entered the main office, and found two gray-haired, well-dressed women behind a counter. They asked what we were looking for, and I replied that I just wanted to obtain some information about the institution and its programs, as I was living nearby and was interested in yoga. I told the women that I would be going to Rishikesh to study yoga and its practitioners and wondered if Omkarananda's ashram there was open for visitors. They regarded us suspiciously, but gave me a selection of literature by Omkarananda. My queries about the whereabouts of the swami were stonewalled; it became clear that prying outsiders were not welcome. At the many other yoga and meditation centers I have visited, the residents have been extremely welcoming; here, however, the cloak of secrecy weighed heavily. I was informed by the very polite (but suspicious) women that if I wanted to meet the swami, I could come on a designated weekend to the Winterthur ashram, and someone would drive me to him. It was impossible, I was told, to visit him on my own or to know his exact whereabouts. I declined.

Sex, Lies, Videotapes and Yoga

While the majority of the "export gurus" emanating from the DLS hub have developed respectable schools of yoga and not generated negative public images, some of Sivananda's disciples have been involved in scandals revolving around sex, money, and violence. These individuals are hardly unique in the history of eastern spiritual teachers and their relationships with disciples of all nationalities.[6]

Of the DLS affiliates accused of scandalous behavior, one who arrived at the DLS ashram in Rishikesh as a teenager comes immediately to mind: Swami Omkarananda. Many anthropologists beginning studies of Hinduism in one form or another have been warned by locals of the coupling of religion and corruption in India (see, for example, McKean 1996; van der Veer 1989). But just where did things go wrong? Omkarananda, like many of Sivananda's early disciples, and indeed the majority of the more recent DLS *brahmacharins* (students/trainees), was quite young when he arrived in Rishikesh. Within the context of available options for young, especially rural, Indian men, the prospect of monastic life appears to be a reasonable choice. By agreeing to obey a few rules, the young DLS initiate will have free housing, food, access to education, the prospect of meeting a wide range of Indian and foreign visitors, and perhaps even working up through the ranks to be able to travel internationally.

I am not questioning the spiritual inclinations or sincerity of belief and practice of these youths, but rather pointing out the material facts that have rarely been acknowledged in relation to the choice of a monastic lifestyle, especially in India. Van der Veer (1989) has discussed the development of priesthood as an occupational niche, but few scholars discuss the job of *brahmacharin-sannyasin* (student-renouncer, skipping the traditional middle phases of the upper-caste Hindu life cycle). Without these young men to do the work, ashrams like the DLS would be unable to carry out their current roster of service and maintenance projects. Yet, as "men of the cloth," their pursuits are clearly considered to be vocations rather than occupations in the ordinary sense. While there are surely downsides to being a monk, the vows and requirements of different sects vary widely (van der Veer 1989) and, of course, not all monks manage to live up to those vows anyway. The business of spirituality, as McKean clearly shows, has two sides: "The premise that spiritual power is transcendent and timeless deflects attention from the contingent and often opportunistic economic transactions which underwrite the social power of religious organizations headed by gurus" (McKean 1996:2).

From Divine Light to Omkarananda International

Omkarananda offers a more interesting case than Satyananda. The history of Omkarananda's Divine Light Zentrum, a completely separate entity from Sivananda's Divine Life Society, highlights the way that efforts to share ideas about universal spirituality can go awry. While the majority of India's "export gurus" have coexisted peacefully with their new neighbors abroad, some high profile groups, like Omkarananda in Switzerland and Rajneesh in the United States,[7] have done much to damage the credibility of Indian spirituality internationally – and, it might be added, at home in India as well. The case of Omkarananda is not widely known, but certainly caused quite a splash in the Swiss newspapers.

According to accounts in the DLS literature of the 1950s, Swami Omkarananda was one of Sivananda's favorite disciples. He came to Rishikesh when he was only 17, and was known as a talented writer and voracious reader of literature and philosophy, both European and Indian; many of Sivananda's major publications were edited by Omkarananda. While most of the other students took the practice of *hatha* or *raja* yoga as their stock-in-trade, Omkarananda had always been intellectually inclined, editing several major publications for the DLS and taking classes at a local college. He was particularly fascinated with Western philosophy and political theory, writing pamphlets on subjects ranging from Shakespeare to dialectical materialism and vedanta. He had been Sivananda's right-hand man in terms of publications, editing or writing a majority of the booklets produced at the ashram during his tenure, including the large volume on Sadhana, subtitled *A Textbook of the Psychology and Practice of the Techniques to Spiritual Perfection* (DLS 1985d).

In 1965, after the death of Sivananda, Omkarananda left Rishikesh, presumably as a result of a less-than-desirable ranking in the inevitable shakedown of organizational hierarchy that followed the loss of the master. Of the immediate post-Sivananda period, little has been documented. According to the official record, the only change was that Chidananda became the DLS president, and a new trustee was appointed in Sivananda's stead. But there were certainly many swamis "on the road" around that time; from an article published in the DLS magazine in 1966 (*Divine Life*, 28(4): 95–98), it appears that many former disciples, and some individuals with no connection whatsoever to the DLS had been making claims that produced negative publicity for the DLS. In defense of their good name, the DLS then published a listing of the "officially sanctioned" DLS affiliates outside of Rishikesh. These included individuals who had left the ashram on their own and started separate organizations which were well thought of by the DLS (e.g. the Chinmaya Mission in Bombay, Swami Radha in Canada, Swami Jyotirmayananda in Puerto Rico), as well as individuals who had been sent by Sivananda to specific locations abroad as representatives of the DLS, such as Swamis Vishnudevananda and Satchidananda. Although these two eventually founded their own organizations, distinct from the DLS, this did not occur until a few years later. Others mentioned in the article included Swamis Venkatesananda, sent to South Africa, and Omkarananda; they were both considered "Headquarters Swamis," available for recall to the home base at any time.

At the request of a Swiss woman who had visited the ashram several times, Omkarananda left Rishikesh for Winterthur, near Zurich, in 1965. There, he built up his own Divine Light Zentrum. While the DLS still considered him to be one of their own, on temporary loan to the Swiss disciples, the official history of the DLZ as given in the pamphlets available at the ashram in Winterthur did not mention the DLS or Sivananda anywhere, but said only that Omkarananda arrived in Winterthur in 1965 and founded the DLZ a year later. Omkarananda, who died in 2000, was by all accounts a charismatic individual who had learned well the strategies for public relations used by the DLS. He followed his leader, Sivananda, in producing scores of pamphlets, often with outrageous titles such as "Dialectical Materialism and the Spiritual Superman." But the Zentrum had difficulty getting along with its Swiss neighbors, and although the exact cause of the dispute is not clear, it seems that, in part, the problem lay in ashramites engaging in loud prayer activities at 4.30 a.m. (per Sivananda's "Twenty Instructions"). Since the ashram consists of a cluster of houses in a very suburban neighborhood, it offers little in the way of privacy or sound insulation.

However, what would appear to be a minor concern escalated dramatically, culminating in a major criminal trial to determine if Omkarananda and his associates were guilty of conspiring against the local government and people through such activities as the stockpiling of poison gas and the deployment of explosive devices (Stürmer 1980).[8] Ultimately, Omkarananda was sentenced to a long prison term, of which he served fourteen years; three of his associates were also sent to jail. Released from the Swiss prison in the late 1980s, Omkarananda was, not surprisingly, asked to leave the country. He went to Austria, and the associates left behind at the Winterthur ashram keep his whereabouts a guarded secret, as I noted earlier; he lived in Austria until his death in 2000 (http://www.rickross.com/reference/general/general164.html).

The story does not end there; instead, it comes full circle back to Rishikesh. Omkarananda was still in prison in Switzerland when his Swiss followers began purchasing land in and around Rishikesh. They worked to develop the organization in this area, and it would seem that while the surface intentions of providing educational services and housing are charitable, there are other underlying concerns. The organization has invested heavily in real estate, and entered into a kind of "return of the prodigal son" competition with Omkarananda's *gurubhai* Chidananda and Krishnananda of the DLS. The term *gurubhai,* or guru-brother, is a fictive kinship term used to designate the degree of association between students of the same guru: membership in the *sampradaya* (the brotherhood of recognized Sivananda organizations) implies the closeness of a kin relationship. Many overtly political moves have been noticed by local Rishikesh residents, such as the naming of a major street after Omkarananda – which takes considerable money and influence to execute – and his appearance on the board of overseers for the Char Dam, the four major pilgrimage sites in the Garhwal Himalaya, and at that time (1992) a major focus for the Uttar Pradesh Ministry of Tourism. The organization purchased prime real estate on the banks of the Ganga; Omkarananda's name began to turn up everywhere. He bought and ran a couple of local schools, mostly English medium, and took over a small temple on the ridge, next to which he built an enormous and elaborate new facility. By 2003, the number of schools owned by the Omkarananda organizations in northern India had expanded to over fifty, along with various other temples and institutions around India.

In 1992, there were about six Swiss people who lived at the opulent new Rishikesh ashram; according to locals who had watched the construction of the facility, these Swiss monks kept to themselves except for necessary shopping outings, but no one had ever seen Swami Omkarananda himself. The service staff of the Omkarananda institutions in Rishikesh are largely native Indians, but the administrators are primarily Swiss citizens of European descent. The combination of the rapidity with which the Omkarananda buildings were erected and institutions set up, along with the lack of visible direction because of Omkarananda's absence, reputed to be the result of tax fraud charges, provoked a fair amount of discussion by local citizens in Rishikesh regarding the insubstantial nature of the organization. Few saw it as anything but a big-money operation, and insisted that it did not belong in the same category as the DLS or other "authentic" religious centers (despite the fact that they, too, are "big-money operations"). However, most people acknowledged that there were a few good side-effects for the community in the form of more schooling opportunities in English.

People in Rishikesh, including a bank employee in charge of Omkarananda's accounts, said that while the service projects were a good thing, the organization itself was merely a front, with no personal substance behind it. The banker also assured me that vast sums were coming into the Omkarananda account from abroad. Although the DLS Sivananda centenary commemorative volume published in 1987 had made no mention of Omkarananda's activities after 1966, declining even to mention where he had gone after leaving Rishikesh (DLS 1987b: 234). His own literature published in Switzerland had mentioned only his stay in "an Himalayan ashram" without naming Sivananda or the DLS. By 1992, however, the two organizations were competing for the most visible presence in the Rishikesh spiritual scene, a not insignificant achievement in such an active religious marketplace. In addition, the association between Sivananda and Omkarananda was finally articulated through such actions as the sale of DLS materials at one of the Omkarananda installations and the participation by high-level DLS ashramites in various activities sponsored by Omkarananda's group. Web searches of Omkarananda-affiliated sites made in 2004 demonstrate active representation of the Sivananda connection (e.g., http://www.omkarananda-ashram.net/POSq1.html). And, though Omkarananda has been dead for several years now, his international institutional legacy is still thriving.

What can we make of such a story? At one level, there seems to be a dissonance between the perceptions of the Swiss and Austrian disciples, who refuse to acknowledge any wrongdoing on the part of their guru, and so continue to provide financial resources in support of his spiritual mission, and the DLS in Rishikesh, which had at least tacitly acknowledged wrongdoing through their complete removal of Omkarananda from their listings of affiliated spiritual leaders for nearly two decades. Yet he was reinstated as a member of the *sampradaya* after demonstration of his considerable financial and political power. While Omkarananda's organizations do not emphasize yoga practices in the way that many of the other DLS affiliates do, the DLZ (now known as Omkarananda Ashrams International), is nevertheless quite similar in at least superficial ways.

Viewing the 1992 "Aims and Objects" of the Rishikesh facility produced a feeling almost of caricature: "The Omkarananda Ashram International is a non-political, non-denominational, non-sectarian, international, spiritual, religious, cultural, scientific, educational, humanitarian, non-profit-making charitable society; it is . . . uncompromisingly dedicated to the untiring selfless Service of individual seekers of the Truth, the community, the nation, and the whole of humanity" (pamphlet, Omkarananda Ashram International 1992: 7); the 2004 website has a much more extensively articulated set of aims (http://www. omkarananda-ashram.org/aims.htm). The observable reality in Rishikesh is that Omkarananda garnered a great deal of money and was engaged in a competitive struggle for influence and spiritual authority in Rishikesh, even while his body remained sequestered in Austria. Even four years after his death, no acknowledgment regarding Omkarananda's *mahasamadhi* had yet been indicated on the ashram's website.

Through the example of Omkarananda, we can see that the transnational pathways linking Rishikesh and Switzerland (that I had myself followed) were fraught with hazards. The apparently simple golden path to fame and fortune that *gurubhai* Vishnudevananda, for example, had followed in his efforts to distance himself institutionally from the DLS while still maintaining a clear-cut and public relationship to the teachings of Sivananda, was rather different than the path taken by Omkarananda. Despite the clashes that the DLZ experienced in their efforts to engage in yoga practices and philosophies, the followers of Omkarananda have remained true to their guru, and seem to have decided that his message was worth promoting, regardless of public accusations and decisions against him.

The DLS Outside of India

When the DLS of Maryland held a retreat in honor of Swami Chidananda coming to the United States in 1993, more than 150 disciples came from across the United States, Europe, Japan, and the Bahamas to participate in a re-enactment of the daily regime at the DLS headquarters in Rishikesh: up at 4.30 in the morning for meditation, followed by a *hatha* yoga class and then breakfast; morning lectures and evening *satsangs* (group prayer meetings) with music and song. At the retreat, I recorded one of the more interesting (though poetically unfortunate) of Sivananda's original songs, sung one morning by Chidandanda. A cautionary tale to would-be social scientists, the Herbert Spencer Song goes like this:

> Be good, do good, govinda, govinda.
> Be cheerful, courageous, tolerant, patient, forgiving, liberal.
> Be moderate in everything . . .
> Do not study Herbert Spencer, this will make you an
>   atheist . . .
> Do not smoke, Govinda, Govinda.
> Do not drink, speak vulgar words, take bribes –
> this is bad, very bad, very, very, very, very bad . . .

Songs and poems of this sort constitute a regular feature of DLS *satsangs*. They are often, as this example shows, practice-oriented, with clear instructions about appropriate behavior and attitude. The Spencer song yields one of the few direct references to an individual Western thinker in Sivananda's writings, as most of his advice is based on broader, less arguable, tenets. While most of the participants were white Americans, a few black and Asian-American families, some native Japanese and Europeans, and several Indian immigrants to the United States (approximately 15 per cent of the group) were also part of this community. Without exception, all were well-educated middle-class people, most of whom had been to India at least once. Many people videotaped the proceedings. Because this retreat preceeded the well-advertised Centenary Parliament of the World's Religions in Chicago, many participants had planned to follow Chidananda there.

In addition to the usual DLS materials available for sale, Chidananda distributed free copies of the book *Essence of Yoga* to all of the retreat participants; it provides a summary of Sivananda's philosophy and the basic precepts of the DLS. This book has been part of the membership package received upon joining the DLS, and before 1992, was not available for sale separately; the edition that I was given explicitly states that it is "for members only." The reason Chidananda gave for distributing it at that time was that "Swami Krishnananda, the general secretary of the DLS, now refuses to take on new *non-Indian* members in the DLS;" since there were very few Indians present, the pointed nature of this gift was rather apparent. This statement, another indication of the ongoing rivalry between Chidananda and Krishnananda for shaping the direction of the DLS, was quite startling, both in its explicit acknowledgement of the rivalry and in its actual content. One of the main tenets of Sivananda's vision centered on the universal aspect of the DLS, and he certainly solicited membership far and wide. Such a push for membership by Indian nationals and Non-Resident Indians (NRIs – Indian citizens with permanent residence in other countries) only is one of the few overt signs of the kind of Hindu nationalist support engaged in by the DLS, but acknowledged publicly only rarely (cf. McKean 1996).

A shift in orientation from primarily international recruiting to broad exclusion, or at least discouragement, of non-Indian membership in the DLS is particularly interesting in light of the development of organizations like those of Vishnude-vananda and Omkarananda as they have become established first outside, and then within India. Just as Vivekananda established his Vedanta Societies first in the West, and only later developed the Ramakrishna Mission in India, these swamis went out from India, established organizations based on yoga and vedanta for specifically Western audiences, and then, in both cases much later, returned to India and created branches there which are now rivaling the mother institution for membership, the SYVCs in urban areas like Delhi, and Omkarananda's organiza-tion in Rishikesh itself. One interpretation of Krishnananda's push for Indian-only membership (aside from the fact that Chidananda is the one to travel abroad, and to acquire foreign disciples, and so it might have the effect of reducing his political power in the organization) would be that the DLS felt a need to strengthen its own position as the authentic Indian heir to Sivananda's empire, as opposed to being on equal footing with other associated institutions known primarily by their non-Indian membership. By capitalizing on the previously de-emphasized Hindu nationalist sympathies, the DLS could better position itself for political favor under conditions of a political scene dominated by right-wing Hindu conservatives of the BJP (Bharatiya Janata Party) and VHP (Vishwa Hindu Parishad).

In 1993, there were officially recognized DLS branches only in two locations – Germany and Belgium. DLS branches are now found in Germany, Austria, Belgium, the Netherlands, Britain, France, Italy, and Spain. The German group was not very open to my inquiries. Although one of their members, whose wife has been living in Rishikesh and translating the writings of Sivananda and other DLS swamis into German, has regularly sent me copies of these translations, my efforts to meet with the group's organizers or to attend functions when Swami Chidananda visited Europe were to no avail. The explanation given to me was that the regular members of the group so rarely see Chidananda that it was not fair to have an outsider take up space at one of the functions. While I can certainly appreciate that line of reasoning (and it should have then applied to the situation in the United States, which was emphatically not the case), I think that the anti-cult climate prevalent in Germany at the beginning of the 1990s, well publicized by articles on the dangers of Scientology and other visible spiritual groups in mainstream magazines like *Der Spiegel*, strongly affected their response to outsiders, even those who were open about their purpose, as I was. I also saw a bit of this sentiment displayed by the lone young woman on duty at the SYVC in Munich. Though Vishnudevananda's centers tend to be extremely public-oriented, holding monthly Open Houses and other regularly accessible programs, and although she was cautiously friendly, she seemed concerned that I would be hanging around trying to learn about the center, even (or perhaps especially!) after I explained that I was an anthropologist. This closed attitude was quite the opposite of what I encountered with the various American and New Delhi groups, who were extremely open to participation by new visitors, whether Chidananda was visiting or not.

The grave concern with being identified as a cult has a rather dark underside in terms of how yoga practice is sometimes understood in Germany today. In the United States, yoga is very much associated with "New Age" spirituality as well as neo-Hindu philosophy, but in Germany, there is a significant distinction made between the practice of *hatha* yoga and any spiritual component associated with Hinduism. A sociology professor then on the faculty of the Free University of Berlin told me that, in several of the yoga classes she had attended, some sponsored by her church and others by one of the *Volkshochschule* (adult education centers), most of the participants, including more than one of the instructors, had not known that the yoga exercises they were doing derived from Hindu philosophy and practice. Rather – and she showed me a class handout to demonstrate – the yoga postures were understood to be explicitly *Aryan* in origin (Shalini Randeria, personal communication, 1993).

The Indo-European Connection: Continental Yoga

One of the key features which distinguishes the early introduction of yoga (late nineteenth and early twentieth centuries) in Germany versus Britain and the United States is the fact that the dissemination of ideas took place almost solely through translated written materials. The charismatic presence of a living teacher was rarely available as was usually the case in the English-speaking countries. What this meant for the German public was that most information about yoga came through the interpretation of a teacher who had read some yoga literature, or who perhaps knew English and had corresponded with a teacher (as had Boris Sacharow, who had based the "First Yoga School in Germany" in the 1940s and 1950s on the teachings of Sivananda as he learned them through postal correspondence with the ashram in Rishikesh). The absence of the direct and personal *guru–shishya* (teacher–student) relationship left ample room for extreme variation in interpretation. The familiar German idea with which yoga could be linked was the search for linguistic and biological roots of "Aryan" northern Europe, which led to Sanskrit and to India; "The craving for the Other identity of the Protestant North middle-class . . . which led in the 1920's to a yearning for the non-national pan-Aryan, leads today with equal ease to a longing to merge with the masses of the Far East" (Bramwell 1989:29). One of the more prominent ways that yoga ideology and practice became known in Germany was through the works of the popular reformer Rudolf Steiner, whose philosophy, which he called Anthroposophy, incorporated elements of yoga into programs of health, education, and personal development.[9]

Among the earliest exceptions to the lack of direct yoga instruction in Germanic Europe was Selvarajan Yesudian. In Switzerland, the yoga studio of Yesudian and Hungarian émigrée Elisabeth Haich stands out as a major influence in the dissemination of yoga in central Europe. A native of south India, Yesudian came to Zurich by way of Hungary just prior to World War II. In Hungary, he met Haich, and with the help of his British passport,[10] they ended up in Switzerland during the war. Yesudian's main influence was Vivekananda, though he professed to have no guru and to espouse no particular philosophy but his own. By all accounts, he was extraordinarily handsome and charming in his youth. Becki described him as the best *hatha* yoga teacher she has encountered over her more than twenty-five years of involvement with yoga in several countries. Her main complaint concerning his pedagogic style concerned his unwillingness to credit any more contemporary (by which she meant post-Vivekananda) spiritual teachers with valuable insights, including Sivananda.

Many Germans came to Zurich to study yoga techniques with Yesudian in the 1940s and 1950s, then returned home to start their own schools. One opened a school in Stuttgart that is now run by his son, a PhD in religious studies who is also the public relations liaison for the German Yoga Teachers' Association. His dissertation discussing the rise of yoga in Germany (Fuchs 1990) provides valuable sociological data on the composition and motivations for German yoga practitioners.

Yoga is taught in most communities in Germany, whether through private schools in the larger towns, or through the *Volkshochschule*, the adult evening/weekend schools which are part of the public education system. In 1989, there were approximately 208,000 students taking part in 12,600 different yoga courses offered at over 750 *Volkshochschule* across former West Germany alone. Of these, 80 per cent of both students and teachers were women between the ages of 30 and 50; there were also about 150 private yoga schools in operation, with similar demographics. The majority of the individuals participating in beginner courses sought to learn relaxation techniques and a better consciousness of their bodies. The advanced students, who had studied for more than three years, were instead more interested in the spiritual component of yoga, as well as increased "self-knowledge" (as opposed to the "body-knowledge" of the beginners (Fuchs 1992:50-52). In 2004, the BDY reported that there are an estimated 4 million yoga practitioners in Germany alone.

One private school that took the notion of "Aryan" origins to an extreme is the "First Yoga School in Germany," based in Bayreuth; this school was started by Boris Sacharow, as discussed previously. The current director of this school, and author of several books, Sigmund Feuerabendt, presents himself in the direct line from Sacharow to Sivananda (http://www.feuerabendt.de/index.html). One of his many books is titled Naked Yoga. Karen, the stressed-out yoga student from Bayreuth whom I introduced in Chapter 1, was the photographer's model for that book. Karen and I had met in Rishikesh, where she had come to learn about the many other traditions of yoga practice available. I was then able to follow up with her after both of us had returned home to Europe. Upon her return to Germany, she decided not to continue taking classes with Feuerabendt, because his practices, seen in the light of the larger Sivananda tradition that she had experienced in India, seemed to her inappropriate. At that time, Feuerabendt was making public statements using the Indo-European linguistic link between Germany and India to assert that yoga was in fact not "Indian" but rather an "Aryan" practice.

During the 1990s, the BDY spent a great deal of energy distinguishing their organization and orientation from that of Feuerabendt, who founded a competing national yoga organization in 1995, the Association of Vidya-Yoga Teachers (BYV) after being removed from the BDY.[11] As the BDY struggled to present yoga as a respectable tool for stress reduction in the modern world, and not part of any cult phenomenon that so incenses the religious right in Germany, Feuerabendt continued to promote Aryan yoga. Interestingly enough, however, the 2004 web presence of the First Yoga School in Germany, still run by Feuerabendt, gives absolutely no indication regarding Aryan roots or nudity as essential components of yoga practice, though he includes an obscure discussion about "Ur-yoga" (original yoga; see http://www.yoga-uryoga.de/) that presumably represents the morphing of Aryan Yoga into a more acceptable format. As with Omkarananda, respectability apparently comes to those who wait.

Rheintal, Germany – April, 1994

The shop was called Siddhartha. Johannes, a young nurse I had met at the hotel in Rishikesh eighteen months before, had stopped nursing and taken up commerce. When I first met him at the hotel in Rishikesh, he was dressed in the white garb of a spiritual student, and could not take in the ambience of life along the Ganga quickly enough. He studied yoga with Swamiji, and later went on a pilgrimage to two of the Char Dam, the four major Himalayan shrines. In the eight months since his return to Germany from Rishikesh, he had opened an Indian import business and begun to teach yoga classes at a nearby ballet school. He returned periodically to Rishikesh, because one of our mutual friends, the owner of the hotel, was also himself trying to develop an export business – a handy arrangement. Johannes brought me news of the hotel swami as well: a world tour was in the works, in association with one of the other Vishnudevananda *gurubhai*, and Swamiji was set to travel to Europe, North America, and possibly Colombia. After I admired the beautiful jewelry and textiles in his shop, we went around the corner to Johannes' apartment for a cup of tea and an interview. He was one of the most earnest spiritual seekers I had encountered in India, yet he was the only person I found who switched from service to commerce. Clearly, the visit to Rishikesh had changed his life.

Reflections on Rishikesh: Creating Community through Practice

In David Miller's analysis of Sivananda and the DLS, he focuses on the concept of the *sampradaya*, which he translates as "teaching tradition," but to which I have added Anderson's (1983) work to include the sense of both imagined and face-to-face community that derives from such shared teachings. According to Miller, the structure of a *sampradaya* consists of "a pattern of ever and ever larger circles moving outward from the center, much as heat waves emanate from a blazing fire.

Yet, at the same time the 'pull' or movement is toward the center. The guru is at the center . . . The further one is from the center and from the guru, the less one feels the intimacy and warmth of the guru" (David Miller 1989:82–83). Miller takes up Bharati's idea of the modern Hindu renaissance as "that kind of Hindu thinking that adopts the language of Western science and technology as a model of communication and persuasion without renouncing traditional religious values" (1989:109). He then adds to that the structural level of the *sampradaya*.

I want to supplement this interpretation with another layer. The DLS *sampradaya* is a modern, ideological community grounded in shared practices which are based on the teachings of one individual, Sivananda. But the disciples who left Rishikesh to found other related yoga institutions or support international branches of the DLS maintained allegiance to Sivananda. Rather than starting new *sampradayas*, their organizations function more as variants of the original, using nearly identical practices and rationales, with only the packaging and catchwords ("Integral yoga" versus "yoga of synthesis," for example) differing. What we have, then, are multiple intersecting concentric circles, like the ripples you might see after throwing a handful of pebbles into a pond. These together comprise a loosely knit community of practice which is nonetheless also an imagined community, as only a small fraction of its participants are able to meet each other at the various conferences and retreats where broader intersections of vectors (individual teachers, practices, writings) within the *sampradaya* might occur.

Upon their return home, all of the visiting yoga practitioners whom I met in Rishikesh continued their yoga activities by themselves, and some, like Johannes, taught yoga classes. They all continued to seek out other people who practiced yoga, for both practical and spiritual support. Beate, for example, would visit the Berlin SYV Center for spiritual activities and attend an Iyengar-style class for technical practice. Just as Karen became uncomfortable with the "Aryan yoga" approach, I found that the people who had experienced yoga in Rishikesh generally sought ideologically similar centers with compatible practice regimes upon their return home, whether or not they had been involved with such groups before their trip. Beate commented that she felt the most "at home" in India when she visited those ashrams and centers that followed Vivekananda's "Science of Yoga" framework, promoting yoga as a rational set of practices that would help solve the problems of modern living, rather than a mystical ideology for removing oneself from society and its problems. This approach to yoga demonstrates an effort to extract the problems or toxins from worldly life, rather than follow the more traditional Hindu strategy of removing the person from the cycle of worldly woe. Using the ideal of the *jivanmukhti* instead of the monastic renunciant, the Vivekananda-influenced Sivananda style of yoga supports the concept of an oasis regime that, unlike a typical holiday (time away from normal routines), is used to develop a new routine to bring back home. By also developing a transnational network of institutions and individuals who belong to the same community of practice, the DLS family of yoga centers provides a way to participate in yoga practice while remaining fully engaged in the travails of everyday life.

When discussing globalization and change, scholars realize both the role of the international media (print, internet, and audiovisual) to create and transmit shared ideas, and the significance of discrete cultures in shaping the interpretation of those ideas. In Chapter 5, we examine how the ideas of health and freedom, embodied in yoga practice, take shared but somewhat different forms in India, Germany, and the United States. One of the outcomes of using yoga to promote the values of health and freedom at the level of the individual has been increased development of the concept of a global community. Such a community, grounded in the shared practice of yoga, has also been supported by other currently popular philosophical and practical programs such as the ecology movement. These two sets of ideology and practices, yoga and ecology, while certainly different in aim, scope, and history, nevertheless have converged at the beginning of the twenty-first century. They can be seen as two kinds of responses to perceived crises of modernity.

–5–

Yoga: A Global Positioning System

Zurich, Switzerland – June, 1994

The OEKO (ecological) Fair is a kind of Mecca for environmentally conscious Swiss. The annual trade show for ecological living draws huge crowds not only of professionals, but consumers from all walks of life. Many of the booths provide information on specific building materials or techniques, while others offer samples of organic food or cosmetics, or show videos relating to solar energy or adventure sports. But there are also a variety of different kinds of products sold which are thought to be of interest to the eco-consumers: gardening tools, outdoor sport specialties, and books. When I inquired about the rationale for devoting at least half of the inventory to books on yoga, Zen, Native American religion, and a host of other spiritual traditions, the proprietor of a specialized ecology bookstore who had brought nearly the entire store contents to OEKO told me that "they simply go together." She gave me a look which clearly said that she thought I was crazy, stupid, or both. The mission statement for the store presents the combined offering of environmental and spiritual information "als Ausweg der globalen Krise," the way out of the global crisis, the path to freedom. Their book catalog gives a list of the topics they cover: consciousness, evolution, women, homeopathy, American Indians, mysticism, nature, ecology, permaculture, solar energy, environment, yoga, and Zen. East and West, material and spiritual, all provide a piece of the answer. The message, though absolutely New Age and characteristically late modern, is one with which Vivekananda would have been completely comfortable.

Yoga and Health: From the Personal to the Planetary

In this chapter, I consider how the propagation of yoga in India, Europe, and North America over the past century represents one example of a broader effort, primarily by educated, middle-class people, to promote an alternative vision of modernity. This alternative can be characterized by its efforts to transcend a number of dichotomies that have persisted since the Enlightenment. It derives from a perceived need for a corrective to the course of modernity, rather than an abandoning of modernity altogether. Yoga as reinvented through the discourses of the Indians Vivekananda and Sivananda, their disciples, and their critics both at home

and abroad, provides a methodology for remaking the world according to a progressive utopian vision that gives primacy to maintaining health and freedom
within a global community.

Over the past century, mass-distributed print media, and more recently electronic media, have increasingly promoted a variety of techniques for improving or
maintaining health in the face of the highly stressful demands of modern living.
One of modernity's most valuable commodities is health, but as I've noted, the
concept of health itself has been changing, even as its importance has remained
constant (H. Green 1986). Health has increasingly come to be seen as a cultural
problem which can only be solved by an appeal to nature. This is not to say that
"nature cures" were unavailable in the nineteenth century – Ascona,[1] an alternative
colony in southern Switzerland, was only one of many places to promote such
treatments – but they were generally supported only by that sector of the educated
middle classes who felt most keenly that urban civilization was to blame for their
ills.

The majority of people in North America and Europe, as well as the rest of the
world, worried about the rapid spread of infectious disease, not the slow malaise
of neurasthenia. But gradually, as the age of infectious disease was seen to pass in
the West, attention focused on chronic illness and its origins in the diet and lifestyle
of modern urban communities (Omran 1971). Around the world, the nineteenth
century brought improvements in sanitary conditions, followed World War II by
the availability of antibiotics and vaccinations, yielding a steady decrease in
infectious disease at least among the more affluent sectors of society. During the
same time period, however, an increase in chronic, often diet and stress-related,
conditions occurred in those same sectors.

While everyone is concerned with reducing stress, the explanations for why
yoga is useful as a stress-reducing, fitness-increasing strategy differ in India and
the West. The American and German magazines emphasize the unification of body
and mind as a way to gain control over stress, and to relax; for Westerners, belief
in the need to integrate the self is essential for relieving the anxiety and tension
demanded by multifaceted modern life. In Indian presentations, however, the focus
tends to be on the scientific proof that yoga's bodily techniques will maintain
physical health and eliminate the physiological stress response.[2]

I want to explore two angles in order to understand the importance of yoga in
relation to the values of health and freedom. The first is to address the ways that
mass media constitute yoga as a desirable health maintenance practice by capitalizing on the promotion of such classic, essentializing dichotomies as body/mind and
the spiritual East/material West. The benefits ascribed to yoga are primarily stress
relief, as a strategy for coping with "modern life" by "connecting" body and mind
to create a unified (thus stronger) person. In the West, yoga is often presented as
a "natural" way to improve health and fitness, while in India, its link with ancient

Hindu culture tends to be the primary focus. The second angle of approach moves from the personal to the planetary level in an effort to understand how the practice of yoga by individuals has been promoted as a tool for improving not only their own health, but also the status of the entire Earth.

Such a claim of identification between the spiritual practices of the individual and the environmental health of the world was made quite explicitly by the woman at the OEKO Fair, quoted at the beginning of this chapter; it is supported by the use of mass media to provide information, rally action, and foster community. One rationale for this linkage between the individual person and the planet can be found in Turner's assertion of the significance of the human body as "the arena of social conflicts and repressive controls, as well as some of the most liberating aspects of contemporary culture and social life" (B.S. Turner 1994:27). Turner suggests that the emphasis on the modern individual's ability to produce him/herself as a particular kind of body and self has, ironically, "unleashed a new collective politics of identity, and an equally collective projection of individual bodily concerns in the form of environmentalist and 'green' movements" (ibid.). Likewise, the use of health-related metaphors, and particularly the notion of flexibility, was stressed by Gregory Bateson as early as the 1970s (Bateson 2000 [1972]).

Yoga appeals to different national audiences for different reasons. While nearly all of the print presentations I evaluated, whether from Indian, German, or American sources, promote yoga as an antidote to the stress of modern living, other "selling points" describe yoga as a technique for strengthening national identity; authenticating (and modernizing) traditional knowledge through scientifically validated health research and practice; creating community; enhancing personal development through control of the body and mind; or recovering mythical romanticized natural origins, thereby undoing the damages done to person and planet by centuries of "following the wrong path," that is, the path of urban civilization.

Yoga is one of those *techniques du corps* (Mauss 1973[1936]) that can be used to develop the self. Yoga practice begins with the management of the individual body, while the ecology movement takes as its focus the management of the planet. Popular representations of both yoga and the ecology movement use the language of health and illness, in both literal and metaphorical modes, to describe the condition of their respective subjects, whether person or planet. Both the popular representation of yoga and the ecology movement profess a holistic approach which refuses to accept dichotomous either/or structures – at least in theory. The primary features the projects of ecology and yoga have in common are the following:

1. *Universality*, defined as inclusivity rather than insistence on a single universal dogma, the making of a category large enough to encompass any opposition –

as Ashis Nandy (1988:99) has said, synthesis is a greater enemy of thesis than antithesis, as it subsumes rather than merely denying.

2. An emphasis on *spirituality* rather than religion, meaning that sentiment which underlies all religious activity, but is not content or context bound.
3. An explicit link between the level of the *person* and that of whole *planet* or even the cosmos.
4. A *praxis orientation* requiring people to practice what they preach, or at least what they read.

Notably, both tend to give more attention to the promotion of agendas which do not necessarily respect the borders of nation-states, but rather emphasize the needs of local communities, larger transnational regions ("the rainforest"), or the world as a whole (global climate change, world peace). By invoking such metaphorical ideals as harmony, health, and balance, proponents of such personal practice-oriented ideologies as yoga and ecology work to reconceptualize the public sphere, creating continuity from personal to global spheres of action. Following the advice prescribed by economist E.F. Schumacher (1990) in his Buddhist-inspired ecology manifesto *Small Is Beautiful* – "Get your own house in order and the rest will follow" – both see the actions of individuals as having a significant potential to affect the "globalen Krise" which so worried the ecology bookstore proprietor in Switzerland described at the beginning of this chapter.

One way to conceive the relationship between yoga and the ecology movement is to subsume them both under the heading of the "New Age," a term I prefer to avoid because it deflects attention from the more specific historical and geographical argument. It is appropriate to bring it up here, however, in order to show how the practice of yoga has been located within the various regional/national traditions, and why these particular places were so receptive. The New Age, as many have ably shown (Albanese 1977; Bramwell 1989; M. Green 1992; Heelas 1996), has a history stretching back to the late eighteenth century with regard to continuity of key principles of self-actualization, healing, connection with self and nature, freedom, and a methodology for achieving all of the above. At various times and places, but most intensively at the ends of millennia (M. Green 1992), individuals have picked up and woven together threads of ideology and practice from available texts and traditions to support these principles. The development of yoga represents one such thread, itself spun of many different strands. The lines of Vivekananda and Sivananda represent only a small portion of the yoga tradition, but they are "good to think with" nonetheless, providing an extended example which is both historically and transnationally significant because of the uses to which it has been put by people from India, Germany, the United States, and elsewhere over the past century.

Central to all of these New Age ideologies, whenever they have occurred, has been the creation of community in one form or another, whether a remote commune like Ascona, or a scattered network of associations like that of Sivananda, or a website like the Global Eco-village Network supported by the Gaia Trust (http://gen.ecovillage.org/); each of these intentional communities, wherever it falls on the scale of permanence to ephemeral associations, can be studied as a matrix, a place where the trajectories of multiple vectors intersect for a time. The power of mass media to create connections has been vital to the sustained existence of these communities. Extending Anderson's (1983) argument for the value of print capitalism in creating national and other supra-local imagined communities, we can see that new types of media representations allow for both the reproduction of core values or practices, as well as the tailoring of these cores to the histories and desires of particular audiences. The increased speed, volume, and multimedia capacities of new communications technologies like computer networks and video cassettes allow for an infinite variety of such representations, all competing for market share and thus attempting to balance universally acceptable messages with specific and unique selling points.

One factor that facilitated the propagation of yoga throughout the world was the existence of an increasingly literate, English-speaking middle class in North America, Britain, and the colonies, including India, during the latter part of the nineteenth century. As we saw in Chapter 2, the press coverage of the Parliament of the World's Religions in Chicago in 1893 was instrumental in making Vivekananda's name and mission known, not only in the West, but also in India. The use of English as a lingua franca permitted a transnational audience which could serve as a vanguard for interest in their respective regional speech communities, and therefore catalyze the process of translation and wider distribution of the various materials. As literacy expanded, the market for inexpensive pamphlets on subjects of health, prosperity and general self-development also increased, and it was among the "target audience" for these booklets that Vivekananda and his yoga practices became known (see Burke 1983, 1984).

Yoga Re-Oriented

The Indian colonial experience created languages and conditions for the interaction of the Indian public with the West, and the transmission and reception of yoga strongly reflects this context of domination. Vivekananda's transnational production of an all-encompassing, universalist yoga system that could seemingly expand to include every religious and spiritual tradition in the world, had the added bonus of dual ratification by the norms of science and the authority of history. As such, this system of yoga provided both Westerners and Indians with a tool for reclaiming personal control against otherwise relentless force of social and/or political domination. In the case of the Westerners, yoga provided an antidote to the stresses of modern, urban, industrial life; for elite Indians, yoga offered an indigenous strategy for resisting colonial institutions and practices.

I use the plural, "languages," to indicate the use not only of English, but also that of Enlightenment science, a speech community unto itself. Vivekananda presented yoga as a science, comparable to the sciences of the modern West, such as astronomy and chemistry. "The science of Raja-Yoga proposes to put before humanity a practical and scientifically worked out method," which he claimed would lead the practitioner to the universal truth of universal unity, not by relying on belief or mere knowledge, but rather on practical knowledge, that is, observation and experience (Vivekananda 1990b:5–6). Vivekananda began this trend of using "science" to validate yoga as philosophy and practice. Presentations of yoga in Indian media today also tend toward use of Western ideas of "science" to explain the value of yoga, as well as to indicate the fact that the Western scientific rationale postdates the original Indian system. The theme of scientific validation can be directed toward Indian audiences, as a way of establishing credibility by showing that yoga is not simply "traditional" and therefore irrational, but has the force of both time and rationality behind it. In this way, science can be used to present yoga to Western audiences, showing that the Western scientists have a great deal to learn from India's traditions.

In a column for *India Perspectives*, published by the Ministry of External Affairs, New Delhi, and distributed at Indian embassies and consulates worldwide, Yash Pal comments that "[l]ong before the modern scientists discovered the endocrine system, the yogis knew about the existence of certain secretions which were responsible for the regulation of various mental and physical functions of the man. The secretions have been rediscovered by modern scientists and are termed as *Hormones*" (*India Perspectives*, August 1992). Yoga provides contemporary Indians with a way of integrating the modern goals of health and fitness geared toward physical manifestation of moral and economic success, formulated largely under the condition of colonialism as protestant ethics, capitalist spirits, and upright bodies, with the "traditional" Hindu pursuit of *moksha* or freedom in the sense of release from worldly bonds; in the spirit of the *Bhagavad Gita*, and as part of *dharma* (duty) one can act without involvement, thereby effecting change in the world without being affected by it.

As the Yash Pal quotation suggests, not only has "science" rediscovered the basic truths known by yogis, but also India has reclaimed yoga. In the English-language magazine *Our Health: Nutrition and Environment* (published in Delhi), a regular column entitled "Yoga and Modern Life" by Dr. Ajit Mistry proclaims that "[s]cience has proved that unless we improve our minds, we cannot improve our bodies, as the mind is the seat of a number of diseases. Hence a commitment to a better life becomes essential in modern times. It is essential that we have control over unpleasant emotions, which build up stress. This can be achieved by committing to the Yoga way of life . . ." (*Our Health*, September–October 1992: 14)). In this approach, references to mystical or spiritual understandings, that is, understandings which are non-rational in the Cartesian sense, are dismissed out of hand. A kind of cognitive dissonance is created in the efforts to maintain both Western (Cartesian) and Hindu understandings of yoga: the idea of embodied knowledge, knowledge obtained through bodily experience, is in some way contrary to, or unexplained by, "rational" models based on separation of subject and object – yet the material or concrete experience of yoga practice seems to offer a way around understandings of yoga as belief in the mysterious Eastern religious system known as Hinduism. For this reason, Dr. Mistry goes on to say that

> It is high time an individual realizes what is available through modern science and what is lacking. What is urgently needed at present is a re-thinking and re-orientation of Yoga as an integral process of education and a way of life. It is wrong to suppose that health is only physical, as prescribed by physicians, or only mental, to be seen to only by psychiatrists, or only spiritual as thought by the sages. It is widely known that total health is the only real health, which is not only physical, but also mental and spiritual. (*Our Health*, September–October 1992: 14–15)

Dr. Mistry is neither anti-science nor anti-modern, but he does subscribe to the use of yoga as a holistic strategy for overcoming the difficulties created by modern life. Such an orientation calls to mind the American "interest in medical systems based on a harmonial [*sic*] interpretation of the relationship between the physical and metaphysical spheres of life" (Fuller 1989:8), characteristic of the late nineteenth century as well as the contemporary New Age philosophy.

Another Indian health magazine, *Fitnesse: A Complete Guide for a Healthy Lifestyle*, begins an article on yoga with the following diatribe:

> Yoga. God, just say the word and see what images come flashing through the mind. Contortions. Fasting. Caves. Austerity. Discipline. Purity. Serpents. Enlightenment. Detachment. Mantras. Observances. No wonder not many find the time! Given the values of the modern age, yoga does not seem to fit. *Misconception*. Given the values of the modern age, yoga is right on time (*Fitnesse Annual* 1992: p. 26)

The article goes on to suggest that yoga is a good way to ease the stress of modern living. A few pages later, an "Executive Lifestyle" profile appears, showing a young manufacturing executive in a variety of yoga poses (ibid.: 34), who attests that yoga helps him concentrate, keeps him physically fit, and eliminates stress from his business and personal life. This young executive is the picture of capitalist success, yet he is portrayed not in a business suit but in a meditative pose. He is presented as a model for exactly the kind of synthesis suggested by Vivekananda one hundred years before – the "material" wealth of the West combined with the "spiritual" wealth of India.

These images, then and now, appeal to a particular segment of Indian society: the educated, but somewhat conservative, middle classes who are looking for a middle way marked by success in both "traditional" and "modern" terms. For this audience, yoga provides a set of ideas and practices which supports a nationalist (though certainly Hindu) rather than a colonially imported, system of physical fitness, but is also supported *by* the findings of "science." Rather than forcing individuals to choose between "traditional" and "modern," this re-orientation of yoga allows them to "go between the horns" of the dilemma. "Ancient truths" can be used to solve modern problems, with success measured in external terms; in this way, indigenous values are not completely subverted, but material goods may be enjoyed.

Suman Seth, the host of an Indian TV program from the early 1980s called *Yoga and Health* (*Yoga aur Swasthya*), produced a newsstand pocket book called *Practical Yoga*, in which she addresses both beginning and advanced yoga students. Using a nearly verbatim quote, she follows Vivekananda's reorientation of yoga in saying that

> yoga is not a religion. It is a pure science, like mathematics or physics or chemistry . . . All religions are based on a system of beliefs but Yoga does not tell you to believe in anything. Just perform it as a scientific experiment . . . And yoga is not Hindu because the Hindus discovered it. Just as the laws of any science are universal, so also Yoga is universal and its laws are equally applicable to all people and at all times. (Seth 1983: xvi)

She goes on to say that the stress and anomie of the modern world is unavoidable, but that yoga offers a way of responding differently to those conditions, therefore negating the consequences of modern stress, even though the stress itself continues.

> The chaos of the outside world is a reflection of that within each one of us. Yoga creates an order within the chaos that we are. Through Yoga, we are able to relate better to ourselves, to other human beings, and to our environment. The feeling of "alienation" disappears and an inner harmony or integration occurs. (Seth 1983 xvii)

Press coverage of yoga in recent years has appeared in tandem with articles on "stress" as the scourge of modernity. Indians tend to see stress as a modern Western epidemic which holds them back and impinges on their freedom to live a good life, a position also held by most Americans and Europeans. Yoga, while presented on one hand as compatible with (and verified by) modern science, is also viewed as the antidote to specific ill effects of modernity, particularly "stress." *India Today*, the major bi-weekly news magazine, ran a major article entitled "The Silent Scourge" (*India Today*, April 30, 1992: 134–140), in which the health effects of a "modern" lifestyle were detailed. The article relies on a number of biomedical studies to confirm the epidemic and focuses on the lifestyles of executives, though it acknowledges the extent of the problem in other socioeconomic groups. "Once thought of as alien to the Indian lifestyle, stress is now a widespread and potentially lethal menace cutting across all socio-economic groups" (ibid.: 134). They comment that medication is the most frequently used treatment, but they also quote a Bombay physiotherapist on other solutions in use:

"People under stress now realize the importance of relaxing by breathing exercises and auto suggestion. A few years ago people would have laughed at the idea" . . . Crompton Greaves [corporation] offers yoga classes all round the year – almost all executives attend . . . Others, such as Telco, have started adventure clubs where executives are put through a mini-boot camp routine of rockclimbing and trekking . . . As the pace of modern living turns even more frenetic, those who are able to combat that feeling in their minds are the ones who will win the battle for a healthier and happier life. (ibid.)

This association of yoga with other health-promoting, back-to-nature activities such as trekking appears in Rishikesh town as well. There, yoga has been packaged with other "adventures" as coming under the purview of those travel agencies specializing in experiential outdoor activities like whitewater rafting on the Ganga and elephant safaris, rather than being promoted by the religious tour and pilgrimage operators. These adventure activities are partly oriented toward foreign tourists, but there is also a growing domestic market, primarily among the educated urban elites, both university youth (e.g., St. Stephen's College of Delhi University) and corporate types. As in the West, such adventures are often packaged as both stress-relieving and confidence-building activities (E. Martin 1994).

In India, yoga is certainly not "exotic." Indeed, its strength there lies in its familiarity, at least at the mythological level, even if often not in actual practice. In addition to ubiquitous textual references in popular oral tradition and literature, audiences in India see yoga as it continues to be represented "in the flesh" by its practitioners. In most Hindu families, according to several of my discussants, the practice of at least some basic yoga postures and breathing techniques continues. But there are still many Indians, like the Bombay businessmen on the train whom I described on the first page of this book, who maintain an idea of yoga that places it as a cultural birthright about which they actually know nothing.

Yoga, because it is also appealing to Western practitioners, has an appeal to Indians that goes beyond the comfort of tradition. The contemporary practice of yoga in India, unlike its original (pre-Vivekananda) identity as a male-dominated technique for achieving strictly religious ends, now has the combined value of countering the stresses of modern urban life (as in the West), identifying with an indigenous spiritual heritage, and also providing the possibility of trumping the Western scientific discourse on health at its own game, by presenting an opportunity for testing ancient practices using modern technologies.

The Indo-European Link: Yoga and German Media Audiences

The reception of yoga in the West, however, has been based on quite different attractions. Part of the difference in how yoga was understood in Germany related to the lack of personal representation. In his documentation of the reception of yoga in Germany, Fuchs (1990:55) suggests that until at least the interwar period, instructional books played a major role in the transmission of information about yoga to the German public; they had no exemplars like Vivekananda in North America and Britain, or the countless yogis in India. The literary genre of moral and medical self-help literature for the improvement of individuals in the middle classes, exemplified in Britain by Dr. Smiles's *Self-Help, with Illustrations of Character, Conduct and Perseverance* (1859) and Mrs. Beeton's *Book of Household Management* (1861), also existed in Germany (Fellman and Fellman 1981; H. Green 1986). By making depersonalized "self-study" books available to a wide audience, the transnational dissemination of *printed* ideas of yoga practice helped to transform the way yoga was perceived.

In the late nineteenth century, the German public was caught up in a nationalist fervor which, through the Romantic ideas of Max Mueller and others, still looked nostalgically back to India as the point of Aryan origin (Rothermund 1986). The ideology and practice of yoga, as presented by Vivekananda and later Sivananda, offered a technique for achieving wholeness and integration. As Bramwell remarks, in the early decades of the twentieth century "India was a place of romance in the German popular imagination" (Bramwell 1989:193; but see also Leifer 1971; Rothermund 1986). Halbfass (1988: 83) suggests that the "Romantic interest in India was inseparable from a radical critique of the European present. The preoccupation with the merely useful, the calculable, rational . . . were seen as symptomatic deficiencies of this present." We can see the application of this interest particularly well in the arena of medicine, where Romantic visions of natural, holistic, harmonious lives were attached to a variety of alternative healing strategies (Proctor 1988).

In the early years of the Third Reich, ideas relating to anthroposophy, ecology, and Indo-Aryan identity were popular, largely due to their promotion by Hitler's assistant, Rudolf Hess (Proctor 1988; Weindling 1989).[3] The initial audience for yoga in Germany therefore included both an academic sector whose interest was grounded in a linguistic (genealogical) link to the Indian subcontinent, and a popular sector whose attention focused on a romantic yearning for the mystical holism of the East: "The very idea of India assumed mythical proportions [within the German Romantic movement]; the turn towards India became the quest for the true depths of our own being, a search for the original, infant state of the human race, for the lost paradise of all religions and philosophies" (Halbfass 1988:72).

Through the first half of the twentieth century, and largely due to the Aryan propaganda of the Nazi era, the German middle classes (though not the most educated sectors) maintained an interest in things Indian. They also supported non-biomedical types of health maintenance because of associations with the land and more "natural" remedies untainted by modern ways. A central issue for the National Socialist (Nazi) revolution was "to replace the mechanistic thinking of recent medicine by a new and more organic (*biologische*), holistic view of the world"; they wanted a medicine that would be "'more Goethe and less Newton' . . . linked with a vision of society supposedly more in tune with nature" (Proctor 1988:223; see also Mosse 1985). Both German and American representations of yoga aimed at Western audiences tend to emphasize the "ancient wisdom" of the Indian yogis, rather than the scientific validation of yoga by Western scientists.

In the popular monthly magazine *Vital: Das Magazin fuer Modernes Leben*, an article on *"Körper Kunst"* ("Body Art", subtitled "Relaxation, Movement/Flexibility, Good Figure": *Vital*, May 1993: 29) exhorts readers to "go to the source" and not follow the exercise fashions: "Who conquers yoga, needs no other exercises. First, you can do nothing better for your body, mind, and soul. Second, many of the centuries-old practices are a regular part of modern stretching and relaxation programs. Yoga is, so to speak, the source." The article ends with a reminder to members of the audience seeking training in yoga: "It's a 'hot number' at the Adult Development Schools!" As we have seen, these adult schools (*Volkshochschule*) are a major part of the German educational system, and yoga is taught at most of them. Yoga has also become a metonym for health in the international language of advertising, as shown in one German magazine advertisement. We see a man wearing a business suit standing on his head with his tie hanging down around his nose, eating yogurt. The copy reads "Vi-thai ist Yoga zum Essen" (Vi-thai [the brand name] is yoga for eating.) The most apparent reading is that headstands = yoga = health, and eating the right brand of yogurt gives the same benefits.[4]

Another popular newsstand magazine, *Der Naturartzt*, ran a piece on yoga which distinguished between the "western people who understand things mostly in their heads, with their intellects, but find a simple feeling quite difficult to deal with" and "the eastern people, for whom the exact reverse is true, their ability to make use of visual images and feelings is more developed than their intellects" ("Yoga aus der Reinheit der Seele", *Der Naturartz*, August 1993: 18–20). In *Amadea* (June 1993: 23), a yoga article focuses on relaxation, and the need for the individual to free herself from the webs of social obligations that hold her prisoner.

Yet in several interviews with Indians in Rishikesh, I was told that yoga is the best method for both getting fit and controlling the intellectual processes, and that it is a completely rational system which would help people to cope with the demands of social life. Here again we meet up with the notion of *jivanmukhti*, living liberation. While Westerners may be searching for a way to escape the bonds of modern life, few of them are actually willing to go as far as renouncing the workaday world. Rather, most – like most Indians who practice yoga – seek an oasis regime, and a way of opting out of daily life for brief periods, measured in minutes, hours, or – at the most – days.

This article from *Amadea* demonstrates how the German popular magazines, directed toward a different sector of the middle classes, see a need for learning the "Eastern" ways of feeling in order to counteract the overemphasis on "reason" in the West. As with other practices connected with the New Age, an anti-rational thread links this ideology with the various Romantic movements across Europe and North America.

Cincinnati, Ohio, and Laramie, Wyoming – February, 2004

Lilias Folan and I have been playing phone tag for months; between the time zone difference, the holidays, and our complex work and home schedules, it was very hard for us to find a few moments for an interview. At last we connected. As she made clear in both our conversation interview and in other records of her start in yoga (Folan 1981; Schneider 2003), she was an American housewife living an almost stereotypical post-World War II suburban dream, possessing every material status symbol that constituted the American ideal, and then some. But she was neither happy nor healthy in her seemingly perfect world, and went to her family doctor for suggestions. His idea of an exercise program coincided with her happening across a popular book on yoga, so she decided to give it a try. Yoga made her feel good; it was as simple as that.

Living in Connecticut gave Lilias access to the nascent New York yoga community, and Swami Jayananda was one of her first teachers. As a householder, a person living in the everyday world of work and childrearing, Lilias fit the parameters that Sivananda had in mind in India in the 1920s and 1930s, except that she was female instead of male. *Jivanmukhti* was the goal; one could practice yoga, live the "divine life" – yet not renounce worldly life, still remain part of the productive middle class society.

Connecting: Yoga in American Media Representations

Lilias found that yoga offered her a kind of physical grounding that allowed her to feel connected to the material world through breathing, stretching of muscles, the feeling of herself in space. But it also provided the option to distance oneself from the world around – stilling, as Patanjali had said, the processes of the mind. Yoga practice was an "oasis regime" that offered the discipline to structure choices, a way to make the path simple. By engaging in yoga practice, one could for a time avoid the escalation of stress, take time out of the busy day without having to renounce everything. With the ecumenical philosophy and practices set out by Sivananda, a Western yoga practitioner had the choice to be Christian *and* do yoga, to be a householder and also be spiritually separate from the quotidian world. Folan says that learning about this option was a huge relief, know that she did not have to give up who she was to learn and practice this new path. After several years of learning yoga from Swami Jayananda and others, and beginning to teach local classes herself, Lilias was offered the opportunity to broaden her audience to through television.[5] Lilias, with her friendly and engaging manner, brought yoga on public television to new heights. In 1972, as the counterculture reached unprecedented heights, this housewife and mother of two from Cincinnati came into the living rooms of middle-class North America to tell her students that it was all right to breathe, that they could feel good without feeling like they had betrayed their upbringing, and that what looked impossible could be achieved by those who worked slowly, carefully, and with faith in their own bodies and minds.

An article from the *Hindustan Times*, shouts the headline "Desperate Americans turn to Yoga." This piece documents the use of yoga by several mainstream American medical institutions, including "the prestigious Harvard Medical School," and proclaims that

> Yoga and meditation are no longer for Eastern mystics or eccentric, vegetarian young men or women: it [*sic*] has arrived in the American mainstream as "alternative medicine" along with acupuncture and homeopathy . . . The reason why yoga and meditation have entered the mainstream and are no longer distrusted as "anti-Western" or "anti-Christian" is that though a person meditating or doing yoga still looks a little odd to many Americans, too many patients are giving testimony to friends to the effectiveness of these techniques. (*Hindustan Times*, October 6, 1992: 20)

The Indian middle classes, like those in the West, see "health" and "fitness" as prerequisites for modern living and success, looking to the Darwinian ideal that "fitness" leads to success. The market-driven American and European societies have promoted this Darwinian ideal primarily through the use of the popular press (Kelly 1981; Weindling 1989). The concept of fitness is crucial because it provides both a metaphor and a physical goal to engage the public. While health is perhaps too broad and utopian a goal to achieve, fitness speaks to the concrete. The publication of Darwin's ideas about natural selection only intensified the nineteenth-century quest for progress at every level, from physical strength to national security. Harvey Green (1986: 322) says that in the United States at least, people were "constantly looking for an 'edge' on the competition, while recognizing that they were always being pursued . . . Health increasingly became one of the advantages one might have, like elocution, [or] education".

In North America, popular stereotypes of yoga practitioners still associate them with left-wing politics, higher education (though perhaps as dropouts from the conventional academic pursuits), environmentalism, and alternative lifestyles (Heelas 1996). The names Emerson and Thoreau come to mind as role models, and indeed the influence of India on the Transcendentalists, and of the Transcendentalists on the American reception of yoga and other holistic health practices (Fuller 1989), are significant. "Like the Hindus, who highlighted the implicit unity of microcosm and macrocosm in an eternal divinity, Emerson and the others thought of the dualism of the manifest and unmanifest worlds as only provisional. At its core, the world was one whole" (Albanese 1977:11). As I discuss later in this chapter, the appeal to wholeness is essential for those, from Sivananda to sociologist Ulrich Beck, who have made the leap from the personal to the planetary.

The American women whom Vivekananda met during his first trip overseas, from 1893 to 1896, impressed him with their social service projects. They influenced his presentation of yoga as not only a means for self-improvement and personal salvation, but also a technique based on selfless service to the wider community, a way of emancipating the whole world. Likewise, Vivekananda's contact with anarchist/socialist reformers like Kropotkin (Halbfass 1988:232–233), along with his own experiences among the poor of India, showed him that spirituality must be accompanied by social and political reform if it is to assuage the wounds torn open in the frenzied rush to modernity. "You will find at last that the easiest way to make ourselves healthy is to see that others are healthy, and the easiest way to make ourselves happy is to see that others are happy" (Vivekananda 1990b:32).[6]

While most of the German publications tend to assume that yoga is known to their audiences as a good thing, even if it is unclear what "doing yoga" actually entails, the American publications direct their attention toward dispelling "yoga myths," with titles like "The New Yoga: No longer the preserve of ex-hippies, this once-mystical discipline is now a total body workout" (*American Health*, July–August 1993: 58–63). The article uses pastel colors and photos of a woman doing *asanas* on a beautiful beach, ocean waves rolling in the background. While debunking myths is the first priority, another theme in the American representations is "connection." Although biomedical research results supporting its recommendations are presented, this article goes on to suggest that

> Perhaps the ultimate attraction is that yoga, which in Sanskrit means union, brings people together. Unlike in aerobics classes, where students jostle for choice spots near the mirror, there's a sense of camaraderie in most yoga studios . . . [it] may be ancient

wisdom, but in the 90's, the idea of striving to connect with others seems thoroughly up-to-date. (ibid.: 63)

This notion of "connecting," is of course part contemporary ecological discourse, on one hand – an extension of the universalist "all men are brothers" concept to the level of global unity, about which more later in this chapter. But it also appears as a central feature of popular psychological thought: in order to realize our potential, we must "connect" with, for example, our "inner child," our *ur*-self as opposed to the insular individual which western capitalist society is said to foster. Thus by describing yoga as a way to "connect" rather than to compete, we see another example of yoga as an antidote to the "bad" aspects of modernity, understood as grounded in western industrial progress. Such an appeal to mutual support and the generation of community can be seen in such corporate slogans as AT&T's "Reach Out and Touch Someone" advertising campaign, as well as the increasing corporate reliance on spiritual/adventure training programs that promote teamwork and flexibility (E. Martin 1994).

In striking contrast with the previous example is an article in the magazine *Men's Fitness* (September 1993: 56–60, 115–117), catering to the men who fall somewhere in between the new men's movement and traditional bodybuilders. The piece is titled "Urban Renewal: Yoga offers the sort of pretzel logic that makes perfect sense to stressed-out men." The author, a woman, draws her audience in with the lure of celebrity names (Kareem Abdul-Jabbar, Jerry Seinfeld, Madonna, and Sting all do yoga, to name but a few), and illustrates its points with a heavily tatooed man, sitting on the pavement in an urban back alley. The article cites a number of medical authorities who now use yoga, and evaluates the compatibility between yoga and weight-training. The author, who has tried out a few yoga classes, reports on the differences. She concludes with a quote from Jerry Seinfeld: "Why do I do yoga? Try limitless energy. Hey, with my work schedule, I'm just trying to stay alive. I'm going non-stop 12-14 hours a day, and there's no way I could sustain this crazy schedule without the yoga. It makes my life better, and, to me, that's what exercise is all about" (ibid.: 117). The macho American version of yoga focuses on what yoga can do for your body, keeping it healthy and minimizing stress. The subtext is that yoga is a rational pursuit, not (just) a feminized or spiritual one, and that real men have nothing to fear from the practice of yoga – it will even help their weight training. A book highlighting this sentiment hit the US bestseller charts in 2003: *Real Men Do Yoga: 21 Star Athletes Reveal their Secrets for Strength, Flexibility and Peak Performance* (Capouya 2003). This focus on masculine rationality is similar to the Indian response, and brings to mind discussions by Tanya Luhrmann (1994) and Ashis Nandy (1988) regarding the feminization of Indian men by their British colonizers and the subsequent struggles after independence to regain a sense of masculinity in their own terms.

The various media representations of yoga discussed earlier, coming from India, Germany, and the United States, demonstrate that neither yoga, nor health, nor even middle-class modernity are monoliths. The particular histories of these locales have shaped the ways that audiences within them have developed, and the media representations that have emerged both reflect and create these audiences.

Rishikesh – May, 1992

Chipko has often been in the news lately. The local Uttarakhand environmental movement, Chipko Andolan has been working hard for several years to stop work on the proposed Tehri Dam. Sunderlal Bahuguna, the leader of Chipko, was engaged in a hunger strike that was having little effect. Periodically, small articles about his health and the Tehri situation appeared in the major newspapers. The *Times of India* reported that Bahuguna had received the Tagore Award, and would use the money to organize *yatras* (pilgrimages) to Gangotri in protest of the dam. The latest news from my friends at the DLS was that Bahuguna, elderly and now quite frail from his fast, was now resting at the DLS ashram, and would have private *darsan* of Chidananda in the morning.

Shades of Green: Ecology and Environmentalism in India and the West

The notion of balance or equilibrium has been used extensively to forge a link between ecology and yoga: "Yoga is intrinsically ecological. All yoga is what I call 'eco-yoga' . . . As the *Bhagavad Gita* (II.48), the oldest yoga scripture, puts it, yoga is balance . . . when we are inwardly balanced, we are also balanced in relationship to our environment" (Feuerstein and Bodian 1993:224). The actual word used in the *Bhagavad Gita* verse cited above, *samatva*, is often translated as "equilibrium," but in the sense of dispassion, neither one thing nor another, of disinterest rather than balance.[4] As with the translation of *moksha* as freedom, the glossing of *samatva* as balance speaks more to the concerns of the stressed-out, modern middle-class individual than to the philosophical goals of Patanjali and others of the yoga tradition's original scribes. Here, then, is another way in which particular English translations have created an opportunity for recasting yoga in a modern light.

Stereotypical images of American and Swiss yoga practitioners often juxtapose yoga/Eastern spiritual philosophy and practice with environmental concern, as we saw in the cartoon of the interview session described in Chapter 4. As Heelas (1996) points out in his massive survey of the New Age, these associations do have a basis in fact, as is often the case with stereotypes. However, although I expected German stereotypes to follow the same pattern as the Swiss and Americans, I found, among my German discussants, other yoga practitioners, and "Greens," quite a strong resistance to the suggestion that members of the German Green party would be inclined toward the practice of yoga or other Asian spiritual practices. Such activities, I was told, were *gegen Vernuenft* – "against reason" – and therefore anathema to the Greens. This finding is also supported by Randeria and Fuchs (personal communication, 1993).

I found this puzzling, and further research produced confirmation that in Germany, one must recognize the strong division that exists between politically active Greens and their leadership, on the one hand, and the average ecologically conscious voter, on the other. The current generation of Green leaders lean more toward socialist/communist ideology – the so-called "Red Greens," while the younger generation of environmentally conscious German citizens are more likely to support the kind of "deep ecology" philosophy promoted by Norwegian phil-osopher Arne Naess and others, whether explicitly or simply in spirit. One explana-tion for the similarity between American and Swiss views (that environmental awareness and eastern spirituality "just go together") could be that the national mythologies of Switzerland and the United States depend more heavily on indi-vidualism than does that of the Germans (Bendix 1992; Dumont 1992).

Ram Guha, chronicler of peasant resistance and the ecological history of the Himalaya, suggests that environmental activist Sunderlal Bahuguna's charisma has made him a modern-day Gandhi in the eyes of many north Indians. He quotes Bahuguna as locating the deterioration of the Himalayan ecosystem "in the [mod-ern] materialistic civilization, which makes man the butcher of the earth" (Guha 1989:179; brackets in original), a position supported by the work of ecofeminist and physicist Vandana Shiva. Shiva seeks to demonstrate the continuity between the "earth body" and the human body that she contends was lost in the patriarchal dualistic shuffle of post-Enlightenment science. In an edited volume, Shiva comments that "there are subtle and complex connections between diseases of the human body, the decay of ecosystems, and the breakdown of civil society, just as there are connections in the search for health at all of these levels" (Shiva 1994:3). Although Bahuguna is not publicly presented as a yoga practitioner, he does visit the Sivananda ashram frequently and appears to support the basic tenets of the DLS. Hindu *advaita* philosophy, as promoted by the DLS and expressed through its practical yoga instruction, has been used by both Indians and Westerners not only as a strategy for personal health and stress-relief, but also as a rationale for a return to an ecological worldview which give weight to the intrinsic value of nature rather than considering only its use-value as an economic resource.

Western attitudes toward the natural environment have tended to fall into two broad categories roughly corresponding with the seventeenth-century philosophies of Spinoza and Descartes, that is, monistic and dualistic models. Monistic models view reality as a singularity, one system, of which humans, like all other aspects of nature, are a part. Dualistic models posit separate thinking human subjects and objectively knowable material environments/objects, opening the way for analyzing the external world without having to include the knowing subject as part of the problem. We can trace the history of environmental thinking along these parallel tracks to two different contemporary Green visions of modernity, represented by Deep Ecologists on one side and scientific conservationists on the other. Anna Bramwell (1989) labels this distinction as one of ecologists versus environmentalists; Warwick Fox (1990: 3) concurs with this distinction, adds the dimension of anthropocentricity versus ecocentricity, and presents an extensive analysis of the various "typologies of ecological and environmental thought." Roderick Nash (1982) contrasts Cartesian dualism and the "objectification of nature" with Spinoza's view of the interrelatedness of all things, which "made it possible for him to place ultimate ethical value on the whole, the system, rather than on any single and transitory part" (Nash 1982:20).

Examples of the dualistic perspective abound; basically, what we consider "normal science" reflects the Cartesian mechanistic approach, assuming differentiation between spirit and matter, and thus between thinking men and their environment. The dualistic model appears in the conservationist and environmentalist movements of the United States National Parks movement at the end of the nineteenth century; the debate between Gifford Pinchot and John Muir over the rational, economically self-interested management of natural resources versus the intrinsic value of nature is often cited. As Giddens puts it,

> It has become a commonplace to assert that the core outlooks of modernity treat nature as instrumental, the means to realize human purposes . . . What is at issue is not just that, with the coming of modernity, human beings treat nature as an inert set of forces to be harnessed to human ends, since this still carries the implication that nature is a *separate domain* from that of human society . . . the development of the created environment – or, another phrase for the same thing, the socialization of nature – cuts much more deeply than this. Nature begins to "come to an end" in the sense that the natural world is increasingly ordered according to the internally reflexive systems of modernity. (Giddens 1991:165)

It is precisely this fear that nature is "coming to an end" (McKibben 1989) that has all along driven the quest for an alternative way of being in the world, a way which disallows the separation of humans from nature. Spinoza's monism was one strand which provided this option within a Western context; the various romantic and other "anti-modern" movements, many of which sought answers in the East, were concerned with the same issues. Yet the East also had traditions of dualism, as the West has its own monist tradition. The essentialization of East and West into first spiritual and material, and then monist/dualist reflected what people on both sides of the self-proclaimed divide were able to find in that greener pasture.

In addition to Spinoza, there were a number of other Western holistic thinkers. For example, Alexander von Humboldt (early nineteenth century) was a naturalist but also read non-dualistic Hindu philosophy as extensively as the times permitted; his brother was an Indologist. In his article on the relation between colonialism and the conservation of nature, Richard Grove points out that, with respect to the colonial administration, "[t]he roots of environmentalism in India were strongly reinforced by the writings of Alexander von Humboldt, [who] promulgated a new ecological concept of the relation between people and the natural world: that of the fundamental interrelation of humankind and other forces in the cosmos" (Grove 1992: 125).

The biologist Ernst Haeckel, who first coined the term "oekologie" in 1866, took Goethe, Spinoza, and others as his inspiration for monistic ecological theory; he was also interested in Buddhism. Bramwell (1989: 53) comments that "Haeckel's most important legacy was his worship of Nature, the belief that man and nature were one, and that to damage one was to damage the other". Haeckel and other nineteenth-century ecologists, though not subscribing to the more dominant dualistic paradigms, were not, however, opposed to other characteristically modern concerns. They "believed in progress (a belief that began to decline in the twentieth century), and in the power of man's will to change himself, so long as his will was used as a 'good' will, that is, in accordance with nature's laws" (Bramwell 1989: 48). Haeckel's application of Darwinian evolutionary theory to the social world of late-nineteenth-century Germany, along with his fundamental monism, also helped support the cause of holistic/natural medicine (Weindling 1989), and thereby provided fertile ground for the promotion of yoga along with other bodily techniques for health, fitness, and the relief of stress through the connection of mind and body, self and world.

Finding the Balance: Eco-Yoga

When we talk about the New Age, it is easy to slip into the either/or dichotomies which so often characterize its internal discourse. Chief among the dichotomies is that of the pro- or anti-modern. Heelas makes the astute observation that, rhetoric aside, the New Age is a thoroughly modern endeavor:

> The New Age belongs to modernity in that it is progressivistic (looking to the future) and constructivistic (things . . . can be changed). More specifically, the idea that one can go [to workshops or seminars], to change for the better, has become so widely accepted that it might be said that our culture amounts to "the age of training." The New Age thus also belongs to modernity in that great faith is placed in the efficacy of specified practices. (Heelas 1996:169)

My own assessment of the rise of yoga as fitting well with the basic orientation of modernity reinforces his analysis. Ulrich Beck and Anthony Giddens have both written extensively about the nature of modernity and concluded that we have not yet, as some suggest, gone beyond modernity and into the postmodern period. Instead, the world has reached a new level of late modernity in which *reflexivity*, our ability to consciously reflect on and respond to conditions of our own making, has become the prime mode of operation. The other two features of late modernity that both Beck and Giddens draw our attention to are first, the increasing *individualization* of primarily Western industrial nations (Beck 1992) or emphasis on *self-actualization* (Giddens 1991), and second, the inescapability of *global interdependence* and translocal effects.

These three characteristic aspects of late modernity are accompanied by an increasing sense of risk, the consequence of living in a science-dominated society which valorizes the control of self and environment, and is forced to reflexively incorporate knowledge about the effects of these various control efforts on future outcomes. Both Beck and Giddens use the example of global environmental threats to make their points about the uses and consequences of scientific knowledge in late modernity. By focusing on the relationship between humanity and nature, they both demonstrate the universality of the problems we face. They also suggest that by shifting our basic approach to interacting with the world around us from a dualist to a monist perspective, we can make progress toward a new and more stable kind of society. Giddens is a bit more optimistic than Beck that this kind of "utopian realism" (Giddens 1990) can be achieved.[7] The convergences and divergences of their ideas, along with those of Scott Lash, are presented in a jointly produced volume entitled *Reflexive Modernization* (Beck et al. 1994).

Both Beck and Giddens are careful to allow for and acknowledge the diversity of both scientific and popular understandings of "the facts" (i.e. empirically verifiable and reproducible data) about the world around us; the widely divergent opinions regarding the global climate change would be one example of this. Indeed, this lack of "absolute truth" is crucial to both of their arguments – neither really allows for the existence of an alternative approach to the underlying relationship between humanity and the rest of the cosmos. They make Science, in the sense of the dominant mechanistic (Cartesian, Newtonian) paradigm, stand as the source and savior of modernity's problems and bring up the idea of alternatives only as part of their theories of the shift from industrial to reflexive modernity. Both Giddens and Beck conflate the histories of environmentalism and ecology in such a way that ecological (holistic) thinking appears only as a recent shift in environmental thinking, one which corresponds with their proposed shift in the stages of modernity. In fact, alternative traditions have coexisted with the dualism of the dominant scientific paradigm, even in the West and certainly in other cultures, for hundreds of years.

Rishikesh, India – November, 1992

Just returned to town after a month of research in Delhi and Calcutta, and it's nice to be home. Walking down the street toward the Sivananda Ashram, vendors wave and say hello, how are you, where have you been? – I guess I've come to be at least expected, if not exactly a local. At the ashram, I stop by the Sivananda Samadhi Shrine for a few minutes on my way to the library. It's always cool in there, and a good place to sit and think. Something seems different, but I can't place it. Then I realize – the signs decorating the walls with Sivananda's pithy rules and goals for the *sadhak* (seeker) are now entirely in English, where previously at least half had been in Hindi. Strange. There were no major international events coming up to account for such a change. After a couple of hours of library work, ever frustrated by the fact that chronological order was not a priority for the library staff, the next task I had to address was picking up an order of DLS publications to bring back to Delhi for stocking the bookstall at the new International Sivananda Yoga Nataraja Center in Delhi.

Located two blocks from the house I boarded at when in Delhi, in the posh neighborhood called East of Kailash, the new center had opened only in September, but seemed to be doing well. Since I was going to return to Delhi later in the month anyway, I had agreed to bring the books, all English titles, back to the city with me. Later that afternoon, I went down to the Omakarananda Ganga Sadhan and found Ram preparing to teach his 4 p.m. yoga class. He was glad to know that I had gotten back from Kolkata, although he had already received a letter from his family saying that I had brought the video and that they had enjoyed it. He didn't seem concerned when I told him about the technical problems or the fact that almost no one there had understood the English interview on the tape. I stretched, warming up for class, and looked out at the river, shiny with afternoon sun.

Rishikesh: Finding the Center

In this book, Sivananda's Divine Life Society and its affiliated organizations have provided a focal point for understanding how people in India and the West have participated in translocal communities of practice which have yoga as their basis. Many people describe the DLS as a neo-traditional organization, in part because it seeks a middle ground, trying to maintain a fundamental (indeed essential) sense of participating in the world of Hindu asceticism while catering to the needs and wants of English-speaking cosmopolitans from India and elsewhere. Ashis Nandy's (1988:74) suggestion that India "is neither pre-modern nor anti-modern but only non-modern" might be better recast as "neo-traditional," for he sees in India's refusal to completely succumb to the supposed rationality of the West a revamping of traditions rather than a return to them. Like many of today's ecologians, Nandy argues for our ability to learn from past experience in a synthetic way, rather than merely replacing the old with the new, solving every problem with a new discovery. India's universalist outlook, Nandy (1988: 75) suggests, "takes into account the colonial experience, including the immense suffering colonialism brought, and builds out of it a maturer, more contemporary, more self-critical version of Indian traditions." Yet following the many threads of global community-making I found at the Parliament of the World's Religions, or almost any of the discussants who were kind enough to tell me about yoga's impact on their lives, I can only conclude that India's universalist outlook is in fact completely modern.

The forms that yoga has taken in the past century are a direct result of its transnational movement, and that is why a multi-local research strategy was required for understanding them. Rishikesh, though geographically located in the Himalayan foothills of north India, is very much a constructed locale, a place created through the mythological and political events of the past few centuries. Rishikesh became the "place to go for yoga" for people around India and across continents through the efforts of many individuals and institutions. Its bucolic setting on the banks of the Ganga, with the first reaches of the Himalayan foothills rising above the glacier-blue river, offers a glimpse into the past with all of the amenities of the future (Figure 10). During the last month of my stay, the promised main trunk telephone lines were installed, and overnight three different telephone/fax centers appeared.

Figure 10 Ganga Dawn (author photo)

Over the past several years, the Government of India has worked hard to bring people to Rishikesh, often using yoga and nature in conjunction to draw in visitors, as with the promotion of an annual Yoga Week which brings well-known instructors together for yoga instruction, in addition to providing recreational adventures like rafting and elephant safaris for participants. Both Rishikesh and yoga have been made over during the past hundred years, and the intertwined histories of these transformations reflect the shift toward a very particular version of modernity, one shared by a cross-section of several different translocal communities. Yoga has become a way to sell the packaged essence of India to tourists both Indian and foreign. In such unexpected sites as a tourist bookstall in the midst of the big red fort at Jodhpur, I found a large picture book on yoga put out by the Sivananda Yoga Vedanta Center standing front and center, surrounded by assorted travel books, about the Ganga and multicolored copies of the *Kama Sutra*. Yoga appears as another desirable commodity, easily detached from its earlier religious context, but not from its value, touted by Vivekananda and scores since, as India's "spiritual gift [for a price] to the world."

Chicago, Illinois – September, 1993

Here I am, in "the field" again, trying to make sense of what is going on around me. Despite being in the same country I had grown up in, I feel nearly as overwhelmed as when I first arrived in Delhi. Walking around at the Palmer House Hotel in Chicago, peering into meeting rooms and watching the people rushing in all directions, I have a hard time taking it all in. The 150-page thick Program of the Parliament of the World's Religions is astonishing in its breadth, with sessions organized around six fundamental themes: Environment/Technology, Social Action, Community/Culture, Myth/Symbol, History of Religions, and Body/Mind. In addition to lectures and films, there were well over fifty exhibitors offering courses, books, spiritual vacations, or simply lifestyle changes for the amassed participants. At the opening ceremonies a few days before, the theme of unity and the fact that the Earth is "the global home of one family," as Swami Chidanandaji stated in his address of the previous day, was everybody's mantra. The next day, Swami Satchidananda, one of Chidananda's *gurubhai* from the DLS in Rishikesh, commented that "one hundred years ago, the world was not prepared for unity. Today we are on the edge, we are ready." He went on to say that "Hinduism is not a religion, it is an ocean, it has all of the religions synthesized inside," and, confirming the general impression that beliefs and values were the primary commodities of the Parliament, concluded with the slogan "Global Harmony – It Begins With You." I needed to get away from all of the talk, so I went off to a yoga demonstration by an Austrian man wearing the latest fashions in Patagonia outdoor wear and Teva sandals. He had grown up in England, Germany, and the United States, spent three years in India, of which a substantial part included Rishikesh as a home base, and then had come back to the United States to start a yoga school in Chicago, which, by the look of his clothes, was doing well.

Yoga and the Good Life: Between the Horns of the Dilemma

This volume has used the ideas and practices of yoga, specifically the version of yoga promoted by Swami Sivananda of Rishikesh, as a tool with which to examine a number of themes. From headstands on an Oriental carpet in Rishikesh to plows in the American heartland,[8] the meanings of yoga have been shifting radically as they traverse nations. Yoga has become entrenched in the global lexicon and its image lodged in the visual imaginary of the world. The re-orientation of yoga by innovators like Vivekananda and Sivananda suggests to Westerners emancipation from material/spiritual dualism, and a way to get themselves and their environment "back on track." To Indians, re-oriented yoga suggests empowerment, using an imagined shared history to create a progressive, self-possessed and unifying identity. In this light, yoga can be understood as part of a methodology for living a good life. It offers a critical practice which encompasses both ends of modernity's personal/global spectrum, the current preoccupation of the middle-class world with personal health and fitness as well as with the ecological health of the planet. Yoga re-oriented is *new* theory with *old* practice. Experientially based, it offers the individual hope that through the practice yoga, they might be freed from the constraints of "taking sides," because yoga suggests the possibility of transcending such essentializing dichotomies as East/West, religion/science, mind/body, culture/nature, and spirituality/materiality. By going between the horns of the dilemma, being free to choose which elements from each side make the most sense to them as individuals, these middle-class yoga practitioners seek a globally relevant model for living a good life.

This model is not static, but dynamic. Yoga offers not only a literate, historically grounded tradition, critical for people who rely heavily on the print media for transmission of authoritative knowledge, but also an active set of practices which, if followed, promise tangible results, spiritual "progress" made visible because embodied. Perhaps more importantly, yoga offers a way to become part of a community of practice, sharing a quest with like-minded others who may be encountered on a daily, weekly, or annual basis, either in person or virtually. Swamis Vivekananda and Sivananda, and their successors, among many others, catalyzed an international wave of interest in self-realization, and provided a framework for individuals seeking emancipation from the bonds of emergent modern society's materialism through a simplified interpretation and re-orientation of the yoga *darsana*.

Yoga: A Global Positioning System

Globalization is often perceived as a negative feature of the modern world, something that has led to the contamination of pristine local or regional cultures. But the history of the world is one of contact. Human communities have always found other groups to interact with, for activities ranging from trade to entertainment to conquest, and now to yoga. By having a similar sequence of postures taught by an internationally linked "school" of yoga teachers, like Swamiji and the others from around the globe who were trained in the tradition of Swami Sivananda of Rishikesh, individuals who travel widely can always find a place to practice their yoga with like-minded others.

Since at least the late nineteenth century, there has been a continuing utopian effort (Kumar 1987) to blend these perspectives in the quest for a lifestyle both good and modern, satisfying the call of nostalgia within the limits required for future sustainability. Yoga has emerged as one transnationally relevant strategy which purports to transcend a host of conflated dichotomies, beginning with East/West and spirituality/materialism, and extending to cover both body and planet. Because damages tend to be perceived as emanating from nations and their economic (materialist) policies and actions, and affecting the well-being of individuals and the global commune, the primary responses to the problems are directed toward eliminating the interests of the nations and promoting the interests of the person and the planet (Roszak 1979). An early issue of the increasingly popular American magazine *Yoga Journal* (October 1981) included a short article by D. Keys on "The Passage to World Community" which suggested that

> we need people who are integral in themselves, who are able to include and not exclude, and who can identify with the planet, planetary life, and human life as a whole . . . We need new kinds of countries for our time as well, nations that embody the same qualities as planetary people. After all, how can a country express something that its citizens are not expressing? (ibid.: 46)

In a strikingly similar vein but forty years earlier, S. Radhakrishnan (who during his career occupied posts in politics, as the second president of the Republic of India, as well as in academia, as Professor of Philosophy at Oxford University) published a collection of essays in 1939 that demonstrated the lasting influence of Vivekananda on Indian society (Das 1992). He spoke as a philosopher in these essays, rather than a theologian or a statesman. Radhakrishnan called for a universal spirituality to complete the project of modern civilization. He felt a responsibility "to give a soul to the growing world consciousness, to develop ideals and institutions necessary for the creative expression of the world soul, to transmit these loyalties and impulses to future generations and train them into world citizens" (Radhakrishnan 1992: viii). The "fundamental insights of Eastern religions," as well as the contributions of the West, would, he thought, be relevant for this effort to develop "a new pattern of living" (ibid.). The globalization process, as the ultimate expression of the increasing tendency toward interdependence, therefore creates its own need for techniques of bodily and social regulation which transcend those required by nation-states.

Swamiji: Going with the Flow

Swamiji's yoga is not just a set of poses. Yoga, he told me, is a science. As such, I must experiment with it, try things out for myself. Like any other science, the practice of yoga can transcend cultural boundaries. Swamiji said once that "yoga is anything you do properly and with complete concentration," so that even participating in other activities, like going for a hike in the mountains, or rafting down a river, could also be a form of yoga. For him, doing yoga meant being in harmony with nature, and that concept extended to his ideas about staying healthy. Swamiji explained that practicing the yoga postures and correctly positioning the body was a skill that could actually be applied to everyday life. Simply by focusing our attention, he said, we can improve every aspect of our lives, from health to work to leisure. I certainly found that my time in Rishikesh, practicing yoga with Swamiji and others from one to five hours daily, left me in the best physical condition I have ever experienced – and that includes the years when I used to run more than 20 miles a week!

But I learned about more than simple physical practices in Rishikesh. Through my ethnographic research experience, including participation in yoga classes as well as other types of spiritual gatherings, walks along the Ganga and into the nearby mountains, interviews with yoga teachers and practitioners, and hours spent in libraries reviewing the writings of yoga teachers like Sivananda, I learned simply to *be*. I learned to let the experiences of others wash over me and infuse my mind and spirit with their knowledge and understanding; to focus my attention on the moment at hand, and to appreciate the singularity of that moment; to see the world through the eyes of people who had traveled a very different road from my own, and to realize that the differences in our lives, though very real in one sense, could sometimes mask the underlying reality of the unity of humankind. All of us sought a good life, a healthy life, a sustainable life.

The image of Swamiji that most embodies his spirit is one I remember from a beautiful day trip up to Shivpuri, a place on the Ganga about 15 kilometers north of Rishikesh. Swamiji had been telling me and my friends about this place for months, and finally we hired a car to take us to see the spot where the spiritual vibrations were so powerful. He and the hotel owner were planning to develop a Swiss-style spa retreat on this site, where yoga would be taught and harried city folk could come for restoration. It was a hot day, and the water of the Ganga was an inviting glacier blue, still quite icy from its trip down through the mountains. Swamiji, orange robes and all, removed his *chappal* (sandals) and waded into the river. Crossing his legs into the lotus position, he floated on his back in the water, a beatific smile gracing his face. Nothing was important save Ganga Ma, the source and sustenance of all.

Afterword: Virtual Yoga

Laramie, Wyoming – February, 2004

I did a web search for Swamiji and found his own personal website. He's living in the eastern United States; his website, however, is hosted in Italy by an Italian yoga teacher who is also one of Swamiji's own students. The site includes links to another yoga teacher in Switzerland, recipes for cooking healthy Indian food, instructions regarding the use of mantras, and stories related to spiritual development. In addition, one link leads to a short treatise on how to apply Swami Sivananda's maxim "Adapt, Adjust, Accommodate" to daily life, using the breathing techniques and physical postures of yoga as an anchor for a balanced life. The Swiss and Italian yoga teachers identify themselves as Swamiji's students in their advertising literature for yoga classes (brochures presented as *.pdf files linked to their respective websites), and so the lineage to the Sivananda tradition is made explicit. However, on his own page, Swamiji also advertises his approach as "Swara Yoga," differentiating himself by focusing on a particular aspect of yoga practice, *swara*, or the use of breathing techniques extended beyond the basic skills generally taught under the heading of *pranayama*. The website also gives contact information for Swamiji, and the interested reader is invited to seek further explanations via email, telephone, or postal mail. Most of the links on the website are unfinished, leaving the primary content of the site limited to the "Adapt, Adjust" statement and a very nice photograph of Swamiji showing his delightful sense of humor shining through laughing eyes and a big smile. He is sitting in lotus position in a spring garden filled with flowers; it is an image that, like the one where he is floating in the Ganga, compels one to look again and again.

Going Global: Sivananda on the World Wide Web

Over the past several years, I tried to find evidence of a web presence for many people whom I had met in Rishikesh, with variable degrees of success. The Divine Life Society and its affiliates have continually refined their websites. Swamiji was never visible to my web-roving eye; the hotel in Rishikesh had a website, but did not mention the availability of yoga instruction, causing me to wonder about what had happened to him. One effort to reach him in the late 1990s by postal mail and fax was to no avail, and after that, I did not try for another few years. Lilias Folan, discussed in Chapter 5, has a website that presents her schedule of workshops and appearances, and gives basic contact information for reaching her; I emailed her myself, and although we did eventually connect in this way, it was clear that electronic communication was not Lilias's preferred mode of interaction, though she felt that it was certainly a useful option.

The DLS itself has had a website for many years. The first version was developed and maintained by a disciple in Kansas, though the site has now been moved to a domain in India and has been upgraded dramatically, adding moving graphics, images, video and audio segments, and full-text downloads of Sivananda's writings (in several languages) and those of his disciples (http://www.sivananda dlshq.org/home.html). One of the most interesting integrations of the older, print-media intensive version of Sivananda's effort to disseminate information about the Divine Life, and the new virtual version can be found among the frequently asked questions (FAQs); such a page is requisite for all institutional websites. The DLS FAQs are not new questions about the website or the institution; rather, they reproduce a list of questions common to spiritual seekers that Sivananda originally published from the 1930s to 1960s.

Vishnudevananda's Sivananda Yoga Vedanta Centers have a rather dramatic website entitled the Sivananda Yoga Om Page™; photos of both Sivananda and Vishnudevananda grace the home (Om) page, and there are clickable links to every aspect of yogic life: publications, FAQs, yoga vacations, and teacher training courses; the site has links to affiliated centers for which the native language is French, Spanish, or German, so that non-English speakers can find out about the institution. Unlike Swami Satchidananda's Yogaville Ashram home page, the SYVC website has no obvious links to consumer goods (notably the "Shop Yoga-ville" button) that give the Yogaville website a decidedly commercial feel.

In addition to strictly informational websites, there are also many ways that one can engage in interactive yoga practice through the World Wide Web. Integral Yoga student Dr. Dean Ornish has a website hosted through WebMD (http://my.webmd. com/content/pages/4/3077_1057) that has a series of five 10-15 minute long video clips of yoga tutorials. Yogaclass.com is another source for online yoga practice; this site makes a point of its non-commercial intentions in the homepage statement that "YogaClass.com is not here to sell our book or video, or some guru. We don't want you to come to our school or ashram in some faraway place. We rather suspect that you came here looking for yoga. So that is what we provide. Of the multi-denominational, therapeutic variety" (www.yogaclass.com); YogaClass.com provides options for practicing postures and breathing techniques, as well as for joining a chatroom or listserve to interact with likeminded others through electronic communication.

What is the potential of the Web for supporting and expanding the international community of yoga practitioners? It is clear that the Web represents a "matrix" of the sort described in Chapter 1; a "sphere of activity" that is contingently located both nowhere and everywhere, as long as an electronic connection has been made. By providing options for speakers of languages other than English, or links to affiliated institutions in a variety of locations around the globe, many of these yoga websites create opportunities for practitioners to find not only teachers and interested others in their home regions, but also in any place to which they might be traveling for business or holiday. One can choose from conferences on yoga that address teaching techniques or health-related therapeutic practices (often available for continuing education credit), as well as workshops, cruises, tropical beach retreats, mountain ashrams and desert spa experiences centered on yoga practice. Whether for personal or professional purposes, it is very easy to use the World Wide Web to connect with other members of the yoga community of practice.

But does this kind of virtual connection replace the direct teacher–student relationship so essential to the transmission of yoga prior to the advent of remote electronic communication? Sivananda, and Vivekananda before him, relied on print media to present his teachings to as wide an audience as possible. He also sent disciples around the world to be personal emissaries of his message, and they, in turn, have followed his lead in disseminating information about the practice of yoga. While the Web offers a new mechanism for this process, it does so in continuity with the previous tradition. What is different about the possibilities engendered by virtual interactions in cyberspace is that there are now many new ways to cross-fertilize the various yogic paths, and for people living in disparate and often remote locations to feel a sense of shared purpose and practice that has otherwise been available only to those who were able to be physically in the same geographic space.

In the end, yoga, like modernity, is an attitude – a way of being in the world. It is a technique that has been proven through time, as pointed out by Vivekananda and Sivananda, to effectively "still the processes of the mind." By bringing a measure of calm to our harried lives, whether through personal or virtual interactive practice, yoga may help us make the world just a little bit better. Anyway, it's worth a try. Om Shanti. Peace be with you.

Notes

Chapter 1 Re-Orienting Yoga

1 See, for example, Eliade (1973 [1958]; O'Flaherty (1984); Varenne (1976); Zimmer (1984[1926]).

2 But see especially Alter (1997) and DeMichelis (2004) for detailed discussions of yoga practices in India in traditions other than that of Sivananda.

3 Most of the scholarly treatments of yoga (Eliade 1973[1958]; B.S. Miller 1996; Varenne 1976) deal primarily with text rather than practice; notable exceptions include work by Alter (1997) and Castillo (1994).

4 These are both philosophical traditions within the broad history of "Hinduism"; the texts include the *Yoga Vashista*, among others.

5 These are the so-called "heretical" paths; the founders of these paths see them as radically distancing from the classical Hindu tradition, although from within the brahmanical position, they are seen as part of the endless variability encompassed within the Hindu context.

6 For extended academic discussions of the use of bodily practices, including yoga, for nationalist purposes, see Alter (1992, 1997, 2004).

7 For an overview, see Kearney (1995). See also Appadurai (1990, 1996); Featherstone (1990); Glick Schiller et al. (1992, 1994); Hannerz (1992, 1996); Rouse (1992).

8 In focusing on yoga, a set of ideas and practices which theoretically transcends caste lines, I am in some ways sidestepping one of the central concerns of South Asian anthropology. Ethnographies of India prior to the 1980s tended to focus on the caste relations in village society (e.g. Marriott 1986[1955]; Pocock 1973; Srinivas 1976; Wiser and Wiser 1971), choosing economic or religious concerns as the central organizing issue. The question of hierarchical ranking of Brahman and Ksatriya (or local dominant caste), Priest and King, posited by Dumont and others, has been bandied about for several decades. In the anthropological literature, we find ongoing debates concerning the relationship between caste and class, and questions about the possibility for a truly non-South Asian example of a caste system. While Dumont (1980) focused on the caste system and its defining feature of ascribed hierarchy as the central concept of Hindu society particularly, and South Asian society more generally (in that even non-Hindus are incorporated into the caste system), others (Appadurai 1988a;

Daniel 1984) have suggested that the dominance of the caste system as a defining concept for South Asian societies is overstated. Triangulating these poles is Raheja (1988), who points out the importance of caste without subscribing to Dumont's Brahman-centered model. I do not wish to negate the importance of caste in many domains of everyday life for an Indian community, but rather to show that there do exist other arenas within which different priorities hold sway.

Following Das (1992) and others, I have structured this study of yoga to demonstrate the interplay between various sorts of textual traditions and lived experience that is vital to South Asian traditions. In addition, by moving away from the social structural studies which characterized earlier work in the anthropology of India, I pursue a trajectory set by Appadurai (1988a), Carman and Marglin (1985), Madan (1987), Raheja (1988) and others, who have worked to qualify Dumont's (1980) hegemonic assertion of the centrality of purity and caste for South Asian cultural studies.

9 Not only does the social scientist seek "authentic" sites for ethnographic research, but so also does the interested layperson. In the case of Rishikesh, the government of India seeks to have the town validated by tradition, scholarship, and tourism as "the place to go for yoga." So, while scholars may seek it out, or be directed there, the same is true for those who simply want to experience "real" yoga, whether they are coming from inside or outside of India.

10 Rolland 1988[1931]; see also Vivekananda's letter of 14 July 1896, from England: "the *Raja -Yoga*, by Longman Green and Co. You can get it at Bombay. It consists of my lectures on Raja Yoga in New York." Letters of Swami Vivekananda, Advaita Ashrama, Kolkata (1989, 298).

11 This is known as *mahasamadhi*, or attaining the next level of consciousness, that of merging into the universal consciousness, Brahman. According to Hindu philosophy, a realized saint (as Sivananda is perceived by his followers to be) is not believed to die, but instead to leave his physical body in an inert and seemingly lifeless state, as his Atman, or soul, merges with the universal Brahman, instead of being reborn into a new physical body. Although Hindu ideology allows for the distinction between soul and body, this distinction is not so neatly separable as the Western Cartesian version (Staal 1983–1984, cited in Alter 1992).

12 Sivananda's original motto also included the words "give" and "purify" but these two elements are no longer represented on the official crest of the Divine Life Society, presumably for the purposes of simplification; with only four words, an easy one-to-one correlation with the four yogas of Vivekananda can be made.

13 The metaphor of oneness, deriving from Vivekananda's primary reliance on Advaita Vedanta, permitted a reading of yoga in both India and the West which

was most easily allied with a kind of non-dualistic "counter-discourse . . . within the general outlines of Enlightened scientific thought" (Reill 1994:347). This counter-discourse can be seen in both Spinoza's response to Descartes's dualistic separation of spirit and substance, which, according to Spinoza, was logically insupportable, as well as in the work of the von Humboldt brothers – Wilhelm, the linguist and Indologist, and Alexander, the naturalist. Reill argues that this counter-discourse sought to avoid the reductionist dualism of both the mechanists and the animists by proposing a "vitalist" paradigm that

> defined matter as a complex conjunction of related parts. There was no such thing as an isolated entity or a simple substance. Rather, everything was related to everything else, everything was joined, *zusammengesetzt* . . . This conception of matter dissolved the strict mechanistic distinction between observer and observed, since both were related within a much larger conjunction . . . The world consisted of a circle of relations, which looked at from the human vantage-point radiated out to touch in varying degrees all forms of matter. (Reill 1994:350)

14 This type of unifying monistic perspective has also been instrumental in the development of ecological thinking over the past few centuries (see Bramwell 1989; Naess 1989; see also Grove 1992 and Halbfass 1988 on the parallels between the biological and humanistic paradigms, particularly as supported by the work of the von Humboldt brothers). For this reason, the conflation of yoga ideology and practice with environmentally conscious thought and action (often invoking planetary or cosmological unity as a basic premise) has frequently occurred. Vivekananda himself linked the *advaita* notion of one-ness with evolutionary theories, pointing out the similarity between these concepts in a speech to the people of Lahore:

> You have heard of the doctrine of physical evolution preached in the Western world by the German and the English savants. It tells us that the bodies of the different animals are really one; the differences that we see are but different expressions of the same series; that from the lowest worm to the highest and most saintly man it is but one – the one changing into the other, and so on, going up and up, higher and higher, until it attains perfection. We had that idea also. Declares our yogi Patanjali: . . . One species – the Jati is species – changes into another species – evolution; Parinama means one thing changing into another, just as one species changes into another . . . The European says, it is competition, natural and sexual selection etc. that forces one body to take the form of another. But here is another idea, a still better analysis . . . [Patanjali says] "By the infilling of nature." What is meant by this infilling of nature? We admit that the amoeba goes higher and higher until it becomes a Buddha; we admit that, but we are at the same time as much certain that you cannot get an amount of work out of a machine until you have put it in in some shape or another. The sum total of energy remains the same, whatever the forms it may take. If you want a mass of energy at one end, you have got to put

it in at the other end . . . Therefore if a Buddha is the one end of the change, the very amoeba must have been the Buddha also. (Vivekananda 1990a: 354–355)

Such juxtapositions are common to both Sivananda and Vivekananda's writings.

15 See, for example Patanjali's Yoga Sutras, as well as the Hatha Yoga Pradipika, the Siva Samhita, Yogatatva Upanisad, and of course the Bhagavad Gita.

16 These translate as "Aapka abhyas kya heh?" in Hindi, "Was machst du denn selbst?" in German, or "You do yoga, don't you?" The intimacy of practice together usually resulted in the use of the informal "du" form with German speakers, even those with whom I would normally be on "Sie" terms; this occurred sometimes in Hindi (use of "tum" versus "aap"), but much less frequently. The linguistic politics of Hindi among the range of people I interviewed were much more conventional than among the German-speaking discussants, perhaps because the Germans viewed me more as a "fellow-traveler" in a strange place than did most of the Indians. Also, the Indians with whom I would most likely have used the less formal address term for the most part wanted to use English, an even greater "leveler."

17 For non-practitioners, especially academics, questions about my practice had a dual purpose: although participant-observation is the norm for ethnographic research, such perceived "New Age" topics as yoga invoke an immediate uneasiness as to the degree of subjectivity, or whether I was "going native" and being unduly influenced by a "guru" or a "cult."

18 The term "discussant" is, I feel, a more accurate way to represent the people usually labeled "informants" in the anthropological literature. Although I initiated the majority of the "official" taped interview discussions, these conversations were generally only one in a long series of dialogues on the subject of yoga and health that I engaged in with these people over the course of my research.

19 India is often a stand-in for the East more generally; see Hay (1970:21).

20 Steven Hay's analysis gives further evidence of the existence of a transnational community of "knowledge workers" who shared a certain degree of status if not always of class (see Weber 1968:302-306) during the late nineteenth century:

Working together, in Tokyo, in Boston, in Peking, or Paris, but most often in Kolkata or London, these Orientophiles formed an international community, a largely English-speaking confederation of rebels against the Westernization of the globe . . . many members of this international fraternity were seized with the conviction that there existed a single entity called Oriental, Eastern, or Asian civilization. (Hay 1970:315)

21 One aspect of the "project of modernity" that has received little attention in discussions of the separation of science, art and morals, is the concept of

health. In *The Birth of the Clinic*, Foucault demonstrated the radical effect of assuming the separation of subject and object on the development of medicine in the post-Enlightenment West. Changes wrought by the medical Gaze on the diagnosis and management of disease have been crucial to contemporary discussions of the power of modern medicine (for discussions of power and biomedicine, see Casper and Koenig 1996; Lindenbaum and Lock 1993; O'Neill 1985; Scheper-Hughes and Lock 1987). But health itself, whether seen as a positively valued commodity, a marker for the achievement of modernity, or simply a citizen's right in the modern world, has not been subjected to this kind of scrutiny.

22 For example, the Government of India produces brochures about Rishikesh which refer to its value for students of yoga, as well as a poster and other supplementary materials promoting an annual International Yoga Week in Rishikesh, with leading yoga teachers from around the country participating.

23 Hindu versus Indian: While yogic traditions are also part of the "heretical" traditions of Buddhism, Jainism and others, and "Hindu" ideas are not the only ones which have shaped the "Indian" approach, I speak here of "Hindu" thought to permit a focus on yoga as it relates to the representations of these ideas by such neo-Hindu thinkers as Vivekananda, Gandhi, Aurobindo, and Radhakrishnan.

24 For a discussion of network theory in the ethnographic study of complex societies, see Hannerz (1980) as well as his later books (Hannerz 1992, 1996).

25 Paul Rabinow put it well when he described the condition of cosmopolitanism as "an ethos of macro-interdependencies, with an acute consciousness (often forced upon people) of the inescapabilities and particularities of places, characters, historical trajectories, and fates" (Rabinow 1986:258).

26 Selye's well-known formulation of the General Adaptation Syndrome (GAS), the relatively uniform physiological response of human bodies to a wide array of stressors, was first developed in the 1930s (Sapolsky 1994). Selye and a host of other medical researchers since then have documented numerous diseases which are created or exacerbated by chronic stress, by which is meant the constant evocation of the GAS: increased heart rate, increased blood pressure, increased flow of blood to extremities, release of epinephrine, and other distinct physiological changes.

27 The concept of the *siddhis*, unusual and seemingly magical powers attributed to many yogis (Eliade 1973), represents an extreme example of this kind of thinking.

28 For India, like every other place in the world today, has developed its own variety of modernity that shares a family resemblance (Wittgenstein 1953) to other modernities, but cannot be fixed in opposition to any one model.

Chapter 2 Lives and Histories: Rishikesh, Sivananda, and the Divine Life Society

1 *Imperial Gazetteer*, Vol. I, p. 252.

2 "Hrishikesh" is the proper transliteration of the Devanagari spelling.

3 Another unusual feature of Rishikesh from an administrative standpoint is that the district boundaries put into place under the British remain in effect today; the impact of this historical artifact is that this community, which looks to outside eyes like a single town, turns out in fact to be administered by three separate governmental offices. Although, as noted earlier, the region recently became its own new state of Uttaranchal, hewn from the very large state of Uttar Pradesh, the cobbling of one community from the intersection of three districts was not altered. The main town of Rishikesh belongs to Dehra Dun district, the sector known as Muni-ki-Reti, where the Sivananda Ashram is located, is a part of Tehri Garhwal district, and the east side of the Ganga, comprising Swaragashram and the eastern side of the Lakshman Jhula, belongs to what is now Pauri Garhwal district. The bridge called Laxman Jhula over the river is at the north end of what is now Rishikesh town; it appears to have existed as a rope bridge in 1889, and been converted to an iron suspension system with a 140 foot span in 1939 (Nest and Wings 1991). Laxman Jhula is indicated on a 1910 map included in Atkinson's *Gazetter of Garhwal Himalaya* (Walton 1989[1910]). It is still in use today, along with another steel suspension footbridge that spans the Ganga from the Sivananda Ashram to Swaragashram. Called at first the Ram Jhula, this bridge was officially renamed the Sivananda Jhula by the Uttar Pradesh government during the celebration of Sivananda Birth Centenary in 1987 (DLS 1987b:268).

4 These numbers reflect official counts (see Sarkar 1985). The unofficial count is nearly double that figure, at 18 million displaces, and over 1 million dead.

5 In addition to visiting Rishikesh, Vivekananda also founded the Advaita Ashram in the Kumaun Himalaya, a few districts east of Rishikesh, in order to have access to what he perceived as a more appropriate environment for the pursuit of spiritual practice.

6 Vivekananda, *Raja Yoga* (1990b: 269), from *Shvetashvatara Upanisad*.

7 For an extended discussion of this concept, see Fort and Mumme (1996).

8 The Fair itself was an extraordinary display of the positive valuation of industrial society's contributions to the world.

9 See, for example, Vivekananda's favorable reference to the similarity between yoga and Spiritualism in his lectures on *Raja Yoga* (1990b:49), indicating that his New York audiences were both familiar with and sympathetic toward Spiritualist practice.

10 Chatterjee's analysis of this group in relation to their "middleness" is most instructive in the context of understanding the impact of Vivekananda on India. "[P]laced in a position of subordination in one relation and a position of dominance in another" (Chatterjee 1993:36), the Kolkata *bhadralok* were simultaneously drawn to the rustic colloquiality of village Hinduism as represented by Vivekananda's master, Sri Ramakrishna, which they could find charming on the basis of a weekly visit (without actually having to go *live* in a rural setting), and to the allure of the nationalist project that promised power and respect in cosmopolitan circles if the British were ever actually overthrown.

11 The philosophic traditions are *advaita, dvaita, tantra*.

12 This vision of the importance of these vows is echoed by Giddens (1991:8) in his analysis of the "close connections between personal aspects of bodily development and global factors" under the terms of high modernity.

13 This sentiment was certainly expressed overtly by the yoga practitioners I interviewed, and many stressed the importance of *my* practice for being able to tell *their* stories accurately; Sumit, one of the yoga teachers I studied with, said that he had seen many reporters give skewed accounts of yoga, and so he was very glad that I was taking the time to learn how to practice myself.

14 Iyer is a very common south Indian Brahman family; the other major Tamil Brahman family surname is Iyengar, a name quite familiar to yoga practitioners worldwide. That these teachers come from these families is not surprising, as Tamil Nadu has a reputation in India for having the most orthodox of Brahman Hindu castes; note the story with which I begin the book, about the Bombay businessmen on the train.

15 The *sannyasin* was a monk of the Saraswati branch of the Dasanami order living at the Kailash Ashram.

16 The story of the pair continued well into the 1970s and was described in novels by both Eliade and Maitreyi Devi (Devi 1991[1977]; Eliade 1993). According to Devi's version of the story, Eliade wrote letters to a friend in Kolkata from the ashram in Rishikesh (Devi 1991[1977]:313), saying that India had bound him, and only India could free him; through the practice of yoga and intense study of the philosophic texts in Sanskrit, he felt himself becoming a "proper Hindu."

17 Eliade's histories, of course, were also somewhat manipulated. In a conversation with Claude-Henri Rocquet, Eliade discusses the relationship between his fictional and academic writings on India. Eliade comments:

> In describing Zerlendi's Yoga exercises in *The Secret of Dr. Honigberger*, I included certain pieces of information, drawn from my own experiences, that I omitted from my books on Yoga. At the same time, however, I added other, inaccurate touches,

precisely in order to camouflage the true data . . . So that if anyone tried to check the plot of the story in concreto, he would find that the author is not acting simply as a reporter, since the setting is an invented one. He would then be led to conclude that all the rest is invented – imaginary – too, which isn't the case. (Eliade 1982:47)

18 Two other major influences on the rise of yoga in Germanic Europe were Selvarajan Yesudian (1916-1998), and his long-time companion and supporter, Elisabeth Haich (1897–c.1989), who taught yoga based strictly on Vivekananda's teaching, and claimed no more recent guru.
19 The tendency, in 1947 as well as in more recent years, is described so well by McKean (1996: 212–275) in her analysis of the 1987 Sivananda Birth Centenary celebration.
20 An interesting aside: a very popular yoga studio in New York City is called Jivamukti for this very reason (see Schneider 2003: 151). The translation of the term used by the owners of the studio, "liberated being," while technically accurate in the sense that both the concept of living liberation, and those individuals who attain that state share the same noun, does not really do justice to the key feature of being in the world but not of it.

Chapter 3 Balancing Acts: Doing Yoga in Rishikesh

1 This was not the only instance of finding a "hotel swami" in India. For example, during the Fulbright program mid-year meeting at an expensive Goa hotel that I was required to attend, I found signs posted about yoga classes, "yoga spots" designated on the beach, and a young "yoga teacher" with book in hand, trying to instruct others in a subject about which he clearly knew nothing!
2 It represents the present time, and can be understood to be modernity itself; after the *Kaliyuga* has run its course, the world will begin anew with a repeat of the first stage Satya-yuga, the golden age of wisdom.

Chapter 4 Moving Out: Yoga for a Transnational Community of Practice

1 Pace William and Charlotte Wiser, whose work *Behind Mud Walls* is a classic in Indian ethnography (Wiser and Wiser 1971).

2 Or, to use Appadurai's (1988a) example, India as "the place for caste."
3 For extended explanations of *guna* theory, see DasGupta (1987[1924]); Iyengar (1979: 46–48); Lannoy (1971:151).
4 The term Integral Yoga was in fact first coined by Sri Aurobindo, a well-known spiritual leader of the nationalist period, in published writings dating from at least the 1930s (Aurobindo 1998).
5 The OAM was created in the early 1990s to explore the potential of unconventional therapies. In well under ten years, the annual budget increased more than six-fold, from under $2 million per year to $12 million in 1998. By 1999, the success of the program led to its demise and rebirth as NCCAM, the National Center for Complementary and Alternative Medicine, which had a 2003 budget of over $113 million (http://nccam.nih.gov/about/offices/od/directortestimony/0302.htm). These funding increases have come from Congress, not the desires of the medical profession; as health care costs skyrocket, consumers have looked for ways to take control of their own health. While these new-old therapies were initially resisted by mainstream American medical professional groups, there has been a sea-change in the past few years, in direct response to the increased research focus. But it is important to note that, despite American vacillation, such "natural" therapies never completely left the mainstream of German medical practice. There, herbal treatments, homeopathy, spa therapies using water and mud, and assorted types of manipulative bodywork maintain a place in the practice of institutionalized medicine. Germany's tradition of naturopathic healing has been linked to larger cultural trends in human–nature interaction, not all of which have yielded positive results.
6 Some swamis have been the subject of numerous claims of inappropriate sexual encounters and cult-like brainwashing over the years. While there has been some press coverage, these allegations have never to my knowledge been successfully prosecuted.
7 The story of Rajneesh, or Osho as he later called himself, became nearly synonymous with the excesses of "export gurus" in the United States during the 1980s. In 1981, Rajneesh's American followers purchased a ranch in Oregon, and persuaded their guru to leave his ashram in Pune to live in "Rajneeshpuram" with them. The amount of money invested in the place and the organization was phenomenal; photographs of a long line of Rolls Royce automobiles along with luxurious grounds and buildings circulated widely in the American press. Sexual and financial scandals followed, and eventually, in 1985, Rajneesh was deported.
8 Accusations of black magic, Tantric practices involving animal sacrifice, and other such extreme activities were also made.
9 Although the influence of yoga was quite clear in Steiner's work at the turn of the century, in later years his organization attempted to erase all connections

with earlier traditions, attributing the anthroposophical framework entirely to the brain of Steiner (Fuchs, personal communication).

10 This was well before 1947, so India was at that time still a British colony.

11 Vidya means "knowledge" in Sanskrit, and is used substantially in fundamentalist Hindu rhetoric to replace the English term.

Chapter 5 Yoga: A Global Positioning System

1 Ascona, a small Swiss village in the southern canton of Ticino, was a center for artists and anarchists from around Europe since just before the turn of the twentieth century. It had gained fame as a nature cure center, and drew a substantial returning crowd of transnational reformers of one sort or another. Individuals like the Russian Count Kropotkin, a well-known anarchist with whom Swami Vivekananda had interacted during his visits to the Continent, frequented the isolated community. The alternative colony at Ascona was founded as a nature-cure center, and ideas about living in harmony with the natural world were central to the lives of many Asconans, whether artists or revolutionaries. Herman Hesse, author of Siddhartha and other novels with Eastern themes, visited Ascona, where he found many others interested in discussing these traditions. Nearly all of the visitors and residents came from middle- to upper-class backgrounds, and were well educated but dissatisfied with the lifestyles available to them in the modern urban centers from which they hailed (Martin Green 1986).

Later, after the heyday of the nature cure center, the facility at Ascona was used for academic retreats. Along with the well-known Orientalist Heinrich Zimmer, both Carl Jung and Mircea Eliade were instrumental in developing the Eranos conferences held at Ascona beginning in 1933. These were annual gatherings for a collection of scholars whose multidisciplinary interests converged at the intersection of Eastern and Western thought which focused primarily on "subjects relating to the history and psychology of religious experience" (Clarke 1994:61). Yoga was in fact the main theme for the first Eranos conference (Martin Green 1986).

2 Here I refer to the physiological definition of stress, as defined by Selye's General Adaptation Syndrome.

3 Later, however, these associations were seen as threatening political stability, and Hess escaped to England (Bramwell 1989).

4 The explosion of yoga and other Eastern spiritual motifs in advertising campaigns worldwide is itself worthy of an entire chapter, if not a monograph.

5 Richard Hittleman, her predecessor by more than fifteen years in this arena, had certainly pioneered the idea of yoga as edutainment (his television show, *Yoga for Health*, premiered in 1961), but since his practice did not derive from the Sivananda tradition, I have not focused on his activities here. Hittleman was influenced by a number of teachers, including Sri Ramana Maharshi and Swami Vivekananda.

6 Coming from a slightly different angle, a magazine called the *PROUT* journal has recently turned up on newsstands. *PROUT*

> is an acronym for the PROgressive Utilization Theory. Conceptualized in 1959 by Indian philosopher Prabhat Rainjan Sarkar, PROUT is a viable alternative to the outmoded capitalist and communist socioeconomic paradigms. Neither of these approaches has adequately met the physical, mental and spiritual needs of humanity. PROUT seeks a harmonious balance between economic growth, social development and cultural expression. Combining the wisdom of spirituality, the struggle for self-reliance, and the spirit of economic democracy, Proutist intellectuals and activists are attempting to create a new civilizational discourse. (*PROUT*, front cover 5(4) n.d.).

Although *PROUT* does not explicitly claim to supply a Hindu version of spirituality, its founder as well as a large percentage of its staff and contributing writers are either South Asian by birth or have adopted a Hindu name and persona (e.g. Ram Dass); references to Sanskrit texts and religious leaders or philosophers like Vivekananda are not uncommon.

The "Principles of PROUT" include neo-humanism; basic access to material needs of food, clothing, shelter, education, and medical care; a balanced economy based on Emersonian self-reliance, local control, and cooperative business; women's rights; cultural diversity; and world government. Of these, the first is perhaps most relevant to the discussion here. By neo-humanism, the Proutists mean to extend "the humanistic love for all human beings to include love and respect for all creation – plants, animals and even inanimate objects. *Neo-humanism provides a philosophical basis for building a new era of ecological balance, planetary citizenship and cosmic kinship*" (ibid.; emphasis added). Of course, the reference to Emersonian ideology also fits with the notion of a transnational community of practice, as the New England Transcendentalists were heavily influenced to change their lifestyles in accordance with the teachings of advaita Hindu philosophy. I stumbled upon this journal, based in the quintessentially New class community of Los Altos, California, quite accidentally at a late stage in my research. I was astonished to find such an encapsulated statement of the precise connections I had been gleaning from a variety of sources, both historical and contemporary.

7 Another theorist who has promoted such a solution to global malaise is Drew Leder, whose analysis of the "absent body" considers the "disembodied"

lifestyle of the modern West (Leder 1990:3) as a function of the "Western valorization of immaterial reason" (ibid.: 152), concluding that the problem can be reduced to the fact that such valorization results in

> certain individuals or groups [being] associated with the body. This includes women, laborers, "primitive" cultures, animals, and nature in general. They are thus defined as Other to the essential self, just as the body is Other. Moreover, insofar as the body is seen as mindless and in need of control, so too its representatives. Subjugation becomes a necessary and a natural prerogative.
>
> Breaking free of this dualist picture is therefore a matter of no little cultural significance. But how? (ibid.: 155)

The answer, Leder suggests, lies in phenomenology, through the application of which we can achieve "genuinely new ways of looking at the world" (ibid.). For example, the notion of the Leib, or lived body, "can help us to be more attentive to experience, uncover phenomena that were concealed, explain what the Cartesian framework renders inexplicable" (ibid.).

8 A cartoon published in *Utne Reader* in 1992, entitled "Yoga for the Heartland," depicts a typical Midwestern "feed-n-seed" farm store with an overall-clad farmer showing his colleagues the yoga pose called the Plow, which entails having one's heels literally over one's head in an inverted posture.

Bibliography

Adams, V. (1996) *Tigers of the Snow and Other Virtual Sherpas: An Ethnography of Himalayan Encounters*. Princeton, NJ: Princeton University Press.

Albanese, C.L. (1977) *Corresponding Motion: Transcendental Religion and the New America*. Philadelphia, PA: Temple University Press.

Alter, J.S. (1992) *The Wrestler's Body: Identity and Ideology in North India*. Berkeley, CA: University of California Press.

—— (1993) The Body of One Color: Indian Wrestling, the Indian State and Utopian Somatics. *Cultural Anthropology* 8(1):49–72.

—— (1997) A Therapy to Live By. *Medical Anthropology* 17:309–335.

—— (2004) *Yoga in Modern India: The Body between Science and Philosophy*. Princeton, NJ: Princeton University Press.

Amit, V. (ed.) (2000) *Locating the Field*. New York: Routledge.

Ananthanarayanan, N. (1987) *From Man to God-Man: The Inspiring Life-story of Swami Sivananda*. Madras: N. Ananthanarayan.

Anderson, B. (1983) *Imagined Communities: Reflections on the Origin and Spread of Nationalism*. London: Verso and New Left Books.

Appadurai, A. (1981) *Worship and Conflict under Colonial Rule: A South Indian Case*. Cambridge: Cambridge University Press.

—— (1988a) Putting Hierarchy in its Place. *Cultural Anthropology* 3(1):36–49.

—— (ed.) (1988b) *The Social Life of Things: Commodities in Cultural Perspective*. New York: Cambridge University Press.

—— (1990) Disjuncture and Difference in the Global Cultural Economy. *Public Culture* 2(2):1–24.

—— (1991) Global Ethnoscapes: Notes and Queries for a Transnational Anthropology. In R. Fox (ed.) *Recapturing Anthropology: Working in the Present*. Santa Fe, NM: School of American Research Press.

—— (1996) *Modernity at Large: Cultural Dimensions of Globalization*. Minneapolis, MN: University of Minnesota Press.

—— and Breckenridge, C.A. (1987) Cosmopolitan Cultural Forms in Late Twentieth Century India. Unpublished manuscript.

Aranya, Swami H. (1983) *Yoga Philosophy of Patanjali*. Albany, NY: SUNY Press.

Asad, T. (1987) On Ritual and Discipline in Medieval Christian Monasticism. *Economy and Society* 16: 159–203.

Atulananda, Swami (1988) *With the Swamis in America and India*. Mayavati: Advaita Ashrama.

Augé, M. (1995) *Non-places: An Introduction to an Anthropology of Super-modernity*, trans. J. Howe. London: Verso.

—— and Herzlich, C. (1995) *The Meaning of Illness: Anthropology, History and Sociology*. Luxembourg: Harwood Academic.

Aurobindo, S. (1998) *Integral Yoga: Sri Aurobindo's Teaching and Method of Practice*. Pondicherry, India: Sri Aurobindo Ashram Trust.

Bahadur, R.P.R. (1992 [1916]) *Garhwal: Ancient and Modern*. Gurgaon, India: Vintage.

Baritz, L. (1989) *The Good Life: The Meaning of Success for the American Middle Class*. New York: Alfred A. Knopf.

Basham, A.L. (1954) *The Wonder that was India*. New York: Grove.

Basnet, L.B., Rey, M. and Rey, P. (1992) *Rishikesh, Hardwar and Surroundings*. Rishikesh: Lamapa.

Bateson, G. (2000 [1972]) *Steps to an Ecology of Mind*. Chicago: University of Chicago Press.

Beck, B. (1976) The Symbolic Merger of Body, Space and Cosmos in Hindu Tamil Nadu. *Contributions to Indian Sociology* 10(2):213–243.

Beck, U. (1992) *Risk Society: Towards a New Modernity*, Ritter, M., trans. London: Sage.

—— Giddens, A. and Lash, S. (1994) *Reflexive Modernization: Politics, Tradition and Aesthetics in the Modern Social Order*. Stanford, CA: Stanford University Press.

Beeton, I.M. (2000 [1861]) *Mrs Beeton's Book of Household Management*, ed. N. Humble. Oxford: Oxford University Press.

Bell, D. (1973) *The Coming of Post-Industrial Society*. New York: Basic Books.

Bellamy, E. (1995 [1888]) *Looking Backward, 2000–1887*, ed. D. Borus. The Bedford Series in History and Culture. Boston, MA: Bedford Books of St. Martin's Press.

Bendix, R. (1992) National Sentiment in the Enactment and Discourse of Swiss Political Ritual. *American Ethnologist* 19(4):768–790.

Benjamin, W. (1968 [1955]) *Illuminations*, trans. H. Zohn, ed. and with introduction by H. Arendt. New York: Schocken.

Berlin, I. (1958) *Two Concepts of Liberty*. Oxford: Oxford University Press.

Berreman, G.D. (1963) *Hindus of the Himalayas*. Berkeley, CA: University of California Press.

Bharati, A. (1970) The Hindu Renaissance and its Apologetic Patterns. *Journal of Asian Studies* 29:267–87.

—— (1976) *The Light at the Center*. Santa Barbara, CA: Ross-Erikson.

Bibliography

Bhardwaj, S.M. (1983) *Hindu Places of Pilgrimage in India: A Study in Cultural Geography.* Berkeley, CA: University of California Press.

Bidney, D. (ed.) (1963) *The Concept of Freedom in Anthropology.* The Hague: Mouton.

Bisht, D.S. (1982) *Guide to Garhwal and Kumaon Hills.* Dehra Dun: Trishul.

Blacking, J. (ed.) (1977) *The Anthropology of the Body.* London: Academic Press.

Boston Women's Health Book Collective (1973) *Our Bodies, Ourselves.* New York: Simon & Schuster.

Bourdieu, P. (1977) *Outline of a Theory of Practice.* Cambridge Studies in Social Anthropology. Cambridge: Cambridge University Press.

—— (1984) *Distinction: A Social Critique of the Judgement of Taste,* trans. R. Nice. Cambridge, MA: Harvard University Press.

Bramwell, A. (1989) *Ecology in the 20th Century: A History.* New Haven, CT: Yale University Press.

Brockington, J.L. (1981) *The Sacred Thread.* Edinburgh: Edinburgh University Press.

Brown, M.F. (1994) Questing for the Spirit in the Self: Religious Dilemmas of the Middle Class. Paper presented at the Annual Meeting of the American Anthropological Association, Atlanta, GA, 30 November – 4 December.

Brownell, S. (1995) *Training the Body for China.* Chicago: University of Chicago Press.

Bruce-Briggs, B. (ed.) (1981) *The New Class?* New York: McGraw-Hill.

Brunton, P. (1989) *A Search in Secret India.* York Beach, MA: Samuel Weiser.

Burbick, J. (1994) *Healing the Republic: The Language of Health and the Culture of Nationalism in Nineteenth Century America.* Cambridge: Cambridge University Press.

Burke, M.L. (1983) *Swami Vivekananda in the West: New Discoveries,* Vol. 1. Calcutta: Advaita Ashrama.

—— (1984) *Swami Vivekananda in the West: New Discoveries,* Vol. 2. Calcutta: Advaita Ashrama.

—— (1986) *Swami Vivekananda in the West: New Discoveries,* Vol. 4. Calcutta: Advaita Ashrama.

Burris, V. (1986) The Discovery of the New Middle Class. *Theory and Society* 15:317–349.

Caldwell, J. et al. (eds) (1990) *What We Know about Health Transition: The Cultural, Social, and Behavioral Determinants of Health.* Proceedings of an International Workshop, Canberra, May, 1989. Canberra: Health Transition Centre of the Australian National University.

Capouya, J. (2003) *Real Men Do Yoga: 21 Star Athletes Reveal their Secrets for Strength, Flexibility and Peak Performance.* Deerfield Beach, FL: Health Communications.

Carman, J. and Marglin, F. (eds) (1985) *Purity and Auspiciousness in Indian Society.* Leiden: E.J. Brill.

Carrier, J.G. (ed.) (1995) *Occidentalism: Images of the West.* New York: Oxford University Press.

Casper, M. and Koenig, B. (1996) Reconfiguring Nature and Culture: Intersections of Medical Anthropology and Technoscience Studies. *Medical Anthropology Quarterly* 10(4):523–536.

Castillo, R.J. (1994) Spirit Possession in South Asia: Dissociation or Hysteria, Part I. *Culture, Medicine and Psychiatry* 18(1):1–21.

Chatterjee, P. (1986) *Nationalist Thought and the Colonial World: A Derivative Discourse?* London: Zed.

—— (1992) A Religion of Urban Domesticity: Sri Ramakrishna and the Calcutta Middle Class. In P. Chatterjee and G. Pandey (eds) *Subaltern Studies VII.* Delhi: Oxford University Press.

—— (1993) *The Nation and its Fragments: Colonial and Postcolonial Histories.* Princeton, NJ: Princeton University Press.

Chattopadhyaya, R. (1993) *Swami Vivekananda in the West.* Houston, TX: R. Chattopadhyaya.

Chen, L., Kleinman, A. and Ware, N. (1994) *Health and Social Change in International Perspective.* Boston, MA: Harvard School of Public Health and Harvard University Press.

Chidananda, S. (1993) *Timely Wisdom.* Keedysville, MD: Divine Life Society of Maryland, for the 1993 Parliament of the World's Religions.

Clarke, J.J. (1994) *Jung and Eastern Thought: A Dialogue with the Orient.* London: Routledge.

Clifford, J. (1997) *Routes.* Cambridge, MA: Harvard University Press.

—— and Marcus, G.E. (eds) (1986) *Writing Culture: The Poetics and Politics of Ethnography.* School of American Research Advanced Seminar. Berkeley, CA: University of California Press.

Conrad, P. (1994) Wellness as Virtue: Morality and the Pursuit of Health. *Culture, Medicine and Psychiatry* 18:385–401.

Costanza, R., Norton, B. and Haskell, B. (eds) (1992) *Ecosystem Health.* Washington, DC: Island Press.

Crooke, W. (1978) *The Popular Religion and Folklore of Northern India,* new edn, Vols I and II. New Delhi: Munshiram Manoharlal.

Csikszentmihalyi, M. and Graef, R. (1980) The Experience of Freedom in Daily Life. *American Journal of Community Psychology* 8(4):401–414.

Csordas, T.J. (1990) Embodiment as a Paradigm for Anthropology. *Ethos* 18:5–47.

—— (1993) Somatic Modes of Attention. *Cultural Anthropology* 8:135–156.

—— (ed.) (1994) *Embodiment and Experience: The Existential Ground of Culture and Self.* Cambridge Studies in Medical Anthropology, Vol. 2. Cambridge: Cambridge University Press.

Daly, H.E. and Cobb, J.B. Jr. (1994) *For the Common Good*, 2nd edn. Boston, MA: Beacon Press.

Daniel, E.V. (1984) *Fluid Signs: Being a Person the Tamil Way*. Berkeley, CA: University of California Press.

Das, A. (1992) *India Invented: A Nation-in-the-Making*. Delhi: Manohar.

Das Gupta, S. (1987 [1924]) *Yoga as Philosophy and Religion*. Delhi: Motilal Banarsidass.

—— (1989 [1920]) *A Study of Patanjali*. Delhi: Motilal Banarsidass.

de Certeau, M. (1988) *The Practice of Everyday Life*, trans. S. Rendall. Berkeley, CA: University of California Press.

Demeny, P. (1968) Early Fertility Decline in Austria-Hungary: A Lesson in Demographic Transition. *Daedalus* (Spring):502–522.

DeMichelis, E. (2004) A *History of Modern Yoga: Patanjali and Western Esotericism*. London: Concordia.

Desai, A. (1995) *Journey to Ithaca*. New York: Alfred A. Knopf.

Deutsch, E. (trans./ed.) (1968) *The Bhagavad Gita*. Washington, DC: University Press of America.

Devi, M. (1991 [1977]) *Liebe Stirbt Nicht*. Berlin: Rutten & Loening.

Dickens, P. (1992) *Society and Nature: Towards a Green Social Theory*. Philadelphia, PA: Temple University Press.

Divine Life Society (1947) *Diamond Jubilee Volume*. Rishikesh: Sivananda Publication League.

—— (1951) *All-India Tour Volume*. Rishikesh: Sivananda Publication League.

—— (1956) *World Parliament of Religions Volume*. Rishikesh: Sivananda Publication League.

—— (1985a, 1985b, 1985c, 1986a, 1986b, 1987a) *Sivananda: His Life and Works*, Vols 1–6.

—— (1985d) *Sadhana: A Textbook of the Psychology and Practice of the Techniques to Spiritual Perfection*. Rishikesh: Divine Life Society. Vol. I: *Sivananda: Biography of a Modern Sage*. Rishikesh: Divine Life Society.

—— (1987b) *The Master, his Mission and his Works*. Rishikesh: Divine Life Society.

—— (2004) *A Steady Light: Swami Gurudevananda, The Life of a Western Disciple*. Rishikesh: Divine Life Society.

Douglas, M. (1966) *Purity and Danger: An Analysis of the Concepts of Pollution and Taboo*. London: Routledge & Kegan Paul.

—— (1982) *Natural Symbols: Explorations in Cosmology*. New York: Pantheon.

Dubos, R. (1965) *Man Adapting*. New Haven, CT: Yale University Press.

Dumont, L. (1980) *Homo Hierarchicus: The Caste System and its Implications*, revised English edn, trans. M. Sainsbury, L. Dumont and B. Gulati. Chicago: University of Chicago Press.

—— (1992) *Essays on Individualism: Modern Ideology in Anthropological Perspective*. Chicago: University of Chicago Press.

—— (1994) *German Ideology*. Chicago: University of Chicago Press.

Dunlap, R.E., Gallup, G. Jr., and Gallup, A. (1993) Of Global Concern: Results of the Health of the Planet Survey. *Environment* 35(9):6–15, 33–39.

Dunn, H. (1959) High Level Wellness for Man and Society. *American Journal of Public Health* February: 786–9.

Eck, D. (1995) Frontiers of Encounter. In D.G. Hackett (ed.) *Religion and American Culture: A Reader*. New York: Routledge.

Ehrenreich, B. (1989) *Fear of Falling: The Inner Life of the Middle Class*. New York: Pantheon.

Eliade, M. (1963) Yoga and Modern Philosophy. *Journal of General Education* 15:124–137.

—— (1969) *Patanjali and Yoga*, trans. C.L. Markmann. New York: Funk & Wagnalls.

—— (1970) *Tales of the Occult*. New York: Herder & Herder.

—— (1973 [1958]) *Yoga: Immortality and Freedom*, trans. W.R. Trask. Bollingen Series. Princeton, NJ: Princeton University Press.

—— (1977) *No Souvenirs: Journal, 1957–1969*. trans. F.H. Johnson Jr. New York: Harper & Row.

—— (1981) *Autobiography, Volume I: 1907–1937 Journey East, Journey West*, trans. M.L. Ricketts. San Francisco, CA: Harper & Row.

—— (1982) *Ordeal by Labyrinth: Conversations with Claude-Henri Rocquet*, trans. D. Coltman. Chicago: University of Chicago Press.

—— (1988 [1934]) *L'Inde*. Mayenne: Les Editions de L'Herne.

—— (1990) *Journal I, 1945–1955*, trans. M.L. Ricketts. Chicago: University of Chicago Press.

—— (1993) *Bengal Nights*. Chicago: University of Chicago Press.

Elias, N. (1994) *The Civilizing Process*, trans. E. Jephcott. Oxford: Blackwell.

Ellwood, R.S., Jr. (1979) *Alternative Altars: Unconventional and Eastern Spirituality in America*. Chicago: University of Chicago Press.

English-Lueck, J.A. (2003) cultures@siliconvalley. Stanford, CA: Stanford University Press.

Erikson, E.H. (1969) *Gandhi's Truth: On the Origins of Militant Nonviolence*. New York: W.W. Norton.

Fardon, R. (ed.) (1995) *Counterworks: Managing the Diversity of Knowledge*, ASA Decennial Conference Series, *The Uses of Knowledge: Global and Local Relations*. London: Routledge.

Featherstone, M. (ed.) (1990) *Global Culture: Nationalism, Globalization and Modernity*. London: Sage.

Bibliography

—— (1995) *Undoing Culture: Globalization, Postmodernism and Identity.* London: Sage.

—— Lash, S. and Robertson, R. (eds) (1995) *Global Modernities.* London: Sage.

Fellman, A.C. and Fellman, M. (1981) *Making Sense of Self: Medical Advice Literature in Late Nineteenth Century America.* Philadelphia, PA: University of Pennsylvania Press.

Feuerstein, G. and Bodian, S. (eds) (1993) *Living Yoga: A Comprehensive Guide for Daily Life.* New York: Jeremy P. Tarcher/Perigee.

Folan, L. (1981) *Lilias, Yoga and your Life.* New York: Collier.

Fornaio, R.J. (1969) *Sivananda and the Divine Life Society: A Paradigm of the "Secularism," "Puritanism," and "Cultural Dissimulation" of a Neo-Hindu Religious Society.* PhD dissertation, Department of Anthropology, Syracuse University, NY.

Fort, A.O. (1996) Introduction. In A.O. Fort and P.Y. Mumme (eds) *Living Liberation in Hindu Thought.* Albany, NY: State University of New York Press.

—— and P.Y. Mumme (eds) (1996) *Living Liberation in Hindu Thought.* Albany, NY: State University of New York Press.

Fortier, A-M. (1996) Troubles in the Field: The Use of Personal Experiences as Sources of Knowledge. *Critique of Anthropology* 16(3):303–323.

Foucault, M. (1972) *The Archaeology of Knowledge and the Discourse of Language,* trans. A.M. Sheridan Smith. New York: Pantheon.

—— (1975) *The Birth of the Clinic: An Archaeology of Medical Perception,* trans. A.M. Sheridan Smith. New York: Vintage.

—— (1984) What is Enlightenment? In P. Rabinow (ed.) *The Foucault Reader.* New York: Pantheon.

—— (1988) *The History of Sexuality, Vol. 3, The Care of the Self,* trans. R. Hurley. New York: Vintage.

Fox, R.G. (1989) *Gandhian Utopia: Experiments with Culture.* Boston, MA: Beacon Press.

—— (ed.) (1991) *Recapturing Anthropology: Working in the Present.* School of American Research Advanced Seminar Series. Santa Fe, NM: School of American Research Press.

Fox, W. (1990) *Toward a Transpersonal Ecology.* Boston, MA: Shambhala Press.

Freilich, M. (1963) Toward an Operational Definition of Community. *Rural Sociology* 28(2):117–127.

Friedman, J. (1994) *Cultural Identity and Global Process.* London: Sage.

Fuchs, C. (1990) *Yoga in Deutschland: Rezeption-Organisation-Typologie.* Stuttgart: Kohlhammer.

—— (1992) Geschichte und Gegenwart des Yoga in Deutschland. In F. Usarski (ed.) *Yoga und Indien.* Materialien 33, Volkshochschulen und der Themenbereich

Afrika, Asien und Lateinamerika; 28-54. Bonn: Deutscher Volkshochschul-Verband e.V., Fachstelle für Internationale Zusammenarbeit.

Fuller, R.C. (1989) *Alternative Medicine and American Religious Life*. New York: Oxford University Press.

Giddens, A. (1975) *The Class Structure of the Advanced Societies*. London: Hutchinson.

—— (1990) *The Consequences of Modernity*. Cambridge: Polity Press.

—— (1991) *Modernity and Self-Identity: Self and Society in the Late Modern Age*. Cambridge: Polity Press.

Glick Schiller, N., Basch, L., and Blanc-Szanton, C. (eds) (1992) *Towards a Transnational Perspective on Migration: Race, Class, Ethnicity and Nationalism Reconsidered*. Annals of the New York Academy of Sciences, vol. 645. New York: New York Academy of Sciences.

—— (1994) *Nations Unbound*. London: Routledge.

Gold, A.G. (1990) *Fruitful Journeys: The Ways of Rajasthani Pilgrims*. Berkeley, CA: University of California Press.

Gomes, M.E. and Kanner, A.D.C. (eds) (1995) *Ecopsychology: Restoring the Earth, Healing the Mind*. San Francisco, CA: Sierra Club.

Gore, A. (1993) *Earth in the Balance: Ecology and the Human Spirit*. New York: Plume.

Gouldner, A.W. (1979) *The Future of Intellectuals and the Rise of the New Class: The Dark Side of the Dialectic*. New York: Seabury Press.

Gowda, R. (ed.) (1991) *Yoga Stream*. Rishikesh: Yoga Study Centre.

Green, H. (1986) *Fit for America: Health, Fitness, Sport and American Society*. New York: Pantheon.

Green, M. (1986) *Mountain of Truth*. Hanover, NH: University Press of New England.

—— (ed.) (1987) *Gandhi in India in his Own Words*. Hanover, NH: University Press of New England.

—— (1992) *Prophets of a New Age*. New York: Charles Scribner's Sons.

Grove, R.H. (1992) The Origins of Western Environmentalism. *Scientific American* 267(1):42–47.

Grover, K. (ed.) (1989) *Fitness in American Culture: Images of Health, Sport, and the Body, 1830–1940*. Amherst, MA: University of Massachusetts Press.

Guha, R. (1989) *The Unquiet Woods: Ecological Change and Peasant Resistance in the Himalaya*. Delhi: Oxford University Press.

Gupta, A. (1992) The song of the Non-Aligned World: Transnational Identities and the Reinscription of Space in Late Capitalism. *Cultural Anthropology* 7(1):63–92.

—— and Ferguson, J. (eds) (1997) *Anthropological Locations: Boundaries and Grounds of a Field Science*. Berkeley, CA: University of California Press.

Gupta, G.R. (ed.) (1983) *Religion in Modern India.* New Delhi:Vikas.

Gusfield, J.R. (1975) *Community: A Critical Response.* New York: Harper & Row.

Hackett, D.G., (ed.) (1995) *Religion and American Culture: A Reader.* New York: Routledge.

Halbfass, W. (1988) *India and Europe: An Essay in Understanding.* Albany, NY: State University of New York Press.

—— (1991) *Tradition and Reflection: Explorations in Indian Thought.* Albany, NY: State University of New York Press.

Haley, B. (1978) *The Healthy Body in Victorian Culture.* Cambridge, MA: Harvard University Press.

Hall, R.H. (1990) *Health and the Global Environment.* Cambridge: Polity Press.

Hall, S., Held, D., Hubert, D. and Thompson, K. (eds) (1997) *Modernity: An Introduction to Modern Societies.* Oxford: Blackwell.

Hannerz, U. (1980) *Exploring the City.* New York: Columbia University Press.

—— (1992) *Cultural Complexity: Studies in the Social Organization of Meaning.* New York: Columbia University Press.

—— (1996) *Transnational Connections.* New York: Routledge.

Hansen, T.B. (1999) *The Saffron Wave: Democracy and Hindu Nationalism in Modern India.* Princeton, NJ: Princeton University Press.

Harper, M. (1972) *Gurus, Swamis, and Avataras: Spiritual Masters and their American Disciples.* Philadelphia, PA: Westminster Press.

Hay, S.N. (1970) *Asian Ideas of East and West: Tagore and his Critics in Japan, China, and India.* Cambridge, MA: Harvard University Press.

—— (ed.) (1988) *Sources of Indian Tradition, Vol. 2, Modern India and Pakistan,* 2nd edn. New York: Columbia University Press.

Heelas, P. (1996) *The New Age Movement.* Oxford: Blackwell.

Herzlich, C. (1995) Modern Medicine and the Quest for Meaning. In M. Augé and C. Herzlich (eds) *The Meaning of Illness: Anthropology, History and Sociology.* Luxembourg: Harwood Academic.

Hobfoll, S. (1988) *The Ecology of Stress.* New York: Hemisphere.

Howell, S. (1995) Whose Knowledge and Whose Power? In R. Fardon (ed.) *Counterworks: Managing the Diversity of Knowledge.* ASA Decennial Conference Series. London: Routledge.

Huss-Ashmore, R., Schall, J. and Hediger, M. (1991) *Health and Lifestyle Change.* MASCA Research Papers in Science and Archaeology, Vol. 9. Philadelphia, PA: MASCA, University Museum of Archaeology and Anthropology.

Huxley, A. (1962) *Island, a Novel.* New York: Harper.

Imperial Gazetteer of India (1984 [1908]) *United Provinces of Agra and Oudh,* Vols I and II. New Delhi: USHA.

Inden, R. (1990) *Imagining India.* Oxford: Basil Blackwell.

Iyengar, B.K.S. (1979) *Light on Yoga,* revised edn. New York: Schocken.

Jacobson, D. and Wadley, S. (1986) *Women in India: Two Perspectives*. New Delhi: Manohar.

Jeffery, P. Jeffery, R., and Lyon, A. (1989) *Labour Pains and Labour Power: Women and Childbearing in India*. London: Zed.

Joshi, S. (2001) *Fractured Modernity: The Making of a Middle Class in Colonial North India*. Delhi: Oxford University Press.

Juergensmeyer, M. (1991) *Radhasoami Reality: The Logic of a Modern Faith*. Princeton, NJ: Princeton University Press.

Jung, C.G. (1975) *Letters*, ed. G. Adler and A. Jaffe, trans. R.F.C. Hull. Bollingen Series XCV:2. Princeton, NJ: Princeton University Press.

—— (1996) *The Psychology of Kundalini Yoga*, Notes of the Seminar Given in 1932, ed. S. Shamdasani. Bollingen Series XCIX. Princeton, NJ: Princeton University Press.

Kaivalyadhama Institute (1975) *Golden Jubilee Souvenir Volume*. Lonavla: Kaivalyadhama Institute.

—— (1984) First International Conference on Yoga and Research, December 1984: Selected Papers. Lonavla: Kaivalyadhama Institute.

—— (1988) Second International Conference on Yoga, Education and Research, January 1988. Lonavla: Kaivalyadhama Institute.

Kapferer, B. (1983) *A Celebration of Demons: Exorcism and the Aesthetics of Healing in Sri Lanka*. Bloomington, IN: University of Indiana Press.

Kaplan, K. (1997) *Questions of Travel*. Durham, NC: Duke University Press.

Kearney, M. (1995) The Local and the Global: The Anthropology of Globalization and Transnationalism. *Annual Review of Anthropology* 24: 547–65.

Keemattam, A. (1997) *The Hermits of Rishikesh: A Sociological Study*. New Delhi:Intercultural Publications.

Kelly, A. (1981) *The Descent of Darwin: The Popularization of Darwinismin Germany, 1860–1914*. Chapel Hill, NC: University of North Carolina Press.

Ketcham, R. (1987) *Individualism and Public Life: A Modern Dilemma*. New York: Basil Blackwell.

Kettani-Hajoui, M.E-C. (1985) Deux discours sur la personne psychologique, biologique et sociale: pyschanalyse et yoga hindou. *History and Anthropology* 2:173–205.

Khare, R.S. (1976) *Culture and Reality*. Simla: Indian Institute of Advanced Study.

Kleinman, A. (1980) *Patients and Healers in the Context of Culture: An Exploration of the Borderland between anthropology, Medicine, and Psychiatry*, ed. C. Leslie. Berkeley, CA: University of California Press.

—— (1995) *Writing at the Margin: Discourse between Anthropology and Medicine*. Berkeley, CA: University of California Press.

Knauft, B. (2002) Critically Modern: An Introduction. In B. Knauft (ed.) *Critically Modern*. Bloomington: Indiana University Press.

Bibliography

Kopf, D. (1979) *The Brahmo Samaj and the Shaping of the Modern Indian Mind.* Princeton, NJ: Princeton University Press.

Kriesi, H. (1989) New Social Movements and the New Class in the Netherlands. *American Journal of Sociology* 94(5): 1078–1116.

—— Koopmans, R., Willem Dyvendak, J. and Giugni, M. (1995) *New Social Movements in Western Europe.* Minneapolis, MN: University of Minnesota Press.

Kripal, J. (1995) *Kali's Child: The Mystical and the Erotic in the Life and Teachings of Ramakrishna.* Chicago: University of Chicago Press.

Kropotkin, P. (1914 [1902]) *Mutual Aid: A Factor of Evolution*, reprinted 2nd edn. Boston, MA: Porter Sargent.

Kumar, K. (1987) *Utopia and Anti-Utopia in Modern Times.* Oxford: Basil Blackwell.

—— (1995) *From Post-Industrial to Post-Modern Society: New Theories of the Contemporary World.* Oxford: Blackwell.

Kureishi, H. (1990) *The Buddha of Suburbia.* New York: Viking Penguin.

Laderman, C. and Roseman, M. (eds) (1996) *The Performance of Healing.* New York: Routledge.

Langford, J. (2002) *Fluent Bodies.* Chapel Hill, NC: Duke University Press.

Lannoy, R. (1971) *The Speaking Tree.* New York: Oxford University Press.

Lash, S. (1994) Reflexivity and its Doubles. In U. Beck, A. Giddens and S. Lash (eds) *Reflexive Modernization.* Stanford, CA: Stanford University Press.

—— and Friedman, J. (eds) (1992) *Modernity and Identity.* Oxford: Blackwell.

Latour, B. (1993) *We Have Never Been Modern*, trans. C. Porter. Cambridge, MA: Harvard University Press.

Lears, T.J.J. (1981) *No Place of Grace: Antimodernism and the Transformation of American Culture 1880–1920.* New York: Pantheon.

Leder, D. (1990) *The Absent Body.* Chicago: University of Chicago Press.

Lehrer, P.M. and Woolfolk, R.L. (eds) (1993) *Principles and Practice of Stress Management*, 2nd edn. New York: Guilford Press.

Leifer, W. (1971) *India and the Germans.* Bombay: Shakuntala and Horst Erdmann.

Leslie, C. (ed.) (1976) *Asian Medical Systems: A Comparative Study.* Berkeley, CA: University of California Press.

Lewis, J.L. (1992) *Ring of Liberation: Deceptive Discourse in Brazilian Capeoira.* Chicago: University of Chicago Press.

—— (1995) Genre and Embodiment: From Brazilian Capoeira to the Ethnology of Human Movement. *Cultural Anthropology* 10(2):221–243.

Liechty, M. (2003) *Suitably Modern: Making Middle-Class Culture in a New Consumer Society.* Princeton, NJ: Princeton University Press.

Lindenbaum, S. and Lock, M. (eds) (1993) *Knowledge, Power and Practice.* Berkeley, CA: University of California Press.

Lipow, A. (1982) *Authoritarian Socialism in America: Edward Bellamy and the Nationalist Movement.* Berkeley, CA: University of California Press.

Lock, M. (1993) Cultivating the Body: Anthropologies and Epistemologies of Bodily Practice and Knowledge. *Annual Review of Anthropology* 22:133–55.

Luhrmann, T.M. (1994) The Good Parsi: The Postcolonial "Feminization" of a Colonial Elite. *Man* 29:333–357.

McKean, L. (1996) *Divine Enterprise: Gurus and the Hindu Nationalist Movement.* Chicago: University of Chicago Press.

McKibben, W. (1989) *The End of Nature.* New York: Random House.

McMichael, A.J. (1993) *Planetary Overload: Global Environmental Change and the Health of the Human Species.* Cambridge: Cambridge University Press.

McQuail, D. (1992) *Media Performance: Mass Communication and the Public Interest.* London: Sage.

Madan, T.N. (1982) *Way of Life: King, Householder, Renouncer.* New Delhi: Oxford University Press.

—— (1987) *Non-renunciation: Themes and Interpretations of Hindu Culture.* Delhi: Oxford University Press.

Marcus, G.E. (1986) Contemporary Problems of Ethnography in the Modern World System. In J. Clifford and G.E. Marcus (eds) *Writing Culture: The Poetics and Politics of Ethnography.* Berkeley, CA: University of California Press.

—— (1992) Past, Present and Emergent Identities. In S. Lash and J. Friedman (eds) *Modernity and Identity.* Oxford: Blackwell.

—— (1995) Ethnography in/of the World System: The Emergence of Multi-sited Ethnography. *Annual Review of Anthropology* 24:95–117.

—— and Fischer, M.M.J. (1986) *Anthropology as Cultural Critique: An Experimental Moment in the Human Sciences.* Chicago: University of Chicago Press.

Marriott, McK. (ed.) (1986 [1955]) *Village India: Studies in the Little Community.* Midway reprint edn. Comparative Studies of Cultures and Civilizations. Chicago: University of Chicago Press.

—— (1989) Constructing an Indian Ethnosociology. *Contributions to Indian Sociology* 23(1): 1–40.

Martin, E. (1994) *Flexible Bodies: The Role of Immunity in American Culture from the Days of Polio to the Age of AIDS.* Boston, MA: Beacon Press.

—— (1997) Anthropological Fieldwork and the Study of Science as Culture: From Citadels to String Figures, in A. Gupta and J. Ferguson (eds) *Anthropological Locations: Boundaries and Grounds of a Field Science.* Berkeley, CA: University of California Press.

Martin, L.H., Gutman, H. and Hutton, P.H. (eds) (1988) *Technologies of the Self: A Seminar with Michel Foucault.* Amherst, MA: University of Massachusetts Press.

Mauss, M. (1973 [1936]) Techniques of the Body. *Economy and Society* 2:70–88.

Mechanic, D. (1994) Promoting Health: Implications for Modern and Developing Nations. In L.C. Chen, A. Kleinman and N.C. Ware, *Health and Social Change in International Perspective.* Boston, MA: Harvard School of Public Health and Harvard University Press.

Memmi, A. (1965) *The Colonizer and the Colonized.* Boston, MA: Beacon Press.

Merchant, C. (ed.) (1994) *Ecology: Key Concepts in Critical Theory.* Atlantic Highlands, NJ: Humanities Press.

Miller, B.S. (1996) *Yoga: Discipline of Freedom.* Berkeley, CA: University of California Press.

Miller, Daniel (1994) *Modernity: An Ethnographic Approach.* Oxford: Berg.

—— (ed.) (1995) *Worlds Apart: Modernity through the Prism of the Local.* London: Routledge.

Miller, David (1989) The Divine Life Society Movement. In R.D. Baird (ed.) *Religion in Modern India,* 2nd revised edn. Delhi: Manohar.

Milton, K. (ed.) (1993) *Environmentalism: The View from Anthropology.* ASA Monographs. London: Routledge.

Morrissey, M. (1992) Review Essay: Historical Sociology and Freedom. *Qualitative Sociology* 15(2):213–217.

Mosse, G. (1985) *Nationalism and Sexuality: Middle-Class Morality and Sexual Norms in Modern Europe.* Madison, WI: University of Wisconsin Press.

Myren, A. and Madison, D. (eds) (1993) *Living at the Source: Yoga Teachings of Vivekananda.* Boston, MA: Shambhala.

Naess, A. (1989) *Ecology, Community, Lifestyle: Outline of an Ecosophy,* trans. D. Rothenberg. Cambridge: Cambridge University Press.

Nandy, A. (1988) *The Intimate Enemy: Loss and Recovery of Self under Colonialism.* Delhi: Oxford University Press.

—— (1990) *At the Edge of Psychology: Essays in Politics and Culture.* Delhi: Oxford University Press.

—— (1995) *The Savage Freud and Other Essays on Possible and Retrievable Selves.* Princeton Studies in Culture/Power/History. Princeton, NJ: Princeton University Press.

Narayan, K. (1989) *Storytellers, Saints, and Scoundrels: Folk Narrative in Hindu Religious Teaching.* Series in Contemporary Ethnography. Philadelphia, PA: University of Pennsylvania Press.

—— (1993) Refractions of the Field at Home: American Representations of Hindu Holy Men in the 19th and 20th Centuries. *Cultural Anthropology* 8(4):476–509.

Nash, R. (1982) *Wilderness and the American Mind*, 3rd edn. New Haven, CT: Yale University Press.

Negt, O. and Kluge, A. (1993) *Public Sphere and Experience*, trans. P. Labanyi, J.O. Daniel and A. Oksiloff. Minneapolis, MN: University of Minnesota Press.

Nest and Wings (1991) *Guide to Rishikesh*. Delhi: Nest and Wings.

Newman, K.S. (1988) *Falling from Grace: The Experience of Downward Mobility in the American Middle Class*. New York: The Free Press.

O'Flaherty, W.D. (1984) *Dreams, Illusion and Other Realities*. Chicago: University of Chicago Press.

Ohnuki-Tierney, E. (1984) *Illness and Culture in Contemporary Japan: An Anthropological View*. Cambridge: Cambridge University Press.

Okely, J. (1996) *Own or Other Culture*. London: Routledge.

Olsen, M.E., Lodwick, D.G., and Dunlap, R.E. (1992) *Viewing the World Ecologically*. Boulder, CO: Westview Press.

Omkarananda, Swami (ed.) (1960) *Sivananda Literature*, vol. I. Rishikesh: Divine Life Society.

—— (1972) *Dialectical Materialism and the Spiritual Superman*. Winterthur: Divine Light Zentrum.

—— (1972) *Aims and Objects of the Omkarananda International Ashram*, Switzerland and Himalayas.

Omran, A. (1971) The Epidemiologic Transition: A Theory of the Epidemiology of Population Change. *Milbank Memorial Fund Quarterly* 49: 509–538.

—— (1974) Changing Patterns of Health and Disease during the Process of National Development. In A. Omran (ed.) *Community Medicine in Developing Countries*. New York: Springer.

—— (1983) The Epidemiologic Transition Theory: A Preliminary Update. *Journal of Tropical Pediatrics* 29: 305–316.

O'Neill, J. (1985) *Five Bodies: The Human Shape of Modern Society*. Ithaca, NY: Cornell University Press.

Ong, A. (1988) The Production of Possession: Spirits and the Multinational Corporation in Malaysia. *American Ethnologist* 15(1):28–42.

Ornish, D. (1990) *Dr. Dean Ornish's Program for Reversing Heart Disease*. New York: Ballantine.

Ots, T. (1994) The Silenced Body – the Expressive Leib: on the Dialectic of Mind and Life in Chinese Cathartic Healing. In T.J. Csordas (ed.) *Embodiment and Experience*. Cambridge: Cambridge University Press.

Parry, J. (1979) *Caste and Kinship in Kangra*. London: Routledge & Kegan Paul.

—— (1994) *Death in Banaras*. Lewis Henry Morgan Lecture Series. Cambridge: Cambridge University Press.

Parsons, T. (1951) *The Social System*. Glencoe, NY: The Free Press.

Patterson, O. (1991) *Freedom*, Vol. 1, *Freedom in the Making of Western Culture*. New York: Basic Books.

Pilgrim (P. Barron) (1990) *Notes of Wandering in the Himmala*. Nainital: Gyanodaya Prakashan.

Pocock, D. (1973) *Mind, Body and Wealth: A Study of Belief and Practice in an Indian Village*. Totowa, NJ: Rowman & Littlefield.

Pollock, S., Bhabha, H., Breckenridge, C. and Chakrabarty, D. (2000) Cosmopolitanisms. *Public Culture* 32: 577–590.

Proctor, R. (1988) *Racial Hygiene: Medicine and the Nazis*. Cambridge, MA: Harvard University Press.

Rabinow, P. (1986) Representations are Social Facts. In J. Clifford and G.E. Marcus (eds) *Writing Culture: The Poetics and Politics of Ethnography*. Berkeley, CA: University of California Press.

Radhakrishnan, S. (1992) *Eastern Religions and Western Thought*. Delhi: Oxford University Press.

Raheja, G.G. (1988) *The Poison in the Gift: Ritual, Prestation, and the Dominant Caste in a North Indian Village*. Chicago: University of Chicago Press.

—— (1996) Caste, Colonialism and the Speech of the Colonized. *American Ethnologist* 23(3):494–513.

Rawat, A.S. (1989) *History of Garhwal: 1358–1947*. New Delhi: Indus.

Rawlinson, A. (1983) Yoga Psychologies. In P. Heelas and A. Lock (eds) *Indigenous Psychologies: The Anthropology of the Self*. London: Academic Press.

Raychaudhuri, T. (1989) *Europe Reconsidered: Perceptions of the West in Nineteenth Century Bengal*. New Delhi: Oxford University Press.

Reich, R.B. (1992) *The Work of Nations*. New York: Vintage.

Reill, P.H. (1994) Science and the Construction of the Cultural Sciences in Late Enlightenment Germany: The Case of Wilhelm von Humboldt. *History and Theory* 33(3):345–366.

Rennie, B.S. (1996) *Reconstructing Eliade: Making Sense of Religion*. Albany, NY: SUNY Press.

Ricketts, M.L. (1988) *Mircea Eliade: The Romanian Roots, 1907–1945*. Vol. I. Boulder, CO: East European Monographs.

Robertson, R. (1992) *Globalization*. London: Sage.

—— (1995) Glocalization: Time–Space and Homogeneity–Heterogeneity. In M. Featherstone, S. Lash and R. Robertson (eds) *Global Modernities*. London: Sage.

Rodrigues, S. (1982) *The Householder Yogi: Life of Sri Yogendra*. Santa Cruz, Bombay: Yogendra Publications Fund, The Yoga Institute.

Rogers, R.A. (1994) *Nature and the Crisis of Modernity: A Critique of Contemporary Discourse on Managing the Earth*. Montreal: Black Rose.

—— and Hackenberg, R. (1987) Extending Epidemiologic Transition Theory: A New Stage. *Social Biology* 34(3–4):234–243.

Rolland, R. (1988 [1931]) *The Life of Vivekananda and the Universal Gospel,* trans. E.F. Malcolm-Smith. Calcutta: Advaita Ashrama.

Rosenberg, C. (1985) The Therapeutic Revolution: Medicine, Meaning and Social Change in Nineteenth Century America. In J.W. Leavitt and R.L. *Sickness and Health in America,* 2nd edn. Madison, WI: University of Wisconsin Press.

Ross, H. and Mico, P. (1980) *Theory and Practice in Helath Education.* Palo Alto, CA: Mayfield. Ross, M.A. (1992) *The Post-Modern and the Post-Industrial: A Critical Analysis.* Cambridge: Cambridge University Press.

Roszak, T. (1979) *Person/Planet.* Garden City, NY: Anchor/Doubleday.

Rothermund, D. (1986) *The German Intellectual Quest for India.* Delhi: Manohar.

Rouse, R. (1992) Making Sense of Settlement. In N. Glick Schiller, L. Basch and C. Blanc-Szanton (eds) *Towards a Transnational Perspective on Migration: Race, Class, Ethnicity and Nationalism Reconsidered.* Annals of the New York Academy of Sciences, vol. 645. New York: New York Academy of Sciences.

Said, E. (1979) *Orientalism.* New York: Vintage.

Saltzman, P. (2000) *The Beatles in Rishikesh.* New York: Viking.

Samuels, M. and Bennett, H.Z. (1983) *Well Body: Well Earth. The Sierra Club Environmental Health Sourcebook.* San Francisco, CA: Sierra Club.

Sangi, V. (1990) *All India Travel Companion,* trans. L. Mazumdar. Calcutta: Asia Publishing.

Sapolsky, R.M. (1994) *Why Zebras Don't Get Ulcers: A Guide to Stress, Stress-Related Diseases, and Coping.* New York: W.H. Freeman.

Sarkar, S. (1985) *Modern India, 1885-1947.* Madras: Macmillan India.

—— (1992) "Kaliyuga," "Chakri" and "Bhakti": Ramakrishna and his Times. *Economic and Political Weekly,* July 18:1543–1566.

Scheper-Hughes, N. and Lock, M. (1987) The Mindful Body. *Medical Anthropology Quarterly* 1(1):6-41.

—— (1990) A Critical-Interpretive Approach in Medical Anthropology: Rituals and Routines of Discipline and Dissent. In T. Johnson and C. Sargent (eds) *Medical Anthropology: Contemporary Theory and Method.* New York: Praeger.

Schetter, R. (1998) Diplomarbeit (MA thesis) *Wellness in Leukerbad,* Universitaet St. Gallen, Switzerland.

Schmidt, W. (1967) *Yoga in Deutschland: Verbreitung-Motive-Hintergruende.* Stuttgart: Kreuz.

Schneider, C. (2003) *American Yoga.* New York: Barnes & Noble.

Schumacher, E.F. (1990a) *Small is Beautiful: A Study of Economics as If People Mattered.* Calcutta: Rupa.

—— (1990b) *A Guide for the Perplexed.* London: Sphere.

Schwab, R. (1984) *The Oriental Renaissance: Europe's Rediscovery of India and the East, 1680–1880*, trans. G. Patterson-Black and V. Reinking. New York: Columbia University Press.

Schwendemann, M.A. (1961) *Yoga for Perfect Health*. Salem, MA: Pyramid.

Sen, A. and Muellbauer, J. (1987) *The Standard of Living*. New York: Cambridge University Press.

Seth, S. (1983) *Practical Yoga*. Bombay: India Book House.

Shils, E. (1961) The Intellectual between Tradition and Modernity. *Comparative Studies in Society and History, Supplement 1*. The Hague: Mouton.

Shiva, V. (ed.) (1994) *Close to Home: Women Reconnect Ecology, Health and Development Worldwide*. Philadelphia, PA: New Society.

Silver, C. and DeFries, R.S. (1991) *One Earth One Future: Our Changing Global Environment*. New Delhi: Affiliated East-West Press.

Singh, G. (1985) *The New Middle Class in India: A Sociological Analysis*. Jaipur: Rawat.

Sinha, A.B.N. (1947) *Siva: The Prophet of the New Age*. Life and Teachings Series no.12. Rishikesh: Sivananda Publication League.

Sivananda, S. (1929) *The Practice of Yoga*. Himalayan Yoga Series Vol. I. Madras: Ganesh.

—— (1979) *Fourteen Lessons in Raja Yoga*, 5th edn. Rishikesh: Divine Life Society.

—— (1983 [1959]) *Yogic Home Exercises: Easy Course of Physical Culture for Modern Men and Women*. Bombay: D.B. Taraporevala sons & Co. Pvt. Ltd.

—— (1984 [1942]) *Lectures on Yoga and Vedanta*, 2nd edn. Rishikesh: Divine Life Society.

—— (1986a) *Triple Yoga*, 5th edn. Rishikesh: Divine Life Society.

—— (1986b) *Yoga in Daily Life*, 6th edn. Rishikesh: Divine Life Society.

—— (1988) *Essence of Yoga*, 13th edn. Rishikesh: Divine Life Society

—— (1991) *Kundalini Yoga*, 9th edn. Rishikesh: Divine Life Society

Smiles, S. (1883 [1859]) *Self-Help, with Illustrations of Character, Conduct, and Perserverence*. Chicago: Belford, Clarke.

Spencer, J. (1995) Occidentalism in the East. In J.G. Carrier (ed.) *Occidentalism: Images of the West*. New York: Oxford University Press.

Spiegelberg, F. (1951) *Spiritual Practices of India*, trans. E.E. King-Fisher. San Francisco, CA: Greenwood Press.

Spivak, G.C. (1988) Subaltern Studies: Deconstructing Historiography. In R. Guha and G.C. Spivak (eds) *Selected Subaltern Studies*, New York: Oxford University Press.

Srinivas, M.N. (1976) *The Remembered Village*. Berkeley, CA: University of California Press.

—— (1993) *Outside in the Teaching Machine*. New York: Routledge.

Staal, F. (1983–1984) Indian Concepts of the Body. *Somatics* 4(3):31–41.

Starr, P. (1982) *The Social Transformation of American Medicine.* New York: Basic Books.

Strauss, S. (1999) Oasis Regimes: Time and the Self in Transnational Health Tourism. Paper presented at the Annual Meeting of the American Anthropological Association, Chicago, IL, November 17–21, 1999.

—— (2000) Locating Yoga: Ethnography and Transnational Practice. In V. Amit (ed.) *Constructing the Field.* New York: Routledge.

—— (2002a) "Adapt, Adjust, Accommodate": The Production of Yoga in a Transnational World. *History and Anthropology* 13(3): 231–251.

—— (2002b) The Master's Narrative: Swami Sivananda and the Transnational Production of Yoga. *Journal of Folklore Research.* Vol. 39, No. 2/3.

—— (2002c) Swamiji: A Life in Yoga. In L. Walbridge and A. Sievert (eds) *Personal Encounters in Anthropology: An Introductory Reader* Mountain View, CA: McGraw-Hill.

Stürmer, E. (1980) *Paradies Rishikesh: Die Hochburg der Gurus-einst und jetzt.* Salzburg: Bergland-Buch.

Tagore, R. (1992) *Nationalism.* Calcutta: Rupa.

Tamney, J.B. (1992) *American Society in the Buddhist Mirror.* Garland Library of Sociology. New York: Garland.

Tönnies, F. (1957 [1887]) *Community and Society,* trans. and ed. C.P. Loomis. East Lansing, MI: Michigan State University Press.

Touraine, A. (1995) *Critique of Modernity.* trans. D. Macey. Oxford: Blackwell.

Treadgold, D.W. (1990) *Freedom: A History.* New York: New York University Press.

Turner, B.S. (1984) *The Body and Society.* Oxford: Basil Blackwell.

—— (1994) *Orientalism, Postmodernism and Globalism.* London: Routledge.

Turner, V. (1981) *The Drums of Affliction: A Study of Religious Processes among the Ndembu of Zambia.* Hutchinson University Library for Africa. London: Hutchinson.

—— (1986) *The Anthropology of Performance.* New York: PAJ.

—— (1987 [1969]) *The Ritual Process: Structure and Anti-Structure.* Ithaca, NY: Cornell University Press.

—— and E.M. Bruner (eds) (1986) *The Anthropology of Experience.* Urbana, IL: University of Illinois Press.

Tyler, S.A. (1986) *India: An Anthropological Perspective.* Prospect Heights, IL: Waveland Press.

Usarski, F. (ed.) (1992) *Yoga und Indien.* Materialien 33, Volkshochschulen und der Themenbereich Afrika, Asien und Lateinamerika. Bonn: Deutscher Volkshochschul-Verband e.V., Fachstelle fuer Internationale Zusammenarbeit.

Urry, J. (1995) *Consuming Places.* London: Routledge.

Van der Veer, P. (1989) The Power of Detachment: Disciplines of Body and Mind in the Ramanandi Order. *American Ethnologist* 16(3):458–470.

—— (1989b) *Gods on Earth: The Management of Religious Experience and Identity in a North Indian Pilgrimage Centre*. London School of Economics Monographs on Social Anthropology. Delhi: Oxford University Press.

—— (1994) *Religious Nationalism: Hindus and Muslims in India*. Berkeley, CA: University of California Press.

van Lisabeth, A. (1992) *Yoga Self Taught*. New Delhi: Tarang.

Varenne, J. (1976) *Yoga and the Hindu Tradition*. Chicago: University of Chicago Press.

Vidich, A.J. (ed.) (1995) *The New Middle Classes: Life-Styles, Status Claims and Political Orientations*. New York: New York University Press.

Vishnudevananda, Swami (1988 [1960]) *The Complete Illustrated Book of Yoga*. New York: Harmony.

Vivekananda, S. (1977) *Complete Works of Swami Vivekananda*, Vol I–VIII. Calcutta: Advaita Ashrama.

—— (1988) *East and West*. Calcutta: Advaita Ashrama.

—— (1989a) *Letters of Swami Vivekananda*. Calcutta: Advaita Ashrama.

—— (1989b) *Memoirs of European Travel*, 3rd edn. Calcutta: Advaita Ashrama.

—— (1990a) *Lectures from Columbo to Almora, 12th edn*. Calcutta: Advaita Ashrama.

—— (1990b) *Raja Yoga*, 19th edn. Calcutta: Advaita Ashrama.

—— (1990c) *To the Youth of India*, 11th edn. Calcutta: Advaita Ashrama.

Wagner, P. (1992) Liberty and Discipline: Making sense of post-modernity, or, once again, toward a sociohistorical understanding of modernity. *Theory and Society* 21:467-492.

—— (1994) *A Sociology of Modernity: Liberty and Discipline*. London: Routledge.

Wallerstein, E. (1974) *The Modern World System: Capitalist Agriculture and the Origins of the European World-Economy in the Sixteenth Century*. New York: Academic Press.

Walton, H.G. (1989[1910]) *A Gazetteer of Garhwal Himalaya*. Dehra Dun: Natraj.

Warnier, J.-P. (1995) Around a Plantation: The Ethnography of Business in Camaroon. In D. Miller (ed.) *Worlds Apart*, ASA Decennial Conference Series. London: Routledge.

Weber, M. (1968) *Economy and Society*, ed. G. Roth and C. Wittich. New York: Bedminster Press.

Weindling, P. (1989) *Health, Race and German Politics between National Unification and Nazism, 1870–1945*. Cambridge: Cambridge University Press.

Werner, K. (1977) *Yoga and Indian Philosophy*. Delhi: Motilal Banarsidass.

WHO/UNICEF (1978) *Primary Health Care: Alma Ata, Report of the International Conference on Primary Health Care*, Alma Ata, USSR, 6–12 September 1978. Geneva: WHO/UNICEF.

Williams, R. (1988) *Keywords: A Vocabulary of Culture and Society*. London:Fontana.

Wiser, W. and Wiser, C. (1971) *Behind Mud Walls, 1930–1960. With a Sequel: The Village in 1970*. Berkeley, CA: University of California Press.

Wittgenstein, L. (1953) *Philosophical Investigations*, trans. G.E.M. Anscombe. Oxford: Basil Blackwell.

Wood, E. (1976) *Seven Schools of Yoga: An Introduction*. Wheaton, IL: Theosophical Publishing House.

Wulff, H. (1998) *Ballet across Borders*. Oxford: Berg.

Young, A. (1980) The Discourse on Stress and the Reproduction of Conventional Knowledge. *Social Science and Medicine* 14B:133–146.

Zarilli, P. (1989) Three Bodies of Practice in a Traditional South Indian Martial Art. *Social Science and Medicine* 28(12):1289–1309.

Zierhofer, W. and Ernste, H. (1994) Individuum, Gesellschaft und umweltverantwortliches Handeln. *Bulletin der ETH-Zurich*. 253:42–44.

Zimmer, H. (1984 [1926]) *Artistic Form and Yoga in the Sacred Images of India*, trans. G. Chapple and J.B. Lawson. Princeton, NJ: Princeton University Press.

Zimmerman, F. (1987) *The Jungle and the Aroma of Meats: An Ecological Theme in Hindu Medicine*. Berkeley, CA: University of California Press.

Index

Note: Page numbers for figures appear in italics.

Abhedananda, Swami, 30
Adapt, Adjust, Accommodate, 43, 141
Advaitananda, Swami, 39–40
Albanese, C. L., 128
All-World Religions' Federation, 42
Amadea, 125
Ambrosia, The, 36
Ananda Ashram, Monroe, New York, 50
Anderson, B., 40–1, 112–13, 119
anthroposophy, 110, 124
Appadurai, A., 8, 16–17, 93
Aryans, Indian origin of, 110–11, 124
Ascona, Switzerland, 116, 154n1
Association of Vidya-Yoga Teachers, 112
Augé, M., 17
authenticity, 58–9

Badrinath, India, 26
Bahadur, R. P. R., *Garhwal: Ancient and Modern,* 27–8
Bahuguna, S., 131
balance
    among the three gunas, 94
    breathing exercises for, 61, 69, 141
    creating wellness, 57–8, 68, 70–1, 74, 99
    as equilibrium (samatva), x, 130
    sequence of yoga postures for, 62, 69
    yoga as, 80, 84
Bangladesh, 28
Bateson, G., 117
Bayreuth, Germany, journal entry, 18
BDY (German Yoga Teacher's Association), 42, 78, 112
Beatles, 29, 49
Beck, U., 134
Become Something, Make Something, 83
Be Good, Do Good, 83
Bellamy, E., *Looking Backward,* 31–2

Bhagavad Gita, 120, 130
bhakti yoga, ix
Bharat Temple, 26
Birch, B., 4
Birth of the Clinic, The (Foucault), 148–9n21
Bodian, S., 130–1
Bombay, India, journal entry, 1
Bourdieu, P., 21
Brahmananda, Swami, 50, 99
Bramwell, A., 124, 132–3
breathing techniques, 10
    for balance, 61, 69, 141
brotherhood, 47
Brown, M. F., 72
Brunton, P., *Search in Secret India, A,* 49
Buddhism, 4, 26

Calcutta, India. *See* Kolkata, India
Canada, media representations of yoga, 126–30
capital, spiritual, 9, 19, 73
Capouya, J., *Real Men Do Yoga,* 129
Carterton, Maryland, journal entry, 49–50
caste system in India, 8–9, 12, 28, 45, 56, 145–5n8
Chicago, Illinois, journal entry, 137
Chidananda, Swami, xiii, 66–7, 87, 107, 137
    rivalry with Krishnananda, 48, 66, 108–9
children
    deciding to have, 70, 74–6
    teaching yoga to, 81
Chinmayananda, Swami, xiii
Chopra, D., 97
Christianity, yoga and, 10
Cincinnati, Ohio, journal entry, 126
classical yoga. *See* Raja yoga
Clifford, J., 16–17
coinciding of opposites, 47
colonialism, 7, 14, 78, 133, 136

communitas, 96
community
  creation of, 119
  ideological (sampradaya), x, 9, 112–13
  imagined, 40–1
community of yoga practitioners, 68, 112–14
  transnational, 39, 54–5, 83–5, 96
    based on print media, 41, 46–9, 119
    oasis regimes and, 90–2
  virtual connections, 143
connection, 128–9
Conrad, P., 68
consciousness, attaining the next level of
  (mahasamadhi), 48, 146n11
cosmopolitanism, 149n25
cosmopolitans, 16
cults, 109
cultural creolization, 96
cultural relativism, xv
cycle of worldly life (samsara), x, 14–15

Darwinism, 127, 133
Das, A., 145–5n8
Datta, N. *See* Vivekananda, Swami
death. *See* consciousness, attaining the next
  level of (mahasamadhi)
death rituals, 56
deep ecology, 131–2
  see also ecology
Descartes, R., 132
Devi, M., 38, 151n16
dichotomies, 22, 116, 138–9
  see also dualism
discipleships, via the post, 41
discussants, 57, 68–70, 148n18
  Ajay, 72–4
  Beate, 74, 98, 113
  Becki, 91–2, 111
  Dr. Arjun Kalwar, 76
  Dr. Gita Kalwar, 76
  Johannes, 112
  John, 71–2
  Karen, 18–19, 22, 111, 113
  Michael, 75–6
  Patricia, 71–2
  Ramesh, 95
  Ram (pseudonym) (Hindi tutor), xiii, 30, 59,
    79–81

  Stella, 87, 90, 92
  Trudi, 70–1
Divine Life Society
  international branches of, 48–9, 109
  Maryland retreat, 92, 107
  officially sanctioned affiliates, 104
  Omkarananda and, 104, 106
  organizational hierarchy, 104
  origins of, 40–1
  Rishikesh, 9, 50–1, *64,* 135, *136*
    Sivananda-style regime, 63, 65
  social equality and, 100–1
  website, 90, 141
Divine Light Zentrum. *See* Omkarananda
  Ashram International
*Dr. Dean Ornish's Program for Reversing
  Heart Disease* (Ornish), 97
dualism, 116, 128, 134, 138–9
  Cartesian, 132
  patriarchal, 131
  see also dichotomies
Dumont, L., 145–5n8
Dunn, H., 58
duty (dharma), 15, 120

ecology, 117
  yoga and, 118–19, 123, 130–3
eco-yoga, 133–4
Eliade, M., xiii, 38–41, 47, 151–2nn16–17
  L'Inde, 39–40
  Maitreyi, 39
  Secret of Dr. Honigberger, The, 39
  Yoga: Immortality and Freedom, 40
Emerson, R. W., 128
English
  as a common language, 15–16, 35, 119
  teaching conducted in, 51, 100
  writings about yoga in, 38, 45–6, 82
environmentalism, 101, 130–3
epidemiological transmission theory, 13
equality, social, 100–1
equal rights, 78
equilibrium (samatva), x, 130
Eranos conferences, 154n1
Essence of Yoga, 108
essentialism, 7
ethnography
  data, 20

Index

field languages, 15–16, 89
interviews, 57, 69–70
  see also discussants
multi-sited fieldwork, 14–18, 63, 88–90, 92–3
participant-observation, xv, 2, 8, 56–7, 60
"Ethnography in/of the World System"
  (Marcus), 88–9, 93
evolutionary theory, 127, 133
export gurus, 45, 67, 95–7, 102–3

fate (karma), x, 15
Ferguson, J., 17
Feuerabendt, S., 42, 111–12
Feuerstein, G., 130–1
fieldwork
  multilingual, 15–16, 89
  multi-sited, 14–18, 63, 88–90, 92–3
First Yoga School, Bayreuth, Germany, 111
fitness, 127
*Fitnesse: A Complete Guide for a Healthy
  Lifestyle,* 121
flexibility, 4, 19, 58, 69, 71, 117
flying swami. *See* Vishnudevananda, Swami
Folan, Lilias, xiii, 92, 126–7
  television yoga classes, 49
  website, 141–2
Foucault, M., 12
  Birth of the Clinic, The, 148–9n21
Fourteen Lessons on Raja Yoga (Sivananda), 55
Fox, R., 101
Fox, W., 132
freedom
  individual, 6, 45, 47, 69–70
    as release from worldly bonds (moksha),
      x, 15, 120
    see also living liberation (jivanmukhti)
  as a key value, 12–13, 31
  national, 69
  see also liberation
Fuchs, C., 78, 124
Fuller, R. C., 121
"Future of India, The" (Vivekananda), 78

Gandhi, M. K., 78
Ganga Ma (goddess), 26
Ganga River, 24
  white water rafting on, 29, *29*
Ganges River. *See* Ganga River

Garhwal: Ancient and Modern (Bahadur), 27–8
Garhwal region, 24–9
  holy places, 26, 105
GAS (General Adaptation Syndrome), 149n26
gemeinschaft, 92
  see also community; community of yoga
    practitioners
General Adaptation Syndrome (GAS), 149n26
German Romanticism, 125
Germany
  media representations of yoga, 124–6
  rise of yoga in, 110–11
German Yoga Teacher's Association (BDY), 42,
  78, 112
Giddens, A., 132, 134
global community. *See* community of yoga
  practitioners, transnational
Global Eco-village Network, website, 119
global interdependence, 134
globalization, 138–9
glossary, ix–xi
good life
  definition, 19, 74–5, 79, 82
  stress preventing, 122
  within modernity, 81–3, 139
  yoga and, 21, 32, 68–9, 87, 138
  see also lifestyle
Green, H., 68, 127–8
Grove, R., 133
Guha, R., 131
Gupta, A., 17
guru-brother (gurubhai), 105

Haich, E., 110, 152n18
Halbfass, W., 45, 124–5
Haley, B., 68
Hannerz, U., 15, 51, 96
Hannover, Germany, journal entry, 87
Hardwar, India, 25–6
hatha yoga, ix, 4, 65, 98
  Hinduism and, 109
  Westerners' attraction to, 94–5
  see also Raja yoga
Hay, Steven, 148n20
health
  definitions, 57–8, 68, 71, 116
  effects of modernity on, 19, 123, 148–9n21,
    149n26

freedom and, 69
as a key value, 12–14, 31, 46
morality and, 68–9
from personal to planetary, 115–19
total, 20
yoga's promotion of, 6, 14, 57
Heelas, P., 130, 133
Hellman, S. *See* Sivananda-Radha, Swami
Herbert Spencer Song, 107
Hess, R., 124
Himalayan mountains, 27
Hindi
teaching conducted in, 50
transliteration of, ix–xi
Hinduism, 26
classical life cycle, 75
cycle of the ages, 82
six philosophies of, 3–4
traditional concepts, 71
Hindus, separation from Muslims, 28
Hindustan Times, 127
Hrishikesh, India. *See* Rishikesh, India
Humboldt, Alexander von, 133

identity, shift in, 92
L'Inde (Eliade), 39–40
India, 11
expansion of yoga in, 100, 120
Independence, 41–2
map, 25
nationalism and, 78
Partition, 28
India Perspectives, 120
India Today, 122–3
individualization, 134
informants. *See* discussants
inner child, 129
Integral Yoga, 49, 97, 153n4
International Sivananda Yoga Nataraja Center, 135
Iyengar, B. K. S., 66
Iyer, K., 36–7
see also Sivananda, Swami

Jainism, 4
Jayananda, Swami (pseudonym), xiii, 20, 49, 98–9
jnana yoga, ix, 9

journal entries
Bayreuth, Germany, 18
Bombay, India, 1
Carterton, Maryland, 49–50
Chicago, Illinois, 137
Cincinnati, Ohio, 126
Hannover, Germany, 87
Kolkata, India, 32–3
Laramie, Wyoming, 126, 141
Rheintal, Germany, 112
Rishikesh, India, 23, 53, 135
Bahuguna and, 130
Ram and, 30, 59
Swamiji and, 55–6, 61–2
yoga classes, 4–5, 61–2
San Francisco, California, 93–4
Washington, DC, 19–20
West Bengal, 79
Winterthur, Switzerland, 102
Zurich, Switzerland, 115
Jyotirmayananda, Swami, xiii, 48

Kabat-Zinn, J., 97
Kailash Ashram, Rishikesh, 27, 29–30, 50–1
Kaliyuga (decadent era), 82
Kaplan, K., 17
karma yoga, x, 9
Kashmir, 28
Keys, D., "The Passage to World Community," 139
Knauft, B., 13
knowledge workers, 148n20
Kolkata, India, journal entry, 32–3
Kriesi, H., 83
Krishnananda, Swami, xiii, 63
rivalry with Chidananda, 48, 66, 108–9

Laramie, Wyoming, journal entries, 126, 141
Lash, S., *Reflexive Modernization,* 134
Laxman Jhula (bridge), 150n3
Lears, T. J. J., 31, 68
Lectures from the 1000 Islands (Vivekananda), 87
Leder, D., 155–6n7
liberation, 15, 45, 47, 120
see also freedom; living liberation (jivanmukhti)
Liechty, M., 73

lifestyle
  Indian monks, 103
  modern, health effects of, 123
  yoga practitioners, 101
  see also good life
Light of Truth Universal Shrine (LOTUS)
  temple, 97
L'Inde (Eliade), 39–40
living liberation (jivanmukhti), ix, 31, 44–7,
  69, 113, 126
Looking Backward (Bellamy), 31–2
LOTUS (Light of Truth Universal Shrine)
  temple, 97
Luhrmann, T. M., 78, 129

McKean, L., 99, 100, 103
Mahabharata, 24
Maharshi, R., 49
Mahesh Yogi, M., 29, 49
Maitreyi (Eliade), 39
Marcus, G. E., 16
  "Ethnography in/of the World System,"
    88–9, 93
Martin, E., 18, 58
master–disciple pair (guru–shishya), 45
materialism
  synthesis with spirituality, 122
  vs. spirituality, 9, 11–12, 35, 51
matrix, definition, 17
media, 114, 116–17
  creating community, 41, 46–9, 119
  print, 30, 45, 104, 138
    as research data, 20, 22
    translation of, 110
  representations of yoga, 78
    American, 126–30
    German, 124–6
    Indian, 120
  see also websites
medicine
  Ayurvedic, 2, 46, 68
  German, 124, 153n5
Men's Fitness, 129
middle class, new (bhadralok), 34
Miller, D., 112–13
Mistry, A., "Yoga and Modern Life," 120–1
modernity
  definition, 12–14, 68

health effects of, 19, 123, 148–9n21, 149n26
key values of, 6, 31
seeking a good life within, 81–3, 139
yoga and, 116–17, 134
monism, 10, 132
  vs. dualism, 134
  see also non-duality (advaita)
"Mother India: A National Anthem"
  (Sivananda), 42
Mueller, M., 124
Muir, J., 132
Muslims, separation from Hindus, 28
mythology, Hindu, 24–7
myths about yoga, 128

Naess, A., 131
Nandy, A., 78, 118, 129, 135–6
Nash, R., 132
National Center for Complementary and
  Alternative Medicine, 153n5
National Institutes of Health, Office of
  Alternative Medicine (OAM), 97
nationalism, vii, 10, 34, 78
Der Naturartzi, 125
nature, qualities of (gunas), 94
Nazi era, 124–5
neo-Hinduism, 8, 45, 109
neo-humanism, 155n6
neo-traditionalism, 135
New Age, 58, 109, 118–19, 133
non-duality (advaita), ix, 10, 35, 131,
  146–8nn13–14, 155n6

OAM (Office of Alternative Medicine), 97
oasis regimes, 21, 54, 57–9, 97, 127
  Sivananda-style, 45, 63, 65, 90–2, 113–14
Occidentalism, 11
Office of Alternative Medicine (OAM), 97
Omkarananda, Swami, xiii, 102–7
Omkarananda Ashram International, 102–4,
  106
  website, 107
Omkarananda Ganga Sadhan, Rishikesh, 59,
  135
Omkarananda Yoga Sadhan Center, Rishikesh,
  68
Omran, A., 13
oneness, 146–8nn13–14

opposites, coinciding of, 47
Orientalism, 7, 11
Ornish, Dean, xiii, 97
　Dr. Dean Ornish's Program for Reversing
　　Heart Disease, 97
　website, 142
Our Health: Nutrition and Environment, 120

Pakistan, 28
Pal, Y., 120
Parliament of the World's Religions, 5, 17, 32,
　119, 137
"The Passage to World Community" (Keys),
　139
Patanjali
　eight stages of classical yoga, 2, 43
　Yoga Sutras, 3–4, 95
pilgrimage, 44, 57
pilgrimage routes, 26
Pinchot, G., 132
postal discipleships, 41
postures (asana) of yoga
　Rishikesh Reihe, 42
　sequence of, 42, 61–2, 93
　sequence of for balance, 62, 69
　Vishnudevananda's sequence of, 99–100
postures (asanas) of yoga, ix
practice (abhyas) of yoga, ix, 6, 7, 10, 54–5,
　151n13
praxis orientation, 118
Proctor, R., 124–5
props, 67
PROUT, 155n6
publications. See media, print
Public Culture, 16

Rabinow, P., 16
Radhakrishnan, S., 139
Raheja, G. G., 8, 145–5n8
Rajaji National Wildlife Sanctuary, 25
rajas (energy, intenseness, movement), x, 94
Raja yoga, x, 9, 43
　eight stages of, 2–4
　see also hatha yoga
Rajneesh, 153n7
Ramakrishna, Sri, xiii, 2–3, 9
　Eliade on, 40
Ramakrishna Mission (RK Mission), 9, 33, 108

Ramayana, 24
Ram Jhula (bridge), 64
Ram (pseudonym) (Hindi tutor), xiii, 30, 59,
　79–81
Real Men Do Yoga (Capouya), 129
Reflexive Modernization (Lash), 134
reflexivity, 134
Reill, P. H., 146–7n13
religion
　Vishnudevananda on, 98
　Vivekananda on, 36
renouncer (sannyasin), 54, 56
　definition, 9, 37
Rheintal, Germany, journal entry, 112
Rishikesh, India
　government, 150n3
　history of, 24–30
　journal entries, 23, 53, 135
　　Bahuguna and, 130
　　Ram and, 30, 59
　　Swamiji and, 55–6, 61–2
　　yoga classes, 4–5, 61–2
　as the place to go for yoga, 2, 14, 27, 54–5,
　　95–6, 146n9
　tea stall, 54
　Vivekananda on, 2–4, 30
　Yoga Week, 137
Rishikesh Reihe
　sequence of yoga postures, 42
　set of practices, 93
Rolland, R., 35
Romanticism, 29, 125

Sacharow, B., 18, 41–2, 110–11
Sadananda, Swami, 48
Sahajananda, Swami, 48
Said, E., 7, 11
San Francisco, California, journal entry, 93–4
Sanskrit
　teaching conducted in, 50
　transliteration of, ix–xi
Satchidananda, Swami, xiii, 49, 96–7, 137
sattva (intelligence, lucidity, calmness), x, 94
Satyananda, Swami, xiii
Schetter, R., 58
Schumacher, E. F., Small Is Beautiful, 118
"Science of Yoga" (Vivekananda), 2–4
Search in Secret India, A (Brunton), 49

Index

Secret of Dr. Honigberger, The (Eliade), 39
self-actualization, 134
self-control, 71
self-development, 59, 83
self-realization, 19
self-reliance, 71, 75, 82
"Serve, Love, Meditate, Realize," 9
service, selfless, 82–3, 101, 128
Seth, S., 122
Shiva, V., 131
Shivapremananda, Swami, 48
Shivpuri, India, 140
Sikh religion, 28
Siva (god), 24
Sivananda, Swami, xiii
 All-India tour, 1950, 43–4
 birth centenary, 40, 99
 commemorative postage stamp, *37*
 early life, 36–8
 influenced by Vivekananda, 3
 lineage, xiii
 motto, 83
 oasis regime of, 63, 65, 90–2
 website, 141
 works, 9–10, 38, 45–6, 113
  Fourteen Lessons on Raja Yoga, 55
  "Mother India: A National Anthem," 42
  Twenty Instructions for Spiritual Success,
   90, 101
  "Universal Anthem, The," 42
  Yogic Home Exercises, 46
Sivananda Ashram, Rishikesh, *64*
 see also Divine Life Society
Sivananda Jhula (bridge), 150n3
Sivananda Publication League, 41, 49
Sivananda-Radha, Swami, xiii, 50, 98
Sivananda Yoga Vedanta Centers (SYVCs),
 48–50
 Delhi, India, 68, 100
 Munich, Germany, 18, 109
 San Francisco, California, 93–4
 Val Morin, Canada, 99
 website, 142
Small Is Beautiful (Schumacher), 118
Spinoza, B., 132, 146–7n13
spirituality, 12, 41, 118, 139
 business of, 100, 103
 synthesis with materialism, 122

vs. materialism, 9, 11–12, 35, 51
Steiner, R., 110
stress
 origins of, 74
 preventing a good life, 122
 produced by modernity, 19, 123, 148–9n21,
  149n26
 yoga as an antidote for, 116–17, 122–3
student-renouncer (brahmacharin-sannyasin),
 ix, 103
Sumit (pseudonym), xiii, *7,* 65–7
Swamiji (pseudonym), xiii, *62*
 biography, 55–6
 Vishnudevananda and, 99
 yoga practices of, 60–2, 67–8, 140–1
Swaroopananda, Swami, 40
SYVCs (Sivananda Yoga Vedanta Centers),
 48–50
 Delhi, India, 68, 100
 Munich, Germany, 18, 109
 San Francisco, California, 93–4
 Val Morin, Canada, 99
 website, 142

tamas (heaviness, inertia, obstruction), x, 94
teachers
 export gurus, 45, 67, 95–7, 102–3
 physical presence of, 47
teaching traditions (sampradaya), x, 9, 112–13
tea stall, Rishikesh, *54*
techniques, bodily, 10–11
television yoga classes, 49, 122, 127
*A Textbook of the Psychology and Practice of
 the Techniques to Spiritual Perfection,* 104
Tönnies, F., 92
tourism, 44, 58, 97
 websites, 57
Transcendentalism, 29, 128
Transcendental Meditation, 29
transnational development of yoga, 1–3, 8–11,
 13, 50–1
transnationalism, xv
True World Order (TWO), 99
Turner, B. S., 117
Turner, V., 96
Twenty Instructions for Spiritual Success
 (Sivananda), 90, 101
TWO (True World Order), 99

United States
  media representations of yoga, 126–30
"Universal Anthem, The" (Sivananda), 42
universality, 117, 119–24, 135
Urry, J., 57
utopian realism, 134
Uttaranchal, 24

Val Morin, Quebec, ashram, 97
Van der Veer, P., 11, 103
vector, definition, 17
vector/matrix concept, 17–18
vedanta (one of six classical Hindu Darsanas),
  xi, 5, 35, 40, 44, 90, 108
Vedanta Societies, 9, 33, 108
Venkatesananda, Swami, xiii, 48
Vishnudevananda, Swami, xiii, 50, 67
  basic principles of yoga, 98
  basic sequence of postures, 99–100
  commodification of yoga, 97–100
Vishnu (god), 25
Vital: Das Magazin fuer Modernes Leben, 125
Vivekananda, Swami, xiii
  four divisions of yoga, 5–12, 14, 33–6
  influencing Sivananda, 3
  motto, 83
  presentation of yoga to American audiences,
    31–3
  on religion, 36
  on Rishikesh, 2–4, 30
  on selfless service, 128
  works
    Eliade on, 40
    "Future of India, The," 78
    Lectures from the 1000 Islands, 87
    motivational speeches, 95
    Raja Yoga, 34
    "Science of Yoga," 2–4
von Humboldt, A., 146–7n13
von Humboldt, W., 146–7n13

Washington, DC
  journal entry, 19–20
wealth, material, 35
  see also materialism
wealth, spiritual, 35
  see also spirituality
websites, 35, 58, 100

Divine Life Society, 65, 90, 141
Feuerabend, S., 111–12
Folan, Lilias, 141–2
Global Eco-village Network, 119
  on Omkarananda, 105
Omkarananda Ashram International, 106–7
Ornish, Dean, 142
Sivananda, Swami, 141
Sivananda Yoga Vedanta Centers (SYVCs),
  142
  tourism in India, 57
  Yoga Journal, 78
wellness, 57–9, 68, 71, 74, 99
West, the, 11
West Bengal
  journal entry, 79
white water rafting on Ganga River, 29, *29*
wholeness, 128
Williams, R., xv
Winterthur, Switzerland
  journal entry, 102
worldviews
  ecological, 131
  therapeutic, 31
Writing Culture (Clifford and Marcus), 16
Wulff, H., 10

Yamuna River, 24
YC (Yoga Center), Rishikesh, 63, 65–7
Yesudian, S., 87, 110–11, 152n18
yoga
  appeal to Germans, 124–6
  appeal to Indians, 120–4
  authentic, 95
  as balance, 80, 84
  as a commodity, 97–100, 137
  definition, 2, 4, 11–12, 55, 80
  ecology and, 118–19, 123, 130–3
  historical context of, 3–4, 28
  with props, *6*
  reasons for practicing, 55, 57
  as a religious activity, 77
  re-orientation of, 5–11, 115–19, 119–24, 138
  Shivananda's style, 62–3
  training in, 30–1
  transnational development of, 1–3, 8–11, 13,
    50–1
  as a universal spiritual system, 68–9

Index

Yoga: Immortality and Freedom (Eliade), 40
Yoga and Health (TV program), 122
"Yoga and Modern Life" (Mistry), 120–1
Yoga Bhavan, Rishikesh, 59, 67
Yoga Center (YC), Rishikesh, 63, 65–7
yoga classes
  on television, 49, 122, 127
  website, 142
Yoga Journal, 78, 139
yoga practice (yogabhyas)
  Iyengar style, 63
  Rishikesh Reihe, 93
  see also oasis regimes
yoga practitioners
  demographics, 2

lifestyles, 101
stereotypes, 128, 130–1
women as, 77–8, 111
see also discussants
Yoga Sutras (Patanjali), 3–4, 95
yoga techniques, 69
  bodily, 9–10, 111, 116–17, 133
yoga vacation, 97
Yoga-Vedanta Forest Academy, 42, 48, 98
Yogaville Ashram, 49, 97
  website, 142
Yogic Home Exercises (Sivananda), 46

Zimmerman, F., 68
Zurich, Switzerland, journal entry, 115